DANGEROUS FRAMES

STUDIES IN COMMUNICATION, MEDIA, AND PUBLIC OPINION

A series edited by Benjamin I. Page and Susan Herbst

DANGEROUS FRAMES

HOW IDEAS ABOUT RACE AND
GENDER SHAPE PUBLIC OPINION

Nicholas J. G. Winter

THE UNIVERSITY OF CHICAGO PRESS

Chicago and London

NICHOLAS WINTER is assistant professor of politics
at the University of Virginia.

Auxiliary statistical models appear in a Web appendix, which is available
at http://faculty.virginia.edu/nwinter/dangerousframes.

The University of Chicago Press, Chicago 60637
The University of Chicago Press, Ltd., London
© 2008 by The University of Chicago
All rights reserved. Published 2008
Printed in the United States of America

17 16 15 14 13 12 11 10 09 08   1 2 3 4 5

ISBN-13: 978-0-226-90236-4 (cloth)
ISBN-13: 978-0-226-90237-1 (paper)
ISBN-10: 0-226-90236-6 (cloth)
ISBN-10: 0-226-90237-4 (paper)

Library of Congress Cataloging-in-Publication Data

Winter, Nicholas J. G.
Dangerous frames : how ideas about race and gender shape
public opinion / Nicholas J. G. Winter.
p. cm.
Includes bibliographical references and index.
ISBN-13: 978-0-226-90236-4 (cloth : alk. paper)
ISBN-13: 978-0-226-90237-1 (pbk. : alk. paper)
ISBN-10: 0-226-90236-6 (cloth : alk. paper)
ISBN-10: 0-226-90237-4 (pbk. : alk. paper)
1. Political psychology—Case studies. 2. United States—Race
relations—Public opinion. 3. Sex role—United States—Public opinion.
4. United States—Politics and government—1989—Psychological
aspects. 5. United States—Social policy—1993—Psychological aspects.
6. Rhetoric—Political aspects—United States. 7. Public opinion—
United States. I. Title.
JA74.5.W56 2008
305.3—dc22
2007036240

Contents

Illustrations

Tables

Preface

This book is about the ways that our mental categories shape our understanding of novel political phenomena. In particular, it explores how political rhetoric can engage our ideas about race or about gender even when the subject at hand has nothing explicit to do with either race or gender — a process I call "group implication." This phenomenon is captured in the subtitle.

With the title "Dangerous Frames," I hope to evoke the power and importance of this phenomenon and to draw attention to the complexity of judging it normatively. I consider these issues at length in the concluding chapter; nevertheless, they bear brief consideration up front. The modern meaning of "danger," of course, is "exposure to harm or injury" (*Oxford English Dictionary*). Group implication is certainly dangerous in this sense: political rhetoric that subtly draws on our ideas about race or gender can — and does — cause harm by mobilizing prejudice, by obfuscating the basis for people's opinions, by reinforcing inegalitarian systems of social stratification, and more. Like another dangerous substance — electricity — it can have powerful effects, and this power is particularly problematic because it is often invisible and because its effects may go beyond what we realize or intend. Also like electricity, however, group implication can be used for positive purposes. In particular, it can facilitate citizen engagement and comprehension and can forge and mobilize egalitarian as well as inegalitarian coalitions.

The origins of the word "danger" shed additional light on group implication. "Danger" derives from the Latin *dominus,* meaning lord or master, which gave rise to an archaic sense of the "power of a lord or master, jurisdiction, dominion; power to dispose of, or to hurt or harm," according to the *Oxford English Dictionary* (of course, the etymological roots of the word make an interesting statement about the nature of hierarchical relationships generally).

This book will argue that our ideas about race and gender are extremely well suited for shaping social and political perception and evaluation and that very subtle language can trigger powerful effects. In a sense, then, we are subject to the power of our own mental categories and to the power of communication to evoke those categories, and avoiding these effects is extraordinarily difficult, if not impossible.

I do not, therefore, end the book with pious calls for the elimination of group implication. Like attempting to envision a world without electricity, we would find it exceedingly difficult to imagine eliminating group implication from our social and political communication. My goal is somewhat more cautious, if perhaps more realistic: that this book will contribute to our understanding of the extremely subtle roles that race and gender frames can play in our understanding of political reality. My first hope is that this understanding will allow us to harness the potential of these frames to facilitate communication while guarding against the dangers they pose, rather than merely whitewashing or ignoring these effects.

* * *

My second hope is that by analyzing both race and gender, we can learn more about each and about their interconnections. As I discuss in chapter 1, the empirical political science literatures on race and gender have developed along curiously different paths. I echo Nancy Burns's suggestion that scholars of gender can profitably draw on the approaches we have brought to the study of race (2007). This intellectual sharing is a two-way street: it is my belief that by examining race and gender simultaneously, we can learn more about each. In thinking about race and gender I am at best dubious about claims that either is somehow the more fundamental cleavage psychologically, socially, or politically. These two hierarchical systems are constructed differently, play different roles in public and private life, and, as I discuss in the concluding chapter, interact with each other in complex ways. Though different, neither is reducible to or more basic than the other. (And, of course, they are both interrelated with yet other axes of difference and power, including class, sexuality, citizenship status, and more.)

Despite this theoretical parity between race and gender, throughout the book I generally discuss race and gender in that order. I do this to foster clarity and to facilitate careful comparison of the similarities and differences between them; I do not mean to imply the primacy of race over gender. As my high school English teacher taught me (and my copy editor reminded me), treating one's topics in a consistent order throughout a text makes for clearer comparisons and contrasts. Throughout the book I take up race and gender in parallel and in that order. Of course, they are not truly parallel, and in the conclusion I return to the question of the relationship between these two dimensions of social stratification and hierarchy. To make a long story short, things are much more complex than that one trumps the other.

Also for the sake of clarity and concision, the tables in the book contain only the most pertinent results from the statistical analyses. In all cases complete results are available in an additional appendix on my Web site. That address is http://faculty.virginia.edu/nwinter/dangerousframes.

Acknowledgments

In the course of this project I have accumulated enormous debts. This book would not have been possible without the emotional, intellectual, and financial support of many people and institutions.

I got my academic start as an undergraduate student at the University of Chicago, where I discovered political science after a brief career as a physicist. I particularly want to thank my mentors Bert Cohler and Marvin Zonis, who nurtured my first forays into political psychology. After college Joel Bradshaw, Beth Sullivan, and my other colleagues at Campaign Design Group helped cultivate the interest in American electoral politics and political behavior that has motivated my scholarly work ever since.

I feel lucky to have benefited from the intellectual community at the University of Michigan, where I did my graduate training and where this project began. For conversations about this project and feedback on my work I am grateful to Chris Achen, Scott Allard, Elizabeth Anderson, Adam Berinsky, Jake Bowers, Ted Brader, Kevin Clarke, Claudia Deane, Doug Dion, Kim Gross, Ashley Grosse, James Hilton, Vince Hutchings, John Jackson, Cindy Kam, Markus Kemmelmeier, Harwood McClerking, Kris Miler, Tasha Philpot, Wendy Rahn, Tom Rudolph, Harvey Schuckman, Denise Sekaquaptua, Nick Valentino, and Kathy Cramer Walsh. I truly appreciate the methods training I received from Chris Achen,

Nancy Burns, Doug Dion, Rob Franzese, Don Kinder, John Jackson, Ken Kollman, and Steve Rosenstone. I learned much from all of them; most important, I learned that the statistics are the easy part — the real social science challenge lies in data analysis and inference.

Five Michigan faculty members played a particularly big role in nurturing both this project and my development as a scholar. I thank Ann Lin for pushing me to be rigorous and thoughtful while offering encouragement throughout my career. Thank you to Liz Wingrove for introducing me to social theory and for encouraging me to take seriously my intuition that abstract social theory and concrete empirical analysis could speak to each other. I thank Don Herzog for introduced me to the joys and challenges of political theory and for offering thought-provoking suggestions on my work ever since. I thank Nancy Burns for tirelessly encouraging me to take seriously all of my interests and to include many of them in this project. She has also helped me master the details of statistical techniques, while also demonstrating and teaching the importance of keeping your eye on the important questions those techniques are employed to answer. Finally, I cannot thank Don Kinder enough. He convinced me to come to Michigan, mentored me in the art of political research, and advised me on every stage of this project from initial idea, through dissertation, to revision into a book. I am grateful to each of you for your time, friendship, guidance, and excellent example.

I also owe great thanks to my colleagues in the Government Department at Cornell University, who welcomed me back to academia and provided an excellent environment in which I converted my dissertation into an initial manuscript. In particular, I appreciate the time that people took to give me advice and/or read sections of the manuscript: Richard Bensel, Allen Carlson, Jason Frank, Michael Jones-Correa, Mary Katzenstein, Jonathan Kirshner, Ted Lowi, Walter Mebane, and Anna Marie Smith. I also thank the "young junior professor types" for support and distraction.

I am also indebted to the Politics Department at the University of Virginia, where I executed major revisions and completed this book. For stimulating discussions I thank Lawrie Balfour, Michele Claibourn, Paul Freedman, Dave Klein, Sid Milkis, Lynn Sanders, and Dave Waldner. I am also particularly grateful to Tim Wilson and Eric Patashnik for reading and offering advice on major revisions to my experimental chapter.

I have benefited from the feedback of participants in the National

Election Studies Fellows Seminar, the Workshop on Race and Gender and Politics at the Institute for Research on Women and Gender at the University of Michigan, and in the work group on political experimentation in the Michigan Political Science Department. I appreciate feedback from audiences at talks I have given at the Cornell Communication Department, the University of Virginia Social Psychology group, and the University of Michigan Center for Political Studies. I also appreciate the advice from Martin Gilens and John Transue, who served as discussants for papers I presented at American Political Science Association meetings, and from Dennis Chong, who discussed this project with me on several occasions.

This research was supported financially at the University of Michigan by the Political Science Department, the National Election Studies, the Center for Political Studies, the Institute for Research on Women and Gender, and the Gerald R. Ford dissertation fellowship; at Cornell by the Department of Government; and at the University of Virginia by the Department of Politics and by Larry Sabato and the Center for Politics.

Earlier versions of chapters 5 and 6 appeared in the *American Journal of Political Science* (Winter 2006) and *Politics and Gender* (Winter 2005), respectively. I am grateful to the respective editors of those journals, as well as to the anonymous reviewers, for advice that improved those articles and also, therefore, the chapters.

I also thank the students who participated in the experiments described in chapter 4. For allowing me to recruit participants in their classes, I thank Kristopher Chrishon, Krista Ham, Vince Hutchings, Tiffiany Murray, Diane Nguyen, Osmara Reyes, and David Winter at the University of Michigan and Ron Herring at Cornell. I would also like to thank the University of Michigan Department of Psychology for allowing me access to their undergraduate subject pool.

I remember my undergraduate years at the University of Chicago fondly, so it is a pleasure to be "returning home" to the U of C Press. I am grateful to the fabulous people there who have made this book happen — John Tryneski and Rodney Powell have been a pleasure to work with from beginning to end. I greatly appreciate the editing work of Mara Naselli, Mark Reschke, and Kathy Swain and the design work of Isaac Tobin. This book has also benefited greatly from the advice of the series editor, Susan Herbst, and from the careful and extensive feedback of two anonymous reviewers.

Most important, I thank my family. My parents, Abby Stewart, David Winter, and Sara Winter, have all served both as family and as colleagues. I would not be the scholar I am today without their influence, and this project would be very different without their input and feedback. My brother, Tim Stewart-Winter, has also always been there with support and interesting thoughts on my work.

To my wife, Tucker, I am thankful for so much. She has believed in me and supported this project for a decade. She has pushed me to make my work as good as it can be, and she also helped me to keep my eye on the big picture whenever I wandered off onto yet another tangent. Finally, I am thrilled to acknowledge Nate and Maggie, whose births were two of the very few moments in my life more exciting than completing this book.

1

Race, Gender, and Political Cognition

I remember well the day my first-grade teacher started to teach me and my six-year-old classmates about the alphabet. She sat us down in a circle and explained that today we were going to learn about letters. "There are two kinds of letters," she began. "Boy letters and girl letters." Holding up a series of cards with various consonants, she introduced us to the boys; she then showed us the much smaller number of girl letters. She explained that although there were not nearly as many, these vowels were nevertheless extremely important "because you can't make any words without at least one girl letter."

That was about as far as the metaphor went, I believe. At one level this was probably an effective way to convey to a set of six-year-olds the idea that there are two different kinds of letters, by drawing on a system of binary difference — gender — that we already understood and took extremely seriously. (I do not recall what, if anything, she said about the letter *Y*, although I am confident that she did not go into matters of intersexuality or transgender — there were limits to her willingness to extend the metaphor.) At another level there is something at least a bit odd about assimilating the gender system to the alphabet merely in service of making the point that there are two types of letters. But in fact we make this sort of leap all the time — even relatively young children have a very easy time classifying all manner of things as masculine or feminine, including toys, colors, types of plants and animals, and even shapes (Bem 1981; Leinbach, Hort, and Fagot 1997). This process is only partly voluntary and is deep enough that speakers of languages that assign grammatical gender to nouns tend to associate gendered characteristics with objects, depending on the gender their language assigns to the noun (Phillips and Boroditsky 2003).

My teacher's metaphor resonated powerfully for me — only several years later did I fully understand that it was not general practice in English to classify letters as male and female, and I still find it easy to think of vowels as being somehow feminine and consonants masculine. After all, the sounds of vowels are softer and smoother, their shapes aren't as hard or pointy, and so on. And isn't Italian — a language with a plethora of vowels — much more feminine than Polish and German, with their profusion of (masculine) consonants? Without much effort we can extend the metaphor almost indefinitely.

* * *

This example illustrates that we have a rich understanding of gender and that we have a powerful ability to map our knowledge of gender onto far-removed new phenomena — even the alphabet. As I will argue in this book, we as Americans have similarly well-developed ideas about race and a similar ability to map those beliefs into unrelated domains or areas of knowledge. The central claim of this book is that these understandings of race and gender, in concert with that mapping ability, can powerfully shape our understanding of political issues.

* * *

Citizens do not do this mapping on their own; they need some help. Political elites — politicians, journalists, interest-group and party leaders, and other political actors — develop frames, or story lines, to convey a particular perspective on political issues; these perspectives come, of course, with suggestions for the best way to understand an issue and for the correct policy course. The central communication challenge for political elites is to find frames that both engage and persuade the public despite the gulf in attention, interest, engagement, and contextual knowledge about politics between elites and the mass public. One way to engage and persuade citizens is to draw on their race or gender schemas.

In this book, therefore, I explore the conditions under which frames can subtly associate an issue with race or with gender and thereby affect opinion. Race and gender are two particularly important stratification systems in contemporary America. Both define appropriate relationships among individuals and between individuals and groups, and both play important roles in structuring society, culture, and politics both today and throughout American (and human) history.

Historically, both race and sex were understood as objective, immutable categories of human beings. Hierarchical social arrangements that turned on racial and gender distinctions were understood as reflections of natural differences. More recently, work on the social construction of race has argued that the concept itself lacks any objective biological meaning. Human societies construct racial categories in relatively arbitrary ways, and the social conventions that are built on the purportedly biological distinctions among races are just that: social conventions. In a similar fashion, feminist theorists developed the distinction between sex and gender to draw attention to the fact that although there are physiological differences between people we classify as male and as female (i.e., sex differences), the elaborate systems of classification and hierarchy that we build on that distinction are neither necessary nor inevitable.

The important point is not that race and gender are not "real" in some fundamental biological sense, because they are very real psychologically and socially. Both race and gender define relevant categories of people, proscribe appropriate attributes and behaviors to those categories, and suggest appropriate relationships among individuals and among social groups. Children are socialized very early to recognize and understand the importance of sex and race differences and to act accordingly, and adults understand and take seriously those distinctions.

Given this centrality, race and gender are well suited to serve as the basis for political communication. People's ideas about race and gender are salient and easy to grasp, and they include strong emotional and normative implications. If political leaders can engage these ideas in a frame (or story line) about a political issue, they can harness them to influence opinion. Gender has rich implications for people's appearance, behavior, and relationships with each other; the right political discourse should be able to piggyback on these implications to motivate opinion on political issues that do not address gender directly. Similarly, race as an ideological system has strong implications for how groups should interact with each other. The right issue frames should mobilize people's ideas about these things and apply them to seemingly unrelated issues. In other words, race and gender structures can both underlie powerful issue frames.

This process happens only under certain fairly specific conditions, however. I draw on cognitive and social psychology and on the literatures on race and on gender in American society to develop a theory of the conditions under which issue frames can unconsciously engage people's ideas about race or about gender. I theorize that when these conditions are met, issue frames can — and indeed often will — resonate with ordinary citizens' ideas about race and gender, even when neither the issue itself nor the framing rhetoric touch overtly on racial or gender matters. Then I explore the implications of this theory, with a combination of experimental research to pinpoint the psychological mechanisms at work and national survey research to demonstrate and explore its importance for American politics.

PLAN OF THE BOOK

Theory

Chapter 2 develops my theory of the "group implication," which is the process by which an issue frame can engage a person's ideas about social categories (in particular race or gender) to shape public opinion. This theory specifies the conditions under which a political appeal (or frame) will resonate with race or gender beliefs and when it will fail to do so. It also allows me to draw together the separate literatures on race and opinion and on gender and opinion.

Group implication is essentially a form of reasoning by analogy. Recent cognitive psychology research suggests that analogical or metaphorical reasoning is an important way people make sense of novel phenomena: we frequently understand new social situations by analogy with familiar domains of experience. This analogical thinking allows us to apply knowledge we have from one domain to a new context and therefore to make inferences and judgments without starting from scratch. When our understanding of the source domain includes normative prescriptions or evaluations, those prescriptions and evaluations are applied analogically to suggest the right evaluation or course of action in the new situation.

An example from the history of the field of psychology helps to illuminate this process. At different times psychologists have employed different analogies or metaphors for the mind; Daugman (1990) classifies these into several categories, including metaphors of the mind as hydraulic systems and as computers. Hydraulic metaphors range from Hippocrates' model of the four humours (phlegm, black bile, yellow bile, and blood) to Freud's model of unconscious libidinal forces. These sorts of metaphors lead us to focus on the hidden forces that lie beneath visible behavior and to expect that as those forces build up, so will pressure for their release. Computer metaphors, on the other hand, draw attention to information processing and specifically to the rules of reasoning and the structures that store information. For our purposes the most important point is that different models or analogies suggest different standards for evaluation. In the case of hydraulic models, the mind is judged in terms of the balance among forces, be they libidinal or humourous. For computer models, on the other hand, we are drawn to evaluate in terms of accuracy, efficiency, and speed.[1]

Political issues, like all multifaceted phenomena, are inherently amenable to more than one analogical association. Consider policy related to alcoholism and drunken driving (Gusfield 1996, 1981). If alcoholism is an illness, then we may draw on our understanding of medicine to develop and evaluate policy options. If, on the other hand, alcoholism is a moral failure, then we would be more likely to draw on moral and religious domains. Moreover, because alcoholism and drunken driving are complex — involving some mixture of genetics, social influence, biological processes, and individual choice — they can be understood in terms that are consistent with both sorts of analogies.

Because different analogies may imply different policy courses, the choice often has important political consequences. Edelman explores this important role for political metaphors:

> Metaphor, therefore, defines the pattern of perception to which people respond. To speak of deterrence and strike capacity is to perceive war as a game; to speak of legalized murder is to perceive war as a slaughter of human beings; to speak of a struggle for democracy is to perceive war as a vaguely defined instrument for achieving an intensely sought objec-

tive. Each metaphor intensifies selected perceptions and ignores others, thereby helping one to concentrate upon desired consequences of favored public policies and helping one to ignore their unwanted, unthinkable, or irrelevant premises and aftermaths. Each metaphor can be a subtle way of highlighting what one wants to believe and avoiding what one does not wish to face. (1971, 67)

The trick, then, is to understand why it is that we choose — consciously or unconsciously — one analogy over another in any particular context. Cognitive science tells us that analogies work and seem apt when the cognitive representation of the source domain and the novel phenomenon share a common structure. For example, war is easy to think of as a game because war and games share a certain structure: two (or more) players, engaged in a common activity but with opposing objectives, each making strategic choices, and so on. Alcoholism is harder to conceive of as a game because it does not fit that basic structure very well.

In these cases the analogical reasoning is explicit — we frequently consider overtly whether a particular analogy is apt for understanding a new situation. We also often reason analogically without realizing it; in fact, some researchers argue that human cognition generally and the process of categorization in particular are fundamentally analogical — that is, that the way we think is *always* by understanding new things in terms of categories we already know (e.g., Hofstadter 2001).

An important goal of communication by political elites is to promote one understanding of an issue over others, precisely in order to promote a particular policy course. This goal is achieved by framing — the process by which political leaders communicate about issues by emphasizing certain features of an issue, downplaying others, and assembling those features into a coherent narrative with clear implications for policy action. A critical feature of issue frames is that they lend structure to political issues.

Our understandings of race and gender each have a structure as well. They are contained in cognitive structures known as schemas, which contain information about race and gender, including our knowledge of common social stereotypes. They also relate this knowledge into a coherent, structured whole. Our understanding of race goes beyond the knowledge, for example, that African Americans tend to be less wealthy than whites, that discrimination occurs, and so on. It also includes links between those bits of information, say, that African Americans are less well-off *because* they suffer from discrimination. Our schemas for both race and gender contain a rich array of knowledge, emotional reactions, and evaluations knit together into a structured whole.

A political issue frame can create an analogy between an issue and citizens' understanding of race or their understanding of gender; this will happen when the frame structures the issue in a way that matches the structure of race or gender schemas. Chapter 3, therefore, takes up in some detail the structure of those schemas. Race and gender schemas share some characteristics, insofar as they both grow out of our understanding of intergroup relations. Nevertheless, they differ in important ways, including in their abstract structure; these differences grow from the distinctive social structures of gender and race and the different ways that each has been enmeshed in society, politics, and culture through American history.

Drawing on theoretical work on race and gender and on research on prejudice and stereotyping, I develop a picture of the key *structural* features of Americans' cognitive representations of gender and race and specify the differences between the two schemas. Outlining the structure of each schema allows me to specify the characteristics of issue frames that will successfully evoke each analogically. If an issue is framed in a way that matches the structure of the gender schema, then people will apply their thoughts and feelings about gender relations to the issue by analogy. If the issue is framed to match the structure of the racial schema, they will instead apply their thoughts and feelings about race relations to the issue.

Moreover, race and gender are particularly likely to serve as sources for this sort of reasoning because both are very important psychologically and socially, because their associated cognitive representations have rich structures, and because these structures provide strong implications for evaluation and judgment.

Experimental Evidence for Group Implication

Chapter 4 presents experimental evidence for race and gender group implication. These experiments demonstrate group implication in action and explicitly compare racialization and gendering. Participants read artificially constructed newspaper articles about three political issues: grandparent-child visitation rights, Social Security privatization, and government involvement in the economy. The experiment included three conditions: a baseline condition, in which the articles simply described each issue; a race condition, which framed each issue to fit racial schemas; and a gender condition, which framed each issue to fit gender schemas.

The construction of the race-condition articles was subtle and covert and did not mention race directly; rather, each issue was discussed in a way that was *structurally* compatible with the race schema. The experimental results for race implication are strong. These subtle framing manipulations cause important changes in the underpinnings of opinion. When participants read frames that match the structure of the racial schema, their racial beliefs influence opinion.

The gender articles, in contrast, varied in their subtlety. Because there is far less prior research on gendering, compared with racialization, the gender articles varied in the explicitness of their gender implication. This variation conditioned the success and strength of the gender-implicating frames in ways consistent with theory. The most effective gender frames were those that were the most symbolic and covert and that drew attention to public-private distinctions and hierarchical role division. Gender implication was *not* induced by explicit references to the gendered nature of policy making; rather, symbolic references that invoked gender metaphorically led respondents to draw on their gender beliefs in constructing their opinions.

Across the issues, then, the experimental findings indicate that nonracial and nongendered issues can be framed in ways that induce people to evaluate them in terms of their racial or gender predispositions; that the process can be subtle and covert; and that the way a frame structures the issue is crucial to the process.

Survey Evidence for Group Implication

Chapters 5 and 6 analyze actual political discourse in recent American politics and show how this discourse has created group implication — that is, has subtly associated issues with racial or gender considerations. While the control afforded by experimentation provides strong evidence of the mechanisms underlying my argument, the analyses in these chapters demonstrate the prevalence of group implication in actual politics and underline its political importance.

Chapter 5 compares and contrasts the racialization of welfare and

Social Security. The chapter begins by reviewing the framing of welfare and Social Security in political rhetoric over the past fifty years in order to show the ways that framing has structured both issues in ways consistent with the racial schema.

Welfare policy has been symbolically associated with blackness — with laziness, lack of personal responsibility, and perverse incentives. At the same time, Social Security has been linked symbolically with hard work and legitimately earned rewards — values and attributes that are associated symbolically with whiteness in most (white) Americans' racial schemas. This linkage has led to Social Security being viewed implicitly as a "white" program, in much the same way as welfare has been branded as "black."

Then, the heart of the chapter draws on national survey data from 1984 through 2000 to show that white Americans associate *both* issues with race. Using a variety of measures of racial predispositions, I find that racially conservative whites are consistently less supportive of spending on welfare, compared with racially liberal whites. At the same time, racial conservatives are *more* supportive of spending on Social Security than are racial liberals. Moreover, the racialization of welfare turns primarily on whites' views of blacks, whereas the racialization of Social Security turns on white Americans' feelings about their own racial group. Those who feel more warmly toward whites as a group are more supportive of Social Security spending. White Americans implicitly view Social Security as a program for themselves, just as they view welfare as a program for the racial other.

The association of Social Security with whiteness is a little-noted phenomenon that is interesting and important in its own right. This analysis also demonstrates the generality of the mechanisms underlying the more commonly reported findings about the racialization of welfare opinion and shows that group implication matters politically. Group implication is not simply a curiosity in the laboratory. Racialization — often studied in the context of welfare opinion — is more subtle, more pervasive, and more implicit than the welfare example alone might suggest.

*   *   *

Chapter 6 focuses on gender implication and explores opinion on health care. Prior to 1993 mass opinion on health care was not linked with gender predispositions. During the 1993–94 debates over the Clinton health care reform plan, however, supporters and opponents deployed a set of frames that served to link health care with gender in new ways. These linkages were subtle and symbolic, and they unconsciously associated people's feelings about gender relations with their thinking about health care reform. Specifically, I argue that health care reform became gender implicated because the frames suggested that government involvement would interfere metaphorically with intimate power relations within the "private" sphere of health care provision; this interference should be particularly troubling to gender traditionalists.

Again turning to national survey data, I then demonstrate that opinion on government involvement in health care is only slightly associated with gender predispositions over the last several decades, with the striking exception of 1994. In that year opinion becomes much more strongly gendered, with gender traditionalists more opposed to a government role than gender egalitarians. Health care opinion became gendered among both men and women; however, the gendering of health care reform in 1994 was especially pronounced among Democratic identifiers, moving gender-traditionalist Democrats against the plan. This finding suggests that opponents' rhetoric was well suited to obstruct the Clintons' coalition-building efforts.

These results reinforce the argument that group implication is caused by a correspondence in structure between elite frames and mass schemas and that race implication and gender implication are in many ways congruent processes. Thus, gendered issue perceptions can be largely or entirely symbolic and metaphorical: the gender implication of health care opinion in 1993–94 turned not on the fact that women and men have different health needs. Rather, the association of health care reform with gender in highly symbolic ways forged the connection with citizens' gender predispositions. The health care case study also demonstrates that the sharp change in elite framing in 1993 led to a similarly sharp change in the underpinnings of opinion.

Implications

The concluding chapter summarizes the findings of the book and sketches some of its broader implications for the study of political communication and psychology, for the study of race and gender, and for American politics more broadly.

This book contributes to several areas of academic inquiry. First, it

adds to our understanding of the political psychology of opinion formation. Specifically, it deepens our understanding of the circumstances under
which people's ideas about two important dimensions of social stratification — those based on gender and on race — will influence their opinions.
Moreover, it demonstrates that the causes of these influences can be more
subtle, and the effects more extensive, than previous accounts suggest.

Second, this political psychological story contributes to our understanding of political communication and framing. Race and gender
implication result from the interaction between elite stories and mass
understanding; group implication will occur only when the frames created by elites resonate with the knowledge structures held by the mass
public. That is, implicit appeals and cognition play an important role in
public-opinion formation, but that role is moderated by the interaction
between communication strategies and psychological structures. Group
implication can have a substantial impact on support for public policies,
and it can reinforce or undermine broad, cross-issue coalitions. More subtly, under some circumstances group-implicating frames may spark citizens' political interest and engagement; under other circumstances they
may also undermine public deliberation and citizens' ability to evaluate
political discourse critically.

Third, this book adds to our understanding of the roles of race and of
gender in recent American politics. Although there exists a large literature on race and politics, and a separate substantial literature on gender
and politics, relatively little work considers both together. I analyze race
and gender side by side, within a framework that specifies common psychological and communication processes, while also taking account of the
differences in the ways that race and gender are structured in society and
therefore in people's minds. This account suggests that race and gender
group implication are both more subtle and more prevalent in American
politics than we might otherwise surmise.

With some exceptions, the majority of the book focuses on separate,
parallel analyses of race and of gender. In the concluding chapter I connect
my findings with research on intersectionality, or the ways that systems of
stratification interact with each other. I argue that we should often expect
to find race and gender implication operating separately. Nevertheless,
intersectional frames, which draw on race and gender together, do exist
and can powerfully affect both policy opinion and our very understanding
of race and gender themselves.

Finally, the book raises an important normative question. What do we think of a political system in which political discourse, and therefore public attitudes, are, in important and subtle ways, shaped by ideas about gender and about race? As I discuss at the end of the book, the answer to that question is complex and ultimately fairly troubling.

PRIOR WORK ON RACE, GENDER, AND PUBLIC OPINION

Before turning to the psychological theory underlying group implication, I wish to discuss in some detail the differences between my approach and most previous work on race, gender, and opinion. Although both race and gender have appeared prominently in research on opinion, they have done so separately, and the two literatures tend to view the intersection of public opinion, politics, and social structure through different theoretical lenses. In addition, most of the work linking race or gender with opinion has done so at a relatively concrete level. Few have explored the more symbolic role of race or gender — the ways that political discourse can mobilize ideas about race and gender in novel and subtle ways to structure political cognition, even without seeming to talk about race or gender.

Work on race and opinion has focused overwhelmingly on the definition and degree of racial prejudice among white Americans and on the impact of that prejudice on white opinion about political issues surrounding race relations. The starting point for much of this work has been the apparent decline in whites' willingness to endorse blatantly antiblack statements, along with continuing white opposition to concrete steps to improve the position of blacks in America (Schuman et al. 1997). This starting point has spawned literatures on the changing meaning and measurement of racism, debates about the relative roles of racial and nonracial opinion antecedents, and more (Kinder and Sanders 1996; Bobo and Kluegel 1993; Tetlock 1994; Sears, Hensler, and Speer 1979; Kinder and Mendelberg 1995; Sniderman and Hagen 1985; Sniderman and Piazza 1993; Sears 1988; Bobo 1988; Sidanius and Pratto 1999; Sears, Sidanius, and Bobo 2000). A smaller but growing body of work explores the antecedents of black opinion in America (Dawson 1994, 2001; Harris-Lacewell 2004; Sigelman and Welch 1991). And a few analysts have compared blacks and whites directly (Kinder and Winter 2001; Smith and Seltzer 2000; Bobo and Kluegel 1993). There also exists some recent work on public opinion among other groups of color, in particular among Latinos and Latinas and Asian Americans (e.g., De la Garza 1998, 1992; De la Garza, Falcon, and Garcia 1996; Garcia et al. 1989; Dominguez 1994; Leal et al. 2005; Cain, Kiewiet, and Uhlaner 1991; Okamoto 2003; Ong et al. 1994; Oliver and Wong 2003; Wong, Lien, and Conway 2005; Aoki and Nakanishi 2001; Wong 2000; Kim 1999).

A slightly different stream of work, and one closer to my own, has explored the role that racial predispositions play as a basis for whites' opinions on two issues that do not relate *directly* to race relations, with particular focus on welfare and crime (Gilens 1999; Mendelberg 1997; Hurwitz and Peffley 1997, 2005; Peffley, Hurwitz, and Sniderman 1997; Peffley and Hurwitz 2002; Fine and Weis 1998). This body of work demonstrates that white Americans' thoughts about race can be mobilized symbolically as a basis for opinion on issues that are slightly removed from race relations per se. The step is a small one, however, because both welfare and crime are issues that most Americans understand to be closely related with race. If our ideas about race — drawn from lifetimes of socialization and lived experience in a racially conscious society — are as deep and psychologically evocative as I argue, then they should be able to serve as resources for much more subtle and symbolic political rhetoric.[2]

* * *

Work on gender and opinion has developed rather differently. Two major approaches to the study of gender and opinion exist, both of which differ substantially from mine. The first focuses on the gender gap, that is, on opinion differences between men and women. This work begins with Shapiro and Mahajan (1986; for an overview and summary of this vast body of work, see Sapiro 2003, 605–10). Substantial work has also been conducted on the gender gap in voting (e.g., Conover 1988; Cook and Wilcox 1991; Gilens 1988; Manza and Brooks 1998).

Focus on gender gaps has been useful insofar as it has drawn attention to the role of gender in structuring opinion and action in realms removed from questions directly related to sex and gender (e.g., Conover and Sapiro 1993; Kaufmann and Petrocik 1999). This work has tried to sort out the source of gender differences in terms of gender socialization, feminine or feminist values, maternal thinking, and other factors. Although this effort has led to significant theoretical work on the ways that gender ideas and ideologies link with opinion, the focus on the gender gap has in many cases drawn attention away from differences among men and among women and away from similarities between them. This lack of attention is somewhat ironic because it reinforces (and probably grows out of) the idea that male and female are natural categories. In addition, by focusing on aggregate differences, work on the gender gap draws attention away from the psychological processes that link ideas about gender (or feminist values, or maternal thinking, or whatever) with thinking about political issues.

The idea of gender implication arises from a fundamentally different assumption, namely, that gender can influence public opinion for both men and women and that it can operate similarly for both. Of course, insofar as men and women differ in their average support for traditional or egalitarian gender arrangements, gender implication can give rise to a gender gap, but this need not be the case. Again, if gender is as fundamental and pervasive a force in society and in our cognition as I argue, then it should serve as a rich resource for interpreting all manner of political issues. We shall see.

The second approach to gender and opinion focuses on people's understanding of their *own* gender and its impact on political beliefs and behavior. Much of this work has explored the roles played by gender identification and consciousness among women (Gurin, Miller, and Gurin 1980; Tolleson Rinehart 1992; Conover and Sapiro 1993). Though important for opinion, especially among women, identification and consciousness are theoretically distinct from beliefs about appropriate gender arrangements (Tolleson Rinehart 1992, 80), although they are related empirically, with identified or conscious women likely to fall at one extreme or the other of the gender ideology scale (Tolleson Rinehart 1992, chap. 4; for an overview of work in this vein, see Sapiro 2003). My approach differs in that it allows for the analysis of women's and men's opinions in a single framework. Whereas identification and consciousness are clearly very different theoretical constructs among women and men (Fiske and Stevens 1993), cognitive *beliefs* about proper gender roles hold the prospect of operating similarly among men and among women. As a theoretical approach, gender implication lets us both explore gender-opinion connections among both men and women and see how beliefs about gender can serve as a symbolic template for interpreting political issues far from the domain of gender itself.

In addition to adding to our understanding of the links between race and opinion and gender and opinion — considered separately — the joint analysis contributes to the underpopulated category of work that considers both in tandem. One important exception to this sharp separation between race and gender is Mary Jackman's book *The Velvet Glove,* on whose work I build (1994). She simultaneously explores people's understanding of race, gender, and class and argues that the structure of people's beliefs about each — their race, gender, and class ideologies — differ in ways that grow out of the different ways that each is structured *socially.* She explores the implications of these differences for people's understanding of various forms of inequality and for the *different* ways dominant ideologies enforce that inequality within each stratification system. I extend these ideas to explore the ways these different patterns of belief about race and gender can be mobilized in frames to affect opinion on issues well beyond the realms of race and gender themselves.

2

Political Rhetoric Meets Political Psychology

THE PROCESS OF GROUP IMPLICATION

The central question of this chapter is when and how citizens' ideas about race or about gender come to affect their opinions on matters of public policy. Obviously, we expect this situation to occur for issues that impinge directly on matters of race or on matters of gender. For example, in the realm of race, when citizens think about busing to achieve racial integration, or about racial affirmative action in school admissions or hiring, or about more-general "programs to help blacks," we are not surprised that their opinions derive in important ways from their more-general beliefs and feelings about race relations — about whites and about blacks.[1] These policies are designed explicitly to address matters of race relations, and citizens draw on their beliefs and feelings about race when they think about them.

Another set of public policies have been associated with race in citizens' minds even though they do not directly and explicitly invoke race. The most prominent examples are welfare and crime policies. The links between whites' racial attitudes and their opinions on welfare policy have been well documented. Scholars have demonstrated the racialized basis of welfare policy design and implementation, the race coding of rhetoric and media portrayals, and the association of welfare policy with racial considerations in white Americans' minds (e.g., Gilens 1999; Quadagno 1994). Similarly, criminal justice policy making has been associated with race, and white public opinion on crime is associated with racial consider-ations in important ways (e.g., Hurwitz and Peffley 1997; Peffley, Hurwitz, and Sniderman 1997).

Gender issues follow the same patterns, although this area is less thor-oughly researched. It stands to reason that beliefs about proper gender relations are an important ingredient in opinions about the Equal Rights Amendment, for example, which sought explicitly to alter relationships between men and women (e.g., Mansbridge 1986). And some evidence suggests that gender attitudes influence opinion on issues that influence men and women differently in obvious ways — such as child care or abor-tion — even if they are not explicitly aimed at influencing gender roles and behaviors (Luker 1984; Tolleson Rinehart and Josephson 2005; for a review of literature on gender and opinion, see Sapiro 2003). All this evidence makes intuitive sense: people's feelings about race and gender influence their stance on issues that deal directly or indirectly with race or gender relations.

We should expect people's feelings about race and gender to have far broader and deeper effects on opinion. We have rich, well-developed understandings of both, which contain profound implications for how we think about behavior, social interactions, and more. Both race and gender condition our experience of social life, and they both play huge roles in structuring personal and social relationships, political discourse, public policy, and popular culture. Each, therefore, has symbolic implications well beyond its literal domain.

Helen Haste argues that the idea of gender difference is so persistent in part because it serves as a sort of master metaphor that gives meaning to myriad dualities at the center of Western culture, including public-private, rational-intuitive, active-passive, hard-soft, thinking-feeling, and many more (1993; see also Ortner 1974). And Evelyn Brooks Higginbotham makes a similar point about the ways our ideas about race have implica-tions well beyond race itself: "Race serves as a 'global sign,' a 'metalan-guage,' since it speaks about and lends meaning to a host of terms and expressions, to myriad aspects of life that would otherwise fall outside the referential domain of race" (1992, 255).

If race and gender are such important social and psychological con-cepts, if they lend meaning to such a wide array of seemingly unrelated things, then surely they can have powerful effects on political cognition as well. Each provides a somewhat different template for understanding relations between individuals and groups, explanations for outcomes, and prescriptions for behavior. Thus, they can serve as metaphors by which we perceive and evaluate a much wider range of political issues. Under the right circumstances, citizens will draw on their beliefs about race or gender when thinking about politics. This chapter explores the ways that political communication and psychological processes combine to drive this process.

THE PROCESS OF GROUP IMPLICATION

"Group implication" is the term I use for the process through which ideas about social groups — specifically, race and gender — can be applied to political issues that do not involve either directly. Group implication occurs in the interaction between political discourse and individual psychology. As I will discuss in some detail below, I use the term "implication" to make clear that the process is frequently implicit: the discourse need not refer explicitly to race or gender, and individuals may be unaware that their opinion is affected by their views on gender or race. Group implication is a form of reasoning by *analogy,* which occurs through the interaction between psychological *schemas* and rhetorical *frames.* It occurs when rhetorical issue frames lead people to understand political issues by analogy with their cognitive understanding of race or of gender.

Schemas

Schemas are "cognitive structure[s] that represent knowledge about a concept" (Fiske and Taylor 1991, 98). They process, store, and organize information and serve as "subjective theories" about the social world (Markus and Zajonc 1985, 145). Schemas play an active role in perception and cognition and allow people to "go beyond the information given" (Bruner 1957) in thinking about a phenomenon. They therefore play a vital role in perceiving ambiguous phenomena of all sorts, including political issues. As summarized by Eliot Smith, "The primary function of an activated schema is to affect the interpretation of related information. The way ambiguous information is construed and the default values that are assumed for unavailable information are influenced by a schema. Through these interpretive processes, schemas will influence evaluations and other judgments about an object" (1998, 403).

When a person encounters a political issue, some schema is brought to bear to understand it; that schema then influences the basis for evaluating the issue (Smith 1998; Fiske and Linville 1980; on its use in political cognition research, see Conover and Feldman 1984; Kuklinski, Luskin, and Bolland 1991; Lodge et al. 1991).

By filling in information, schemas can lead us to attribute stereotyped characteristics to people on the basis of only their group membership.[2] Research on racial stereotypes has found, for example, that many Americans' schemas for "black person" include such attributes as poor, lazy, aggressive, athletic, and so on (e.g., Dovidio, Evans, and Tyler 1986). In a classic study of the effects of these stereotypes, Duncan found that whites rated an ambiguous shove by a black person as more violent than the same shove by a white person (1976; Sagar and Schofield 1980).

Similarly, gender stereotypes affect perceptions and inferences about men and women. For example, Dunning and Sherman explored people's recall of such sentences as "When Jack found out that his friend had been murdered, he became very upset." People who read that sentence about Jack tended to recall (incorrectly) that he was described as *angry*, whereas people who read an equivalent sentence about "Jill" recalled her as *sad* (1997).

Schemas include the objects in the domain, attributes that describe those objects, and a set of relationships among those attributes that provide structure to the schema. For example, white Americans' schemas for understanding race contain an understanding that white and black racial groups exist (the objects) and contain *attributes* of those racial groups, including those drawn from common cultural stereotypes: that whites are rich, that blacks are athletic, that discrimination occurs against blacks, that whites are hardworking, that blacks are lazy, and so on. Although people vary in their endorsement of these views, it is important to note that everyone is aware of those attributes—prejudiced and unprejudiced alike. Devine, for example, shows that both highly racially prejudiced people and less-prejudiced people are equally aware of cultural racial stereotypes (1989; Devine and Elliot 1995).

For some, this schema also includes a relationship or structural linkage that suggests that blacks are poor *because* they face discrimination and limited opportunities. This linkage leads to structural explanations for poverty that hold individual blacks less responsible for their situation. Others' racial schemas include a different structural link that suggests whites are rich because they work hard and blacks are poor because they are lazy (Wittenbrink, Hilton, and Gist 1998); this linkage tends to lead to an individualist understanding of poverty that holds blacks responsible for their situation (Wittenbrink, Gist, and Hilton 1997). This difference in schema structure will lead people who differ along these lines to make different inferences and evaluations about situations that they perceive in terms of their race schemas.

One important feature of schemas is that they operate implicitly, outside of our conscious awareness (Smith 1998). Greenwald and Banaji draw a distinction between explicit and implicit cognitive processing: explicit thought is that which we are aware of, whereas implicit processing occurs outside of awareness (1995).[3] Explicit and implicit are not completely separate, however. Implicit cognitions can affect our conscious thoughts — they would be of little interest if they did not — but we are not aware of those effects and, therefore, have little if any conscious control over them. For example, people who have their racial schemas primed, or cognitively activated, are more likely to judge ambiguous actions by an African American as aggressive, compared with people whose racial schemas are unprimed (e.g., Sagar and Schofield 1980). This schematic influence happens without the people noticing the effect of their racial predispositions; moreover, it happens without them even being aware of the priming, which can be done subliminally (Greenwald and Banaji 1995).

Schemas, then, are the cognitive structures that contain our knowledge about concepts. These structures play an active role in our perception of phenomena and, in so doing, can influence our understanding and evaluation of those phenomena. Our schemas affect perceptions of people and situations, but they do this unconsciously, so we are not aware of their effects.

Frames

An issue frame is a "central organizing idea or story line that provides meaning to an unfolding strip of events, weaving a connection among them. The frame suggests what the controversy is about, the essence of the issue" (Gamson and Modigliani 1987, 143). An issue frame fits a set of considerations together into a coherent story about the issue. This story, in turn, has implications for how the issue should be evaluated, which considerations are relevant, and which considerations are immaterial.[4]

In short, frames lend structure to political issues. From the mass of undifferentiated facts, perspectives, and other considerations that might plausibly relate to any political issue, an issue frame constructs a narrative with actors, a plot, and a structure. In this process some considerations are put on center stage; others are pushed to the background or left offstage entirely. Most important, the facts of the issue are linked together into a coherent account with implications for how we think about the issue. This process is, in Dennis Chong's words, "the essence of public opinion formation" (1993, 870).

Framing is an important political strategy because frames affect the public's understanding and evaluation of issues. Political elites seek to reorient political conflict in order to build new and larger winning coalitions (Riker 1986). Often they do this by developing new issue frames, which emphasize new or different dimensions of conflict over issues. For example, Jacoby finds that when discussing government spending, Republicans emphasize general appeals, whereas Democrats focus on specific programs (2000). These frames lead to different opinions: when citizens think about spending in general terms, they are substantially less supportive of government spending, compared with thinking about specific programs (Jacoby 2000; see also Feldman and Zaller 1992). There is broad evidence that frames matter for public opinion: people think about issues differently — and come to different opinions on them — depending on the framing they encounter.[5]

We can draw a distinction between explicit and implicit frames, depending on whether they invoke explicit or implicit cognition. Many frames consist of explicit arguments that an issue should be understood in a particular way. For example, the debate surrounding Clarence Thomas's Supreme Court nomination involved explicit framing: activists advocated not just different outcomes but also explicitly for different ways of understanding the issue. Some suggested the issue should be understood in terms of race (a "high-tech lynching," in Thomas's words); others proposed that it should be seen in terms of gender and sexual harassment; still others suggested that it be understood in terms of partisan conflict, judicial philosophy, and more (Morrison 1992).[6] Moreover, these different interpretations — or frames — mattered for the public's understanding of the issue and evaluation of Thomas (Thomas, McCoy, and McBride 1993; Sapiro and Soss 1999). Similarly, many contemporary debates about tactics in the "war on terror" turn explicitly on whether they should be understood in terms of civil liberties or in terms of threat and security. In the current debate, as in past debates about civil liberties, the choice between these two frames matters for opinion (Davis and Silver 2004; Marcus et al. 1995; Chong 1993).

In other cases frames operate more subtly. People use frames to construct a coherent, compelling story about an issue by emphasizing some points and downplaying others while drawing certain connections. In doing so, they need not be explicit about the process. In the context of racial communication, Mendelberg defines explicit racial appeals as messages that "[use] such words as 'blacks,' 'race,' or 'racial' to express anti-black sentiment or to make racially stereotypical or derogatory statements." Implicit racial appeals, on the other hand, "convey the same message as explicit racial appeals, but they replace the racial nouns and adjectives with more oblique references to race. . . . In an implicit racial appeal, the racial message appears to be so coincidental and peripheral that many of its recipients are not aware that it is there" (Mendelberg 2001, 8–9).

More generally, then, an implicit frame is one that has implicit effects, that is, a frame that affects the basis for judgment without the recipient being fully aware of that effect.[7] An implicit gendered frame is one that leads people to evaluate an issue through their gender schema without realizing it; an implicit racial frame leads people to evaluate an issue through their race schema without realizing it.

In fact, frames may be more effective when those promoting them do not emphasize the fact that they are engaged in persuasion. Insofar as the speaker conveys the idea that that a particular frame is the natural and obvious way to view an issue, the frame will be all the more effective. Implicit frames can be quite powerful because people are unable to defend against frames they do not notice.[8]

Joining Frames to Schemas by Analogy

But how do we frame something implicitly? Explicit frames are simple: they involve some more or less outright statement that "the issue must be understood this way." Implicit frames must be more subtle. They work, I suggest, by evoking a particular schema and triggering analogical reasoning that makes people transfer evaluations from the schema to the issue. Schemas, then, are the psychological counterpart of issue frames; the two are joined through analogy. In explaining how this works, I draw from literature on both analogy and metaphor interpretation because both share fundamentally similar cognitive processes.[9]

Analogical or metaphorical reasoning is an important strategy we use to understand and evaluate new situations. When we encounter something we do not understand — such as a new political issue — we attempt to understand it in terms of some other context we do understand. To do this we map knowledge from a source domain to the target we seek to understand. Analogical reasoning, therefore, goes well beyond such standardized test puzzles as "word : sentence :: hand : _____."[10]

Analogy is fundamental to cognition; it is the "ability to think about relational patterns" (Holyoak, Gentner, and Kokinov 2001, 2; see also Hofstadter 2001). Lakoff and colleagues argue that our fundamental perception of reality occurs in terms of basic conceptual metaphors. For example, we generally understand time passing in terms of objects moving through space; this understanding influences both the language we use to talk about time as well as our basic comprehension of what time actually is (Lakoff and Johnson 1980; Lakoff and Turner 1989).

Moreover, people cannot help thinking this way. Glucksberg and colleagues show that people find metaphorical meanings in statements even when they are instructed to consider only literal meaning (Glucksberg, Gildea, and Bookin 1982; see also Glucksberg 1998). In Holyoak and Thagard's words, "Metaphorical interpretation appears to be an obligatory process that accompanies literal processing, rather than an optional process that occurs after literal processing" (1995, 219).

Analogical reasoning is also central to political discourse. One of the central challenges for political leaders is to communicate with the mass citizenry, because for many citizens politics is a remote, abstract, uninteresting, and mysterious terrain (Converse 1964; Delli Carpini and Keeter 1996; Kinder 1983). Leaders who use analogies may help citizens understand abstract political issues in terms of better understood and more interesting domains, making them both comprehensible and compelling (Thompson 1996). For example, President George H. W. Bush deployed a "Saddam-as-Hitler" analogy in the run-up to the Gulf War of 1991. This analogy made a relatively obscure issue much more immediate and concrete for many citizens. It also made clear the correct course of action, not least due to the strong negative emotions people have toward Adolf Hitler (Spellman and Holyoak 1992).

Political analogies frequently draw on domains further removed from politics itself. Blanchette and Dunbar (2001) studied the analogies deployed in political discourse surrounding the 1995 referendum on Québec's independence, for example. They found that the analogies generally relied on the translation of structure from the source domain to the target of the referendum. For example, in the analogies "Québecers don't want to feel at home in the rest of Canada, what they want is to build their own home" and "It's like parents getting a divorce, and maybe the parent you don't like getting custody," there is considerable translation from the domains of construction and of family life, on the one hand, to the politics of confederation on the other.

The "Québec independence as divorce" analogy also highlights the ways that analogies can invoke both cognitive and emotional reactions — another advantage for a political tool. Thagard and Shelley (2001) describe the process by which analogies can transfer both inferences and emotions from source to target in order to produce a positive or negative "gut reaction" to the target phenomenon. They suggest that persuasive arguments — in particular those in politics — trade in these sorts of analogies precisely because emotional transfer creates strong opinions. Thus, the advocate who describes Québec's independence as a divorce intends to draw not just on citizens' cognitive knowledge of divorce — that children's school performance suffers, say — but also on citizens' emotional reactions to divorce as well. (Of course, some people associate divorce with the termination of a painful and dysfunctional relationship that hurts everyone involved; they would presumably draw a different lesson from the analogy. Group implication involves exactly this sort of polarization in the context of implicit, rather than explicit, analogical reasoning.)

We can also see emotional analogies at work in famous historical political communication. For example, delegates to the 1896 Democratic Convention no doubt had strong emotional reactions on hearing the famous words, "We will answer their demand for a gold standard by saying to them, you shall not press down upon the brow of labor this crown of thorns, you shall not crucify mankind upon a cross of gold."[11] For a Christian follower of the Democratic Party in 1896, hearing that the gold standard is a crown of thorns and a cross of gold (two related analogies) is likely to be powerful and compelling and is likely to attach strongly negative thoughts and feelings to it. Certainly William Jennings Bryan knew what he was doing when he used this imagery, rather than focusing solely on the gold standard's effects on inflation, interest rates, and the availability of easy credit for farmers.

* * *

Cognitive science tells us something about the conditions that govern analogical reasoning. The centrally important consideration is that the relational structure of the source and target domain must match. That is, in forming an analogy from a source domain to a target, the important objective is *not* that the two domains are particularly *similar;* rather, the structure of relations among the elements of each domain must be congruent. Thus, for example, Gentner points out that we understand the relation "2:4" as analogous to the relation "3:6" not as the result of any similarity between the numbers 2 and 3 (or between 4 and 6) but rather because the relationship between the first pair (the second is twice the first) is the same as the relationship between the second pair. This structural congruence is why the analogy "two inches is to four inches as three gallons is to six gallons" makes just as much sense as one that deals only in length. Similarly, we understand an analogy such as "an electric battery is like a reservoir" not in terms of the basic similarity between the two but in terms of congruence in the relations among the elements in the domain of batteries and the domain of reservoirs. "The essence of the analogy between batteries and reservoirs is that both store potential energy, release that energy to provide power for systems, etc. We can be quite satisfied with the analogy in spite of the fact that the average battery differs from the average reservoir in size, shape, color, and substance" (Gentner 1983, 156).

When we draw analogies, "whole systems of connected relations are matched from one domain to another" (Holyoak, Gentner, and Kokinov 2001, 3), and the more complex the system that is mapped, the more we are satisfied with the analogy and the more we believe that we understand the target domain (Holyoak and Thagard 1995, 131). When this mapping occurs, the things we know about the one domain are transferred to the other domain. This sort of reasoning "conveys a system of connected knowledge, not a mere assortment of independent facts" (Gentner 1983, 162). It is this *system* of knowledge that makes analogical reasoning useful and interesting for political cognition, because the system often includes causal attributions, positive or negative evaluations, and emotional reactions, all of which can influence the opinion a citizen adopts on an issue.

When Spellman and Holyoak (1992) explored President Bush's 1991 Saddam-Hitler analogy, they found that it led people to map a whole set of objects and characteristics between the geopolitical situations in 1938 and 1991: Saddam was mapped to Hitler; Bush to Churchill; the U.S. to Britain; Kuwait to Poland (or Austria); and Saudi Arabia to France. Of course, part of Bush's purpose in proposing the analogy was to suggest a mapping of attributes — in particular the mapping of such attributes as "expansionistic," "violent," and "genocidal" from Hitler to Saddam. Still, the analogy works not simply to the extent that Saddam is perceived as sharing attributes with Hitler but to the extent that the *set of relations* among the objects in the 1938 system (Hitler, Germany, Poland, and so on) mirror the set of relations among the objects in the 1991 system (Saddam, Iraq, Kuwait, and so on). Equally important, the "Munich schema" also contains a causal argument, that appeasing Hitler led to World War II; when people make the analogy, this causal argument is also transferred to the situation in the Middle East in 1991. This transference generates the inference that if the United States did not respond aggressively, Saddam would continue imperialist expansion in the Middle East in 1991.[12]

Tourangeau and Sternberg's work on metaphor comprehension explores further the way that knowledge is translated from one domain to the other (Sternberg, Tourangeau, and Nigro 1993; Tourangeau and Sternberg 1981; Tourangeau and Sternberg 1982). The authors suggest that people understand concepts, or mental categories, in terms of physical dimensions. For example, they find that people organize the category "land mammals" along dimensions of size, aggressiveness, prestige, and "humanness." Mice are small, not very ferocious, low prestige, and not very human; tigers are medium sized, quite ferocious, high prestige, not very human, and so on. Each animal can be located in terms of these dimensions. Other categories have their own structures, often with at least some of the same dimensions. The category "things that fly," for example, shares the dimensions of size and aggressiveness (hawks and ICBMs are aggressive, blimps and sparrows are not). The authors' experimental studies suggest that people perceive a metaphor as *apt* insofar as the source and target items are located similarly on similar dimensions. Metaphors are *aesthetically pleasing* insofar as the source and target domains are very different from each other.

Consider this example, based on Tourangeau and Sternberg (1981), of three analogies that relate mammals, birds, and world leaders. The relevant dimensions of the subspaces for this example are aggressiveness and prestige:

1 The eagle is the lion of birds.
2 Ronald Reagan is the lion of world leaders.
3 Ronald Reagan is the squirrel of world leaders.

The first is relatively apt, because lions and eagles share relatively high prestige and aggressiveness — that is, the lion is located in the mammal subspace at a point very close to the location of the eagle in the bird subspace. The analogy, however, is not very aesthetically pleasing or insightful because the categories "mammal" and "bird" are quite similar to each other. The second is also apt, because Reagan is also prestigious and aggressive, but it is more insightful than the first because the mammals and world leaders are rather different from each other. The third is not particularly apt, because the squirrel is quite far from Reagan in terms of prestige and aggression.[13] Thus, for an analogy or metaphor to feel apt, the source and target must share important structural dimensions.

Those dimensions, however, can undergo considerable symbolic translation in the application of the metaphor (Tourangeau and Rips 1991). This translation happens trivially in the "Reagan is a lion" example because aggressiveness in the context of lions (a propensity to attack physically) is not literally the same as aggressiveness among leaders, at least not usually. These transformations can be more substantial. For example, Tourangeau and Sternberg studied a metaphor about a fictional politician: "Donald Leavis is the George Wallace of Northern Ireland." Participants took this statement to mean that Leavis was anti-Catholic — this is a translation of Wallace's racism into the Northern Irish context, despite the fact that Wallace was not himself anti-Catholic (Tourangeau and Sternberg 1982).

MAKING GROUP IMPLICATION HAPPEN

Now we have the building blocks for group implication in place: *schemas,* the psychological entities that hold our race and gender predispositions and lend them structure; *frames,* rhetorical devices that lend structure to political issues; and *analogical reasoning,* the cognitive process that transfers inferences and evaluations from one domain to another, such as from a schema to a political issue. I draw on Price and Tewksbury's model of framing to understand how these come together (1997). They argue that two things are necessary for a particular predisposition to influence opinion: it must come to mind, and it must be relevant to the issue. In the case of group implication through implicit framing, I argue that a schema is more likely to come to mind if it is *cognitively accessible,* and it is more likely to seem relevant if the frame constructs the issue to *fit the structure of that schema.* When these two things occur, evaluations from the schema transfer analogically to the issue and influence opinion.

Coming to Mind: Cognitive Accessibility

Cognitive accessibility refers to how easily and quickly a particular schema comes to mind. The more accessible a schema, the more likely it is to affect perception and evaluation. Schemas can be highly accessible for two reasons: because they are chronically accessible for a given individual or because they have been recently activated.

Race and gender schemas are more or less chronically accessible for different people (Bargh and Pratto 1986; Higgins, King, and Mavin 1982; Lau 1989). For some, the gender or race schema is psychologically very prominent and serves as a central organizing principle for much of social reality; these people are described as "schematic" for race or gender. For others, race or gender is less central; these people are less inclined to perceive social settings in terms of gender or race.[14] Sandra Bem finds, for example, that gender schematics tend to recall random words in groups on the basis of gender (e.g., bikini, butterfly, and perfume) rather than semantic category (e.g., bikini, trousers, and sweater), suggesting that they code the words into memory in terms of their gender connotations (1981; see also 1993; Frable and Bem 1985). In the racial domain, Fazio and Dunton show that individuals vary in how likely they are to categorize a target stimulus along a racial dimension (1997), and Levy found that children's race schematicity affects their memory for stereotype-consistent and stereotype-inconsistent features of drawings (2000; see also Runkle 1998).

A schema may also be more or less accessible at any one moment. When we use a particular schema, it is then temporarily more accessible for future use (Smith 1998, 408–9; Fiske and Taylor 1991). Recently activated categories are more likely to be used in subsequent perception and evaluation of ambiguous behaviors (Srull and Wyer 1979, 1980); this effect has also been demonstrated in political contexts both in and out of the laboratory (Iyengar and Kinder 1987; Krosnick and Kinder 1990; Valentino 1999; see, though, Lenz 2006).

Relevance: Structural Fit between Schema and Issue

An accessible schema is more likely to affect issue perception and evaluation. But mere accessibility is not enough; for one thing, many schemas may be accessible at a particular moment for any one person, yet only one will play a role in issue perception. When framing is explicit, an individual can consider and decide the relevance of a particular way of evaluating an issue. For implicit framing and evaluation, the relevance or applicability of a particular schema is conditioned by the congruence between the structures of the schema and the issue. Implicit framing works, therefore, by constructing the issue in a way that is congruent with a particular schema. This allows an implicit analogy to be created between the issue and the schema; this analogy transfers evaluations from the schema to the issue, affecting opinion.

Wittenbrink and colleagues conducted an intriguing experiment that demonstrates this sort of reasoning in the context of an extremely subtle framing that drew an implicit analogy across very different domains (Wittenbrink, Gist, and Hilton 1997). After priming racial stereotypes for some participants, they showed them a series of animated videos involving the interaction of a single fish with a larger group of fish. These videos involved conflict between the fish and the group, but were ambiguous as to the individual fish's and the group's motivations (to the extent, of course, that animated fish can be said to have motives). They found that participants' racial beliefs affected how they interpreted the videos. Those who believe blacks are lazy tended to hold the individual fish responsible for the interactions; those who believe blacks are discriminated against held the group responsible. What was crucial was that structural congruence between schema and situation mattered: racial stereotypes did *not* influence interpretation of a different video that did not involve conflict among the fish.

This study makes clear the extent to which a schema can influence evaluation of a situation that bears little or no surface resemblance to the contents of the schema. In their example, the race relations schema contains cognitions about white and black Americans and the nature of and causes for their interactions. This schema affected interpretation of a cartoon about some fish. Two elements were necessary: accessibility and fit. First, the effect held only among participants who were primed for race — that is, who had the race schema activated and therefore made more accessible than it otherwise would have been. Second, the schema only influenced interpretation of a video that shared a structure with the schema. The race schema includes elements representing minority and majority groups and conflict between those groups. It also has a causal attribution for that conflict and corresponding evaluations of the majority and minority groups. When participants saw a video with that same structure (minority and majority groups of fish and conflict), they applied the schema and transferred the attributions and evaluations from the race schema. When they saw a video with a different structure (no conflict), they did not apply the schema.

*   *   *

This experiment dealt in animated fish videos and racial predispositions. This same basic process can occur for political perception and race or gender predispositions — a process I call group implication. Group implication occurs when a subtly crafted issue frame shapes an issue to match the structure of a cognitively accessible race or gender schema. The issue is then mapped analogically to the race or gender schema, and feelings about race or about gender are transferred back to the issue, influencing evaluation of the issue. The structure of Americans' gender and race schemas are therefore crucial because the match — or lack of match — between structure and rhetoric governs group implication. In the next chapter, I consider the structure of these schemas.

3

American Race and Gender Schemas

This chapter turns to the nature of Americans' race and gender schemas. In the prior chapter I argued that people can engage a schema in perceiving and evaluating a political issue if the issue is framed in a way that makes it match the structure of the schema. The task of this chapter, therefore, is to specify the abstract structure of these two important schemas. These structures reflect the ways — often implicit — that Americans understand and think about race and gender. In other words, the race and gender schemas depend on popular ideologies of race and gender.[1]

A long line of psychological research makes clear that humans have some basic cognitive machinery for making sense of social groups. Social identity theory argues that we develop our sense of self in terms of the groups to which we belong and in contrast to the groups to which we do not. The mere fact of categorization triggers a psychological process of differentiation that leads people to identify with and feel warmly toward the in-group and perceive the out-group negatively (Tajfel and Turner 1979; Tajfel 1982).

Muzafer Sherif demonstrated in his notorious "Robbers Cave" experiments that groups of boys placed in zero-sum competition very quickly and easily develop group identity and strong in-group/out-group effects (1988). Henri Tajfel documents a syndrome of in-group/out-group effects in which people systematically discriminate against an out-group, even at an absolute cost to their own group. Moreover, it takes surprisingly little to get these effects off the ground: even random group assignment can do the trick (1981). He argues that "the reason for this cognitive, behavioral and evaluative intergroup differentiation is in the need that individuals have to provide social meaning through social identity to the intergroup situation, experimental or any other; and that this need is fulfilled through the creation of intergroup differences when such differences do not in fact exist, or the attribution of value to, and the enhancement of, whatever differences that do exist" (1981, 276).

This basic psychological process is only the starting point. The social meanings of race and gender (and of other dimensions of social categorization) go well beyond simply valuing the in-group and derogating the out-group. Rather, these dimensions of social categorization give rise to broad intergroup ideologies. These ideologies are elaborated stories that explain, justify, and normalize the social relations among groups. Although the basic social identity processes are fairly constant across types of groups, the stories that develop out of them can vary considerably.

Intergroup ideologies are shaped in the first case by the structure of relations among groups. Tajfel argues, for example, that a permeable social hierarchy can lead to ideologies of individualism and social mobility in which members of a devalued group seek to join the dominant group, rather than vilify it. Conversely, rigid hierarchy can foster paternalistic or "separate but equal" ideologies that mask the inequalities in very different ways. In explaining intergroup ideologies, Tajfel lays heavy emphasis on the patterns of the social hierarchy and on the perception of the stability and permeability of that hierarchy (1981, 276–87).

Beyond the effects of objective social structure, intergroup ideologies are further shaped through a social process of meaning formation in which members of a culture develop and maintain a shared understanding of group relations. Ideologies of group relations are socially constructed (Berger and Luckmann 1966). This social construction means that the details of particular intergroup beliefs cannot be deduced solely from the psychology of group identity formation. Rather, within a set of psychological constraints, these ideologies develop gradually through time as members of a society attempt to understand and reshape group relations. Their precise structure, therefore, will depend on the objective social structure of group relations, on the strategies pursued by social actors to reshape those ideologies, and on accidents of historical development.

We should expect, therefore, some similarities in intergroup beliefs about race and gender because both have their roots in basic processes of social differentiation and identity development. Nonetheless, we should also expect race and gender beliefs to vary in several ways. The social structures of gender and race are quite different, which constrains their respective ideologies to take different forms. Also, beliefs about race and about gender are the products of different histories of intergroup relations and political action. The particular details of beliefs about race and about gender are the product of centuries of conceptual evolution that compound the basic structural differences between them.

Thus, we should expect race and gender ideologies to differ in important ways cross-culturally. It is well documented that different societies structure race in significantly different ways (Omi and Winant 1994); we would not expect beliefs about the relationships among races and about the nature of race itself to be the same across these contexts. In addition, different societies have different histories of social and political development and attach different salience to group-based categories such as race and gender. All these variations will lead to subtle and not-so-subtle differences in the nature and structure of citizens' beliefs about those groups.

For example, Brazilian and American race relations are structured quite differently. Many analysts have characterized race relations in Brazil as relatively harmonious compared with the United States. Although Brazil certainly has racial stratification and inequality, it has less segregation, more intermarriage, and less hostility between races. Moreover, racial categories themselves are constructed very differently, with much more flexibility and diversity — the "single drop" rule that defines as black anyone with any black heritage is uniquely American.

Much debate surrounds the antecedents of these differences, with analysts drawing attention to historical differences in demographics, economics, the organization of slavery, political action, religion, and democratic ideals (Freyre, Putnam, and Hendrickson 1946; Tannenbaum 1946; Omi and Winant 1994; Winant 2001; Marx 1998; Degler 1971; for a helpful though somewhat dated review of this literature, see Drimmer 1979). And some recent work suggests that Brazilian racial ideologies may not be so benign (e.g., Reichmann 1999; Twine 1998). Nevertheless, the basic points remain that Brazilians' ideas about racial categories and race itself are constructed quite differently from corresponding American ideas and that those differences grow out of historical differences in social structure and processes of social construction.

In addition, we should expect intergroup ideologies to evolve over time. Many analysts have explored the ways that racial categories in the United States have evolved over time in response to social, economic, political, governmental, and institutional changes. Omi and Winant trace changes in the ideology of race — what they call "racial formation" — through American history (1994). Others have explored changes in ideas about who counts as white and have traced that evolution to changes in the political economy of work (Roediger 1999, 2005) and government policy (Brodkin 1998; Katznelson 2005; see also Nobles 2000).

Although important changes occur over time, we should expect them to be relatively gradual, perhaps punctuated by greater change during periods of broader social change or political action.[2] For my purposes, then, I can treat the ideologies of race and of gender as essentially constant. We should keep in mind, however, that nothing is inevitable or transhistorical about either. Although I refer to "the race schema" or "the gender schema," it should be clear from the discussion that follows that each is particular to a greater or lesser extent to the contemporary American context. In the concluding chapter, I will return to the question of how we might expect these schemas to vary cross-culturally and historically and whether and how we might therefore expect them to change in the future.

We should note that to say these schemas are social constructions is not to suggest they are not, simultaneously, "real"; rather, it is to say that there is nothing inevitable about the particular details of their construction and that that construction will reflect the social, cultural, and institutional history of their development. Saying they are constructed does not imply infinitely plastic, nor does it imply unstable; our society's constructions of race and gender are very real in the sense that they *feel* real and that people act on them.[3] Ruth Frankenberg makes this point well: "Race, like gender, is 'real' in the sense that it has real, though changing, effects in the world and real, tangible, and complex impact on individuals' sense of self, experiences, and life chances. In asserting that race and racial difference are socially constructed, I do not minimize their social and political reality, but rather insist that their reality is, precisely, social and political rather than inherent or static" (1993, 11).

At the elite level these structures could be called ideologies of race and gender; at the mass level they are absorbed as a part of race and gender schemas. Because these structures are absorbed implicitly, people may not be able to articulate the logic of the ideology. Nevertheless, this logic will affect perception and evaluation.

Although race and gender schemas should differ from each other, we should expect each to be relatively homogenous because the sources of these schemas are similar for most Americans. An important source for our understanding of race and gender is childhood socialization — as we grow up we are exposed to relatively consistent messages about what race and gender mean (Stockard 1999; Katz 1982; Holmes 1995). We constantly construct and reconstruct race and gender in our day-to-day lives; we are always "doing gender" and "doing race" (West and Zimmerman 1987; Lorber and Farrell 1991). This production is broadly similar for most Americans. And, of course, the media and elite political discourse shape our mental categories as well and play an important role in creating and reinforcing our notions of race and gender categories (Entman and Rojecki 2000; Holtzman 2000).[4]

These points have two important implications for my theory. First, we should expect race and gender to have different structures in our minds; that is, they should have differently shaped schemas. Second, we should expect those schemas to reflect differences in the social structure of race and gender; in the political, cultural, and social discourses that have surrounded each; and in the treatment of each by institutions in American society.

To spell out those structures, therefore, I draw on work on race and gender relations in the United States to lay out what I take to be the centrally important particularities of race and gender schemas (that is, of modern American race and gender schemas). In doing so, I will sketch the schemas at a middle level of abstraction, because my interest is in the ways those abstract structures can be mapped metaphorically to other domains. In this discussion, I will lay out the reasons we should expect each to have a particular shape and the reasons we should expect them to be distinct from each other. The empirical analyses in subsequent chapters will afford the opportunity to test the reality of these distinctions.

STRUCTURE OF THE RACE SCHEMA

There are four important aspects of the racial schema: a division of the world into in-group and out-group that are fundamentally separate from each other; a sense that the groups are different, unequal, and in competition; hostile, negative emotions between the groups; and a dimension along which people vary in their evaluation of this configuration. My discussion and analysis focus on the schema for black-white race relations in contemporary America. As I discuss below, there are good reasons to expect this schema — as opposed to a more general, multiracial one — to be important for political cognition. Nevertheless, an important avenue for future research concerns the effects of racial contexts in society on racial schemas and therefore on issue racialization.

The first major element of this racial schema is the division of the world into in-group and out-group. The tendency to categorize social groups in these terms is psychologically central (Tajfel 1982; Sherif 1988), and although an us-them distinction is not unique to racial schemas, it is an important component (e.g., Hirschfeld 1996; Hamilton and Trolier 1986). American racial segregation imposes a physical, and therefore also a social, distance between whites and blacks. This separation facilitates and reinforces the sense of racial groups as separate and fundamentally different from each other. The white Americans who view the world through the race schema see social groups as divided distinctly into in-groups and out-groups — into "us" and "them." (As we will see, this characteristic sharply contrasts with gender, where the physical proximity and functional interdependence of men and women limits this sense of "us" and "them.")

Second, the white-black racial schema is more than just in-group and out-group: these groups stand in a certain relationship to each other and come with particular attributes. In the American racial schema, one central relationship between whites and blacks is the belief that whites are better off socially and economically compared with blacks. In addition, each group has a series of stereotyped attributes: blacks as lazy, dependent, and poor and whites as hardworking, independent, well-off, and potentially prejudiced (Fiske 1998; Devine 1989; Dovidio, Evans, and Tyler 1986; McCabe and Brannon 2004). These associations have deep roots. Work — and the independent ownership of the fruits of that labor — has historically been at the center of what it has meant to be white in America (Roediger 1999; Harris 1995), and it is by contrast with "black" that the category "white" has evolved over time (Warren and Twine 1997; Brodkin 1998). For whites, these attributes both add to the perceived contrast between racial in- and out-groups and reinforce in-group favoritism.

Moreover, American society is starkly segregated racially, and racial groups are relatively economically and socially independent of each other (Massey and Denton 1993). As I discuss above, this physical and social separation reinforces the idea of group difference. It also facilitates the development of a sense of zero-sum competition between groups, in which gains by one group are seen as necessarily entailing losses for the other.

Third, the perception of zero-sum competition between "us" and "them" leads to hostility and negative emotions between the groups. In a context where people believe that a gain for the out-group means a loss for one's own group, it is understandable that they come to regard members of that group with suspicion and hostility and to view them not simply as different but as a threat. Because whites and blacks are not generally dependent on each other in any direct way, there is no need for the development of ideologies of warmth and compatibility between racial groups. Rather, American racial understanding is dominated by hostile, negative emotions and a sense of zero-sum competition (Entman and Rojecki 2000; Jackman 1994; Sigelman and Welch 1991).[5]

Finally, the race schema includes a set of attributions that link together ideas about work, success, and prejudice and discrimination into a coherent story.[6] These attributions fall into one of two basic patterns. On the one hand are racial conservatives,[7] who attribute inequalities in outcomes between in-group and out-group to individual-level factors such as merit and effort. This "color-blind" perspective denies that race in and of itself means anything, and this group believes, therefore, that African Americans could do just as well as whites if they would only work harder (Gotanda 1995; see also M. Brown 2003; Bonilla-Silva 2003). On the other hand are racial liberals, who are more apt to recognize the existence and impact of white prejudice and of other structural and contextual barriers to achievement and less likely to conceive of racial conflict as inherent or zero sum. They are thus less likely to attribute blacks' position to individual merit or effort; differences are due, in other words, to the continuing effects of historical and current barriers faced by African Americans in American society.

Thus, Americans' racial schemas include implicit arguments about *why* unequal outcomes occur that draw on common stereotypes about black and white Americans. Racial conservatives trace the shortcomings of the out-group to the failures of its individual members. They get what they deserve because they fail to live up to proper standards: in particular, those who fail are likely lazy and dependent, and claims of discrimination are simply an excuse for personal failings. Conversely, the in-group members' individual hard work explains their success. Racial liberals, in contrast, trace the out-group's position to a different set of stereotypical attributes, such as malicious action or neglect by the in-group or institutionally racist practices. Conversely, they do not attribute the in-group's successes to individual moral superiority. For racial liberals, individual-level attributions for the out-group's failures amount to blaming the victim.

Of course, individuals can fall somewhere in between these two ideal types — that is, Americans' racial schemas vary along a dimension that answers the question of why blacks and whites do not achieve equal outcomes. Aside from this variation, however, the race schema should be reasonably homogenous among white Americans, who are all socialized to understand race similarly, are immersed in a relatively consistent culture, and are exposed to largely the same media. Different people will vary in their location on the evaluative continuum — from racial conservatism to racial liberalism — but they should share the same basic schematic structure.[8]

Moreover, mainstream political discourse has reinforced this way of understanding race for decades. Matters of race have been a central feature of recent American political discourse (e.g., Kinder and Sanders 1996); scholars have also explored the ways that racial considerations have subtly permeated the discussion of elections (Mendelberg 1997; Mayer 2002; O'Reilly 1995), issues including welfare and crime (Gilens 1999; Quadagno 1994; Hurwitz and Peffley 1997), and partisan conflict generally (Carmines and Stimson 1989; Edsall and Edsall 1992). White citizens have therefore learned to use it to judge racial issues, to understand political campaigns, and to think about domestic politics generally. All of this means that this racial schema should be cognitively accessible for most white Americans most of the time.

* * *

I expect, therefore, that this schema, or interpretive lens, should help people understand even issues that have nothing to do with race, as long as they are framed to fit the schema. A frame will create this fit when it emphasizes an "us-them" distinction and links the in- and out-groups with attributes and arguments from the racial schema. The key is not that race be mentioned explicitly in conjunction with an issue. Rather, the racial reference is in the structure of the appeal: the competitive us-them dynamic, attributions regarding work and outcomes, and the invocation of a standard of judgment that symbolically links with traditional stereotypes.

Within the racial schema, black Americans are the out-group, and white Americans are the in-group. As I discuss above, however, when the schema is used to perceive a political issue, the characteristics are generalized — the "us" and "them" need not refer to racial groups. The critical factor is the structural mapping. In the case of the race schema, this mapping will involve in-group and out-group with differential outcomes, controversy over individual versus social attributions for outcomes, and negative affect. Once the racial schema is applied to an issue framed in this way, people will apply their beliefs and judgments about race relations — that unequal outcomes are rooted in individual moral failure or in discrimination — to the issue.

STRUCTURE OF THE GENDER SCHEMA

The gender schema has a somewhat different structure, which means it will be engaged by different frames. I focus on four central aspects of the gender schema: the centrality of individual and functional difference, the importance of power, patterns of positive emotional interdependence, and variation in the evaluation of difference and power.[9]

First, the idea of difference between individuals has been central to theoretical understandings of gender for centuries. Because men and women generally inhabit the same physical space, this difference has been elaborated in terms of functional differences rather than in terms of physical distance and separation. Thus, the idea of gender difference gives rise to beliefs about appropriate roles and spheres of activity for men and women and ultimately underlies the distinction between public and private (e.g., Epstein 1988). The mass public also understands gender in terms of difference. Children learn at a very young age about sex differences and are socialized early and often to understand and respect gender differences (Stockard 1999), and the power of the idea of fundamental gender difference is evident in the resilience of the claim of biological bases for all manner of observed sex differences (e.g., Fausto-Sterling 1992).[10]

Second, a central point of feminist theorizing is that gender is more than mere difference; it is fundamentally also about power and dominance. Catharine MacKinnon argues that "construing gender as a difference, termed simply the gender difference, obscures and legitimizes the way gender is imposed by force. . . . The idea of gender difference helps keep the reality of male dominance in place" (1987, 3). Gender is "deeply embedded in the politics of family relations" (Goldner et al. 1998, 556)—it defines appropriate roles, behavior, and power within the family sphere and between the public and private spheres. In turn, dominance relationships in the family sphere both reflect and support dominance relationships in politics and society (e.g., Phillips 1991, 102–4). This supremacy is codified and enforced in laws and in the design and implementation of public policy (Tolleson Rinehart and Josephson 2005, sec. 2; Epstein 1988, chap. 6; Fraser 1989; Mettler 1998; Skocpol 1992). Moreover, people's day-to-day experiences of gender serve to normalize structures of power, dominance, and inequality (e.g., West and Zimmerman 1987; Goffman 1977).

Also important, and in contrast with race, this difference is *not* understood as involving a necessary conflict of interest between men and women. The social structure of gender puts men and women in close contact and makes them economically and socially interdependent. This facilitates the development of a paternalistic ideology that couches the dominance and power relationship as a benign one in which men and women work together — each in his or her assigned role — for the betterment of both. For example, the folk expression "Behind every successful man is a woman" reflects this sort of assumption that, although the man may traditionally be in front, he and his woman work together and both benefit.

Simone de Beauvoir discusses the ways that this intimate construction of gender and the idea of interdependence make it particularly difficult for women to organize politically:

> The reason for this is that women lack concrete means for organizing themselves into a unit which can stand face to face with the correlative unit. They have no past, no history, no religion of their own; and they have no such solidarity of work and interest as that of the proletariat. They are not even promiscuously herded together in the way that creates community feeling among the American Negroes, the ghetto Jews, the workers of Saint-Denis, or the factory hands of Renault. They live dispersed among the

males, attached through residence, housework, economic condition, and social standing to certain men — fathers or husbands — more firmly than they are to other women. If they belong to the bourgeoisie, they feel solidarity with men of that class, not with proletarian women; if they are white, their allegiance is to white men, not to Negro women. (1989, xxv)[11]

This characteristic of close contact and interdependence gives rise to the third element of the gender schema, which relates to the emotional ties spanning the gender divide. Because men and women are generally in close proximity to each other and are dependent on each other, belief systems surrounding gender emphasize positive emotions. Thus, ideas of romantic love, as well as traditional paternalistic beliefs, emphasize the compatibility of men and women, the positive feelings each should have for the other, and the ways that the separation of their functional roles benefit both. This positive emotionality serves to mask patterns of domination and potential (and actual) conflicts of interest between men and women (Jackman 1994; Fiske and Stevens 1993; Glick and Fiske 1999).

The final element of the gender schema turns on an evaluation of the first two: (1) the centrality of individual differences and the articulation of these differences into appropriate spheres of conduct, and (2) the power relationships that operate within and between these differences. Analysts have long noted the centrality of prescription in gender beliefs: these are beliefs not just about how men and women differ but how they *should* differ (Fiske and Stevens 1993). For supporters of traditional gender arrangements, the difference between men and women is fundamental. For some, this fundamental difference springs from divine intention; for others, the root is biological. In fact, these two views are often conflated, as in this 1980 statement by the British minister for social services, quoted by Lewontin and colleagues (Lewontin, Rose, and Kamin 1984, 6): "Quite frankly, I don't think mothers have the same right to work as fathers. If the Lord had intended us to have equal rights to go to work, he wouldn't have created men and women. These are biological facts, young children do depend on their mothers." Whatever its root, gender traditionalists see gender hierarchy as a natural, necessary, and positive outgrowth of that difference.

In contrast, gender egalitarians believe that "the artificial division [of gender] is neither fair nor functional and that it promotes an unfair and unjust system" (Sigel 1996, 15). In short, they point out the dominance and exploitation involved in the paternalistic system of gender relations.

Catharine MacKinnon characterizes these opposing interpretations of gender difference in contrasting her perspective with Phyllis Schlafly's: "We both see substantial differences between the situations of women and of men. She interprets the distinctions as natural or individual. I see them as fundamentally social. She sees them as inevitable or just — or perhaps inevitable *therefore* just — either as good and to be accepted or as individually overcomeable with enough will and application. I see women's situation as unjust, contingent, and imposed" (1987, 21).

The public is also divided along this axis of evaluation. Despite liberalization in gender norms, considerable public debate still exists about gender equality and especially about changes in actual gender arrangements (Huddy, Neely, and LaFay 2000; Sanbonmatsu 2002). Moreover, this axis of disagreement structures political conflict over explicit gender issues, including the Equal Rights Amendment (Mansbridge 1986) and abortion (Luker 1984) and serves as an organizing principle for both liberal and conservative women's organizations (Dworkin 1983).

We can expect men and women to share a common gender schema structure for several reasons. Both men and women undergo similar socialization (boys and girls are taught to assume different positions in the gender system, but they are socialized to the same system), are immersed in essentially the same culture, and watch largely the same media. Moreover, the fact that the social structure puts men and women in close and intimate contact with each other should limit the degree to which they develop radically different understandings of what gender *is*.[12] Men and women may differ in their average location on the evaluative continuum, but they should share the same basic schematic structure.[13]

We should also expect gender schemas to be relatively accessible for most Americans. Matters of gender have made a frequent appearance on the political agenda, including not only the Equal Rights Amendment and abortion, as mentioned above, but also equal pay and family and medical leave (Mathews and De Hart 1990; Luker 1984; Adams 1997; Evans and Nelson 1989), and they have been the focus of partisan conflict as well (e.g., Delli Carpini and Fuchs 1993; Wolbrecht 2000; Sanbonmatsu 2002). Political actors, therefore, do plenty of priming of gender concerns. Thus, although Americans likely vary substantially in the chronic accessibility of their race and gender schemas, both schemas are invoked frequently enough in politics that they should be fairly accessible for a broad cross section of people at any given time.

In summary, then, the gender schema consists of four interconnected elements: (1) beliefs about the centrality of individual differences and the articulation of these differences into appropriate spheres of conduct; (2) beliefs about the power relationships and hierarchy; (3) warm, positive emotions across the lines of difference; and (4) a dimension of evaluation of the first two. Gender traditionalists fall at one end of this dimension; they believe that the differences are natural and that the hierarchy is appropriate, and they therefore oppose change. Gender egalitarians fall at the other end; they believe that the differences are socially constructed and that the hierarchy is inappropriate. Others fall somewhere in the middle.

People may draw on this schema to understand political issues — even issues that have nothing to do with gender — when those issues are framed to fit the gender schema. The key is not an explicit reference to gender; it is in the *structure* of the appeal: the invocation of difference, of power relations, of positive emotions, and of appropriate roles within and across spheres.

SUMMARY OF SCHEMA STRUCTURE

Patricia Hill Collins identifies basic themes that run through American race and gender (and class) ideologies. These ideologies all include the idea of either-or dichotomies in which each part of the dichotomy gains meaning from its relationship to the other. These dichotomies are understood in oppositional terms; the "other" is objectified; and they all involve the domination of one group and subordination of the other (1990, 67–68). Thus, at a very abstract level, race and gender schemas share much: they are both sets of ideas, or ideologies, or stories, about the nature of differences between social groups, about the level (individual or group) at which those difference exist, and about the reasons for and consequences of them. Both ideologies normalize systems of power and inequality. Finally, both schemas include an evaluative dimension along which individuals vary.

Beyond these broad conceptual similarities, though, race and gender ideologies are elaborated in significantly different ways, because they reflect different structures of social relations and different histories of media portrayal, government policy, and political action. The implicit ideology of race grows out of spatial segregation and emphasizes hostile zero-sum competition between groups. Citizens' implicit ideology of gender, on the

TABLE 3.1   Summary of Schema Structures

	RACE SCHEMA	GENDER SCHEMA
Central dimension of difference	In-group/out-group	Individual difference
	Separate physical spheres	Separate functional spheres
Relationship across difference	Different attributes and unequal outcomes	Power, hierarchy, and dominance
	Zero-sum competitive; opposed interests	Interdependent; shared interests
Emotional valence	Hostile (negative and cold)	Paternalistic (positive and warm)
Evaluative dimension	Attribution: Individual vs. structural	Differences: Natural and appropriate vs. artificial and inappropriate

other hand, grows out of the close, intimate nature of much gender inter-action and, therefore, emphasizes individual over group, draws attention to confluence of interests, and veils power and dominance in a shroud of paternalistic warmth. The schemas associated with each ideology also include a dimension of individual variation in which individuals differ in their evaluation of the causes and legitimacy of the state of racial and gender affairs.

The important structural features of the two schemas are summa-rized in table 3.1. In the two schemas the central idea of difference is con-structed in very different ways. Within the racial schema, difference is constructed in terms of physical separation of groups, whereas in the gender schema difference is not really about "us versus them" at all. This difference gives rise to very different constructions of the relationship between groups. Race is understood in terms of competition between incompatible groups, whereas gender is understood in terms of the mutual interdependence of different types of people. Finally, these differences lead to the cold emotional tenor of racial ideologies and the warm nature of gender ideologies.

Both race and gender schemas are psychologically important, and both are available for symbolic, metaphoric association with novel social phenomena, including political issues. Because the schemas differ sig-nificantly in their structure, however, we should expect rather different metaphoric appeals to tap each. In the chapters that follow, I test these expectations.

4

Group Implication in the Laboratory

In chapter 2 I argued that people perceive ambiguous phenomena, including political issues, through schemas. The unconscious choice of schema affects their understanding of the issue, and the schema may suggest grounds for evaluation as well. People can draw on a schema far removed from the stimulus at hand if the issue is framed in a way that structures it to be analogous to the relational structure of that schema. When this framing occurs, the feelings and evaluations from people's schemas can be applied to the issue. We have seen, for example, that study participants' race schemas can even influence their evaluation of a group of fish (Wittenbrink, Gist, and Hilton 1997). But can this happen for political issues? And does it happen in contemporary American politics?

I use two different approaches to answer these two questions. In this chapter I take up the first question: whether group implication can occur when people are exposed to appropriately structured issue frames. Through a set of carefully constructed experiments, I demonstrate that the right sorts of frames do indeed create group implication. Then, in the next two chapters, I take up the second question. Here I use a very different analytic approach: the analysis of nationally representative survey data. These analyses will show that group implication actually happens and that it matters politically. Each of these chapters will explore the frames that have been used in American political debate and will analyze their effects on public opinion. Both approaches — experiment and survey analysis — have strengths and limitations; taken together they reinforce each other to give us a more complete picture of the process and effects of group implication, both psychologically and politically.

This chapter begins with an explanation of the unique advantages of experimental methods for making clear inferences about causes. That is, my experimental results can demonstrate clearly that subtle alterations in issue frames substantially alter the ways people construct their opinions. Then I discuss the artificial (but realistic) frames that I constructed to induce racial and gender group implication and present the specifics of the experiments I conducted. Then, in the heart of the chapter, I present the results, first for racialization and then for gendering. These results have some nuances, though overall they strongly support the claim that very subtle implicit frames can induce group implication.

After presenting the racialization and gendering findings, I conclude the chapter with two additional analyses that put the basic results into broader context. The first further isolates the central mechanism of group implication: structural fit between schema structure and issue frame. This analysis confirms that merely bringing race or gender schemas to mind is *not* enough to cause group implication. Rather, structural fit really is crucial.

The second additional analysis takes up the question of the distinctiveness of the structure of the race and gender schemas. In chapter 3 I argued that the two schemas have different structures. In the final analysis of this chapter, I present direct evidence to support this claim. The subtle racial frames in my experiment do *not* evoke the gender schema, and the subtle gender frames do not evoke the race schema.

EXPERIMENTATION IN POLITICAL PSYCHOLOGY

As I discuss in chapter 2, my theory suggests that different rhetorical issue frames can induce people to perceive issues through different psychological schemas. The schema people use to perceive the issue matters because it suggests the grounds for evaluating the issue. Every political issue is amenable to multiple interpretations. A citizen who thinks about Social Security, for example, might view it in terms of thoughts and feelings about many different things, including the elderly, government spending

in general, intergenerational equity, actuarial imbalance, partisan conflict, and—as I show in chapter 5—race. These different interpretations
matter because they can lead to different opinions for individuals. When
Social Security is framed as a program to help the elderly, citizens who feel
sympathetic toward the elderly will tend to be more favorable toward the
program, and those who are less sympathetic will be less favorable. In contrast, when the program is framed as an example of rampant government
spending, then fiscal conservatives will become less favorable toward
it. Frames also matter because different frames lead to different lines of
opinion cleavage among the public as a whole. The "help-the-elderly"
frame will divide those who are sympathetic toward the elderly (who will
be relatively more favorable toward Social Security) from those who are
less so (who will be relatively less favorable); the "government spending"
frame will divide fiscal conservatives from those who are more supportive
of generous social spending. In short, both people's opinions and the lines
of cleavage on an issue depend on the schema people use to think about it.
The schema used, in turn, depends on the framing of the issue.

This chapter explores this process by looking directly at whether
exposing people to particular issue frames causes them to evaluate issues
differently than they would otherwise. The crucial characteristic of an
experiment is that the investigator controls two elements: the different
materials, or treatments, that different groups of study participants
encounter, and the random assignment of participants to receive one
treatment or another. As noted by Kinder and Palfrey, "By creating the
treatments of interest, the experimenter holds extraneous factors constant and ensures that subjects encounter treatments that differ only in
the designed ways. By assigning subjects to treatments randomly, the
experimenter can be confident (within the limits established by statistical inference) that any differences observed between subjects assigned to
the different treatment conditions *must* be caused by differences in the
treatments themselves" (1993, 11; on experimentation in political science,
see also Druckman et al. 2006; McDermott 2002).

Specifically, I want to demonstrate that certain sorts of frames—those
that implicitly invoke race or gender considerations—alter the *basis* for
opinion. I am not directly concerned, at this point, with whether racialized or gendered frames shift overall opinion (a persuasion effect). Rather,
I am interested in the ways that racialized or gendered frames alter the
conceptual lens through which citizens view a policy and, therefore, the

sorts of predispositions that shape their opinions on that policy. In particular, I expect a racialized issue frame to induce people to evaluate the issue — perhaps unconsciously — in terms of their beliefs and feelings about race, and I expect a gendered frame to induce people to evaluate the issue in terms of their beliefs and feelings about gender. Thus, when an issue becomes racialized, I expect the opinions of racial liberals and racial conservatives to be pushed in opposite directions, creating opinion polarization between these groups. In an analogous way, when an issue becomes gender implicated, I expect gender traditionalists and gender egalitarians to become more polarized on the issue.

To explore this theory I constructed artificial newspaper articles on three different political issues: grandparent visitation laws, Social Security privatization, and government intervention in the economy. I chose these issues because they meet several criteria: they do not deal explicitly with race or gender relations, they were the subject of moderate levels of political debate at the time of the experiment, and they are complex enough to allow for multiple frames, yet not too esoteric for ordinary people to develop and express opinions.

For each issue I constructed three frames, which are contained in three different versions of each article. One set of articles subtly framed each issue to match the relational structure of the race schema; these are the racial treatment. These articles did not mention race explicitly. Rather, they framed each issue in ways that should make it analogous to race schemas — by drawing a distinction between in-group and out-group, suggesting unequal outcomes and negative emotional tenor, and posing controversy over individual or group attributions. The second set of articles subtly framed each issue to match the gender schema. With one exception — discussed below — these articles did not mention gender directly. Instead, they framed each issue in terms structurally consistent with the gender schema: in terms of differences in appropriate spheres of action, power and dominance, and so on. Finally a third, otherwise parallel, set of articles omitted both racializing and gendering content. These articles served as the baseline or control frames.

I assigned study respondents randomly to one of these three conditions: racialized, gendered, or baseline. Because of this random assignment, any systematic differences among the groups must be due to the different treatments they received. In this case, I expect particular sorts of differences. The racial frames should induce participants in the race condition to perceive and evaluate the issues through their racial schemas. Similarly, the gendered frames should induce participants in the gender condition to perceive and evaluate the issues through their gender schemas. The control condition gives us a baseline for comparison with the race and gender conditions.

Though it is impossible to observe directly the schema that people draw on to think about a political issue, we can make inferences about this schema by examining the differences in the relationship between race or gender predispositions and opinion among participants in the different conditions. When a frame leads people to perceive and evaluate an issue through their race schema, for example, then their opinions on the issue will map from their schematic beliefs about race relations. That is, the relationship between racial predispositions and opinion will be systematically different for participants in the racial condition, compared with those in the baseline condition. When exposed to the racial frames, racial liberals and racial conservatives should polarize differently than they do absent those frames. In an analogous fashion, if the gendered frames invoke the gender schema, then the relationship between gender predispositions and opinion should be systematically different for participants in the gender condition, compared with those in the baseline condition.

RACE- AND GENDER-IMPLICATING ISSUE FRAMES

I drew on language from actual newspaper coverage of the issues to construct each version of the articles. The articles were formatted and duplicated to appear as if they came from the *New York Times*.[1] The baseline version of each article included background information about the issue and basic arguments for each side. The race and gender versions added additional discussion of the issue. This additional material invoked race or gender schemas symbolically; with the exception of the gendered economic article, they did not make direct reference to race or gender. Rather, they were designed to make the issue structurally consistent with either the race or gender schema. All the articles had a relatively neutral tone and presented arguments on both sides of each issue. In the sections that follow, I describe the treatments; the full text of all the articles appears in appendix 1.

Issue One: Grandparent Visitation Rights

The visitation issue is based on *Troxel v. Granville,* a 2000 Supreme Court case. At issue was the constitutionality of a Washington state law that allowed a court to grant visitation rights to grandparents or other nonparents who have a significant relationship with a child. I measured opinion on this issue with a Gallup question about support for a possible visitation law in one's state.[2]

The racial article frames the issue in terms of the need to deal with incompetent parents. Visitation laws, the article suggests, are a way for more-responsible adults to have a hand in raising a child. In this account the incompetent or irresponsible parents are described in a way that is structurally resonant with stereotypes about the irresponsibility of African Americans, albeit without any explicit references to race. In this framing, racial liberals should oppose visitation laws as meddling, whereas racial conservatives should favor these laws. The link to race is veiled, but thinly so, through the use of such words as "cities" and "crime." For example, the article states that visitation laws address "parental drug use and crime" and suggests that supporters fear the Court might block "well-thought-out, court-approved visits with other responsible relatives who could provide stability to a child's upbringing." This treatment links visitation with (symbolically white) intervention in (symbolically black) dysfunctional family dynamics.

My expectation, therefore, is that the effect of racial predispositions on policy opinion will differ between the baseline and race conditions. Among those exposed to the racial framing, I expect racial liberals to be more opposed to visitation rights and racial conservatives to be more supportive, compared with those exposed to the baseline article.

The gender-condition article, on the other hand, frames the issue in terms of historical changes in family relationships. It portrays visitation laws as a mechanism to give a legal basis for newer, nontraditional relationships between children and the adults in their lives. Gender liberals should support these changes to traditional family structures and therefore support visitation laws; gender conservatives should oppose them. The article does not mention gender or sex, but the gender framing is thinly veiled because the discussion focuses on families and parenting — topics that are closely linked with gender schemas. For example, supporters of visitation laws are described as fearing that the Court might block "well-thought-out, court-approved visits with former stepparents and others who have a strong relationship with the child, such as ex-partners who cohabitated with the parent and child." This sort of language associates visitation with nontraditional family structures — something gender egalitarians should support and gender traditionalists should oppose. Thus, compared with those in the baseline condition, in the gender condition I expect gender egalitarians to be more supportive of visitation and gender traditionalists more opposed.

We should note that the race and gender treatments for visitation work in opposite directions. That is, compared with the baseline condition, the gender treatment should make gender egalitarianism more positively associated with opinion, and the race treatment should make racial liberalism more negatively associated with opinion. Because race and gender predispositions are correlated, this helps us to disentangle them and to be sure that the effects really are distinct, a matter I return to later in this chapter.

Issue Two: Social Security Privatization

For the second issue, Social Security privatization, the articles focus on the looming funding shortfalls for the program. The articles discuss two possible solutions: either privatizing the program or devoting money from the (then substantial) federal budget surplus to the program.

The survey included three questions to assess opinion for this issue. The first asks whether respondents support a privatization plan that would "take about a third of the Social Security tax now paid by a worker and employer and put that money into a private individual savings account for retirement." The second question asks respondents who they think should manage individual stock market accounts: the government or individuals themselves. Finally, as part of a battery of questions about federal spending levels, the third question asks whether overall spending on Social Security should be increased, decreased, or kept the same.

In the race condition, the article frames Social Security in symbolically white terms. In terms quite similar to the actual framing of Social Security I describe in chapter 5, this article plays up the notion that Social Security is a benefit that hardworking Americans earn. This account is quite symbolic: it describes Social Security recipients in the first person plural to emphasize the in-group link and characterizes them in terms that are symbolically (but not explicitly) racial. For example, the race treatment describes the following testimony before a Social Security reform commission:

> "As baby-boomers approach retirement, we need to devote some of the surplus to Social Security, to ensure that we are all taken care of," suggested Mark Johnson, of the Coalition to Safeguard Our Retirement, a Washington advocacy group. With the first surplus since before World War II, "let us use that money, rather than creating some other new do-gooder government program," he continued. "There is no need to break — and no justification for breaking — the sacred covenant between those of us in the working generation and the retired generation of Americans by privatizing Social Security. . . .
>
> "Social Security is one of the few programs that actually works. It benefits all working Americans. It is a contract we've made with retired Americans and future retirees: if you've worked as a productive member of society, and you have contributed to the Social Security trust fund, then you can get yours back. You will be supported in your golden years."

The article suggests that the program can be saved in either of two ways: by devoting the surplus to Social Security or by privatizing, which would free up the surplus for other programs. Thus, this frame implies that privatization would take public funds away from the Social Security program.

This frame should make Social Security particularly attractive to racial conservatives. Therefore, I expect that this frame will move racial conservatives to favor Social Security spending increases, compared with those in the baseline condition. Conversely, I expect racial liberals who read the race-condition article to favor spending cuts compared with those who read the baseline article.

By suggesting that privatization will take public money away from Social Security (and free it up for "other programs"), the article should move racial conservatives against privatization, compared with the baseline article. Racial liberals who read this article, on the other hand, should favor privatization more, compared with those in the baseline condition. Thus, in the race condition compared with the baseline condition, racial liberalism should be more positively related to support for Social Security privatization and more negatively associated with support for spending on Social Security.

We should note that this mapping of racial conservatism with opposition for privatization runs counter to the traditional opposition of *political* liberals. I did this intentionally in order to have the racialization and gendering operate in opposite directions and to make it easier distinguish the effects of racial and ideological predispositions. I have no theoretical expectations regarding government versus individual management of privatized accounts, so I omit that item from the race analysis.

In the gender frame, as opposed to the racial frame, the article implies symbolically that Social Security is emasculating because it limits people's (implicitly men's) autonomy to care for themselves and their families. The article suggests that privatization would allow people to care for their own and to have control over their own destinies, an argument that should be particularly appealing to gender conservatives. On the other hand, this article also presents the argument that Social Security has helped to equalize the position of various economically vulnerable groups, including women. This claim should be relatively appealing to gender egalitarians.

This account is quite symbolic: it relies on images of power, control, and emasculation and has only limited reference to actual gender or gender relations. This frame is illustrated by the section of the gender treatment that corresponds to the quotation from the race treatment:

> John Bowers, a steelworker from Monroeville, Penn., argued forcefully for privatizing Social Security. "I've provided for my family since I got married as a young man," he said in testimony before the commission. "I don't see why I should be forced to depend on the government to make decisions about my retirement."
>
> His point was echoed by Philip Milkey, a policy analyst with Privatize Now, Inc., who testified that "those who oppose privatization are saying to America's workers, 'some bureaucrat in Washington can decide better than you how to invest your nest egg.' One of the best things about Americans," he continued, "is their independent initiative and self-reliance. We should harness that, not stifle it."

Thus, in the gender condition (compared with the baseline), I expect gender conservatives to be more supportive of privatization, more supportive of individual (rather than government) management of Social Security investments, and less supportive of Social Security spending. Gender egalitarians should demonstrate the opposite pattern. In other words, in the gender condition, gender egalitarianism should be more negatively associated with privatization, and more positively associated with government control and with increased spending, all compared with the baseline condition.

Issue Three: Government's Role in the Economy

The final issue focuses on a central dimension of the New Deal party alignment: the appropriate scope of the government's economic role. The articles discuss the government's appropriate economic role in the context of the strong economy prevalent at the time of the study. I used two questions to measure opinion on this issue: an item from the American National Election Studies (ANES) (2005) that asks about the government's responsibility to ensure people a good job and adequate standard of living and a question about raising the federal minimum wage.

The race frame revolves around whether we as a nation should take public action to extend American prosperity to the poor. Although the targets of this public action are not identified racially, the article positions them in ways that are structurally compatible with racial stereotypes and builds on the racialized discourse on poverty that has existed for a generation or more. The argument in favor of greater government effort suggests that we owe it to society's less fortunate to help them; the argument against more government effort suggests that those who need help despite the strength of the economy probably do not deserve our help. The article therefore implies that the strength of the economy means that the unemployed have only themselves to blame:

> "We don't need the government to be more involved in the economy, because anyone who wants a job and is plausibly attractive to employers can find a job within a half-dozen weeks of searching," argues Philip Russell, of the research group Concerned Americans, "and once those people are absorbed into the labor force, they will gain work experience that will prove attractive to future employers and help them weather the next recession. The private economy is providing opportunity for anyone willing to grasp it."

Thus, racial liberals should support economic intervention, and racial conservatives should oppose it, as always compared with the baseline condition. This pattern means that racial considerations should be more positively linked with support for economic intervention in the race condition, compared with the baseline condition. This frame is relatively heavy-handed; although it does not make explicit reference to blacks and whites, it does position the targets of government help in ways compatible with racial stereotypes, and it uses the racially coded terms "cities" and "poverty."

The gender frame for this issue is different from the other gender frames in that it makes explicit mention of gender. This article indicates that government intervention gets more women into the workforce and suggests that this intervention both promotes equity and sustains the economic expansion. The article presents arguments on both sides of the issue, but both sides frame the debate in terms of women's role in the new economy. Thus, the article quotes a lobbyist who opposes more government effort:

> "We don't need the government to be more involved in the economy. The government has no business pushing mothers — or anyone else — into the work force," said Philip Russell, of the lobbying group Concerned Americans. He cited a poll conducted by *Glamour* magazine, which found that 84 percent of women who were employed full or part time agreed with the statement "If I could afford it, I would rather be at home with my children."

Gender egalitarians, therefore, should be more supportive of government intervention in the economy; gender traditionalists should be less supportive, because it might interfere with traditional family structures. In other words, in the gender condition, gender egalitarianism should be more positively associated with support for government economic intervention, compared with the baseline condition. This issue involves the most explicit invocation of gender: the article frames the issue directly in terms of the effects of government intervention for women and for gender roles.

Explicit versus Implicit Group Implication

As this discussion suggests, the race frames are all fairly implicit. None mentions race; rather, each frame is *structured* to resonate with racial schemas. On the basis of prior research on race and American political discourse, I have strong expectations that relatively subtle and implicit racial frames should work to evoke racial schemas, insofar as they highlight group division, unequal group outcomes, and controversy over individual- versus social-level causes for that inequality (Gilens 1999; Kinder and Sanders 1996).

In contrast, little empirical work has been conducted on how gender ideologies are assimilated metaphorically to political issues, so it is less clear that such subtle gendering frames will work. On the one hand, my theory leads me to expect that schematic effects are unconscious and that implicit frames can effectively shape issues to resonate with gender schemas. On the other hand, subtle gendering in American politics is less well documented and perhaps less prevalent than racialization, so it may take a more blatant frame to forge connections between political issues and gender.

I varied the explicitness of the gender frames to allow a crude test of the most effective gendering strategy. The framing of the economic issue is explicit; the article discusses the effects of government economic intervention on women and on families. Thus, this treatment makes an explicit link to the policy's different impact on men and women, rather than creating a more symbolic structural alignment with the gender schema. The visitation framing is somewhat subtler; although the article does not discuss gender relations explicitly, the nature of the issue inevitably brings up consideration of family. Finally, the framing of the Social Security article is most symbolic and implicit. It does not refer to gender; rather, the treatment indirectly refers to themes of masculinity and self-determination. This rough-and-ready variation in explicitness does not allow for definitive answers, but it does maximize the chances of observing *some* gendering and may give some hints about relative effectiveness.

EXPERIMENTAL PROCEDURES

The articles were embedded in a paper-and-pencil survey that ostensibly concerned selective perception. Participants were assigned to one of the three conditions (baseline, race, or gender) by a random and double-blind procedure, so neither the participants nor I knew which condition they were in. Each respondent read the three articles in a random order.[3]

The Treatments

As I discussed in chapter 2, two preconditions for group implication are that the relevant schema be cognitively accessible and that the frame match the structure of the schema. The treatment—the aspect of the experimental materials that varied across conditions—therefore included two parts to meet these conditions: a multiquestion *prime* to ensure that the relevant schema was cognitively accessible, followed by the three articles that *framed* the issues to match the schema.[4] Thus, the experiment simultaneously manipulated both schema accessibility and the fit between issue and schema. I did this to maximize the amount of data available to discern relatively subtle effects, although it prevented me from testing directly the independent roles of accessibility and fit. Nevertheless, I will present indirect evidence on the importance of fit later in the chapter.

After reading the articles, participants answered several questions about their opinion on each issue (the dependent variable in the analysis) and about bias in the articles (to reinforce the cover story for the experiment). The survey then continued with a long set of additional questions that measured race and gender predispositions, various political predispositions, political knowledge, and basic demographics. Appendix 2 presents the complete question wording and summary statistics for all the survey questions.[5]

Measuring Race and Gender Predispositions

I measured participants' race and gender predispositions using multiple-item measures that capture the structure of each schema and respondents' position on its evaluative dimension (see appendix 3 for a more in-depth discussion of the measurement of race and gender predispositions). For race I used the racial resentment scale (Kinder and Sanders 1996), which captures the complex ways that concerns about race have become written into modern political rhetoric. It taps into a range of elements of the racial schema, including the sense of unequal outcomes, different attributes, and zero-sum competition, and it measures respondents' attributions—individual or structural—for this state of affairs. I measured racial predispositions using a four-item racial resentment battery. For clarity in the discussion that follows, I reversed this scale, and I call it "racial liberalism," rather than racial resentment.

For gender I relied on the Sex Role Egalitarianism Scale (SRES), which measures beliefs about the appropriateness of traditional gender arrangements in contemporary American society (King and King 1997; Beere et al. 1984). These items capture important aspects of the gender schema, including the ideas of difference between the sexes, hierarchical arrangements between men and women, warm confluence of interests, and so on. The SRES also has the advantage, unlike many measures of gender predispositions, of focusing on men *and* women's roles, rather than only on one or the other. The complete SRES includes two different sets of ninety-five items. I used a subset of thirteen items (see appendix 2) in order to keep the survey reasonably short and to avoid tipping respondents off to my particular interest in gender attitudes.

Study Participants

The experiment was completed in the spring of 2000 by 313 University of Michigan undergraduate students. The participants were recruited from introductory and advanced courses in political science and psychology.[6] About two-thirds of the participants were women, three-quarters were white, and the average age was just under twenty.[7] Respondents varied in political affiliation, with about half identifying as Democrats, a quarter as Republicans, and a quarter as independent.

Use of a student sample raises obvious questions about how far I can generalize the results of this study; the concern is that college students are different from the general population in ways that matter for my inferences (Sears 1986). Although one wants to be cautious in generalizing recklessly from any study, I have several reasons to believe that the results from this experiment — college students and all — should be taken seriously. First, although my sample differs in some ways from the nation as a whole, it in fact reflects national variation in race and gender predispositions. Compared with the nation, my participants are younger, less Republican and more independent, more female, and more Asian and less Latino, and they vary less in education (all having completed some college).[8] On the other hand, the distributions of racial and gender predispositions are quite comparable between my participants and national samples.[9]

Second, we are on stronger ground generalizing about the relationships between variables (as opposed to their levels) and in particular about changes in those relationships in response to the treatments.[10] I would not generalize confidently about the average *level* of policy opinion from the experiment to the general population. But this is not my goal. I do not even seek to generalize about the baseline relationship between gender or race ideology and opinions. Rather, I am interested in the ways that different frames engage — or fail to engage — race and gender schemas and thereby change the relationship between race and gender predispositions and opinion. Therefore, my interest is in the way these frames *change the relationship* between predispositions and opinion.

Thus, these experiments that rely on college students are well suited for the task at hand, which is to demonstrate how group implication can be induced by subtly crafted issue frames. This sort of experimental evidence — no matter what the sample — cannot tell us whether and how often these sorts of frames actually occur in political discourse and, if they do, whether they have politically important effects. To answer these important questions, in the next two chapters I will explore two different cases of group implication in action in recent American politics. But first, let us continue with the prior question: whether and how subtly crafted issue frames can induce group implication at all.

Statistical Model and Empirical Expectations

As I discuss above, my basic expectation is that the treatments will change the basis of evaluation for a policy. To test gendering, for example, I run a statistical model that calculates the relationship between gender predispositions and opinion separately among two groups: those in the baseline condition and those in the gender treatment condition. The difference between these relationships indicates how the gender treatment changes opinion formation. This process directly tests the impact of group-implicating frames.

These relationships can be interpreted most easily in graphic form. Figure 4.1 gives a hypothetical example of the sort of plots I will present for the results. It shows the probability of supporting a policy as a function of gender egalitarianism, separately for respondents in the control condition and in the gender condition.[11] The solid line shows this relationship for participants in the control condition. In this example, this line slopes

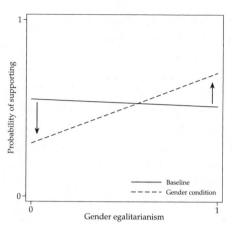

FIGURE 4.1 Example of Gendering of a Hypothetical Issue

slightly downward as we move from gender traditionalists (on the left) to gender egalitarians (on the right). This result indicates that gender egalitarians are slightly less likely than gender traditionalists to support this policy, although the difference is very small. The dashed line shows this same relationship among participants in the gender condition — among, that is, those participants exposed to the gender-implicated framing. In this example the line has a sharp upward slope, indicating that when the issue is framed this way, gender egalitarians are substantially more likely than traditionalists to support this issue. The arrows emphasize the direction of this change — in this case the gender framing had a positive effect on the relationship because the dashed line has a more positive slope than the solid line.

I also report the results of the statistical models themselves in terms of two coefficients. The first, b_1, represents the relationship between the gender ideology and opinion among those in the baseline condition. The second, b_2, represents the *difference* in that relationship among those in the treatment condition. For example, if I predict that the gender condition will lead gender egalitarians to support and gender traditionalists to oppose a policy compared with the control condition — as depicted in figure 4.1 — then I expect the coefficient b_2 to be positive. Conversely, if I expect gender egalitarians to be less supportive of a policy in the gender condition (and gender traditionalists more supportive), again compared with the control condition, then b_2 should be negative. Of course, the

TABLE 4.1   Hypothesized Sign of B_2 Coefficients

	FAVOR VISITATION LAWS	PRIVATIZE SOCIAL SECURITY	GOV'T MANAGE SOC. SEC. ACCOUNTS	INCREASE SOCIAL SECURITY SPENDING	RAISE MINIMUM WAGE	GOV'T JOBS AND STD OF LIVING
Race	−	+	n/a	−	+	+
Gender	+	−	+	+	+	+

analysis of racialization is exactly parallel and involves comparing participants in the race condition with those in the baseline.[12]

Table 4.1 summarizes my expectations for the sign of coefficient b_2 for each model; each of these signs indicates the expected direction for the difference in slopes between the baseline (solid) and treatment (dashed) lines in the figures. For the visitation issue, I expect gender predispositions to be more positively related to opinion under the gender condition than under the baseline condition (just as depicted in figure 4.1). For the race treatment on this issue, conversely, I expect the opposite. Racial considerations should be related to opinion more negatively in the race condition — racial liberals should be less supportive of visitation and racial conservatives should be more supportive of visitation in this condition, compared with the baseline condition.

I need to make two points here. First, I do not necessarily expect the treatments to affect the overall level of support for each policy. That is, my expectation is that they will affect who supports and opposes each policy — the degree of polarization by racial or gender ideology — but not necessarily that they will have a direct persuasive effect. Although group implication will lead some respondents to favor a policy more and others to favor it less, the fact of this polarization is the key. Thus, I do not expect or care whether the dashed line is systematically higher or lower than the solid line. (And, in fact, the treatments had little direct persuasive impact: overall opinion is essentially the same for each issue across the three conditions.)

I also do not have expectations about the baseline relationship between predispositions and opinion — that is, about the slope of the solid line. If the control treatment is truly neutral, then the baseline slope will reflect the degree to which the issue is already gendered (or racialized) for these participants. My interest, rather, is in the difference between the two lines, as indicated by the arrows that show the altered slope.[13]

TABLE 4.2   Experimental Racialization Results

	FAVOR VISITATION LAWS	PRIVATIZE SOCIAL SECURITY	INCREASE SOCIAL SECURITY SPENDING	RAISE MINIMUM WAGE	GOV'T JOBS AND STD OF LIVING
Racial liberalism (b_1)	0.524	−0.650	1.158	0.583	2.500
Racial liberalism × race condition (b_2)	−1.168	0.836	−1.196	1.231	0.315
Hypothesized sign for b_2	−	+	−	+	+
One-sided p for b_2	0.036	0.094	0.045	0.033	0.317

Note: Entries are ordered probit coefficients. B_1 is the coefficient for the baseline condition; b_2 is the change in the impact of racial liberalism on opinion between the race and baseline conditions. Number of cases varies from 210 to 211; complete results are in the Web appendix.

RACE FINDINGS

Table 4.2 summarizes the results of the racialization analysis. The table reports, for each opinion measure, the coefficients b_1 and b_2, the expected sign of the b_2 coefficient, and the one-sided p-value for the coefficient b_2.[14]

The overall pattern of results is encouraging. All the b_2 coefficients are in the expected direction. For all but the government jobs and standard-of-living item, the coefficients are substantively quite large and approach or reach traditional levels of statistical significance. These findings mean that without invoking race explicitly, the treatments influenced the basis of opinion. Those respondents who read the race articles drew on their racial predispositions differently when considering these issues, and they did so in the ways I predicted.

Figure 4.2 translates the coefficients from the first column of the table into the predicted probability that respondents will support visitation. The solid line slopes moderately upward, meaning that in the baseline condition racial liberals are somewhat more likely than racial conservatives to support visitation laws. The dashed line represents the relationship between racial liberalism and visitation opinion among respondents in the race condition. This line slopes downward, indicating that in the race condition racial liberals are somewhat less likely than racial conservatives to support visitation.

The key test is the difference between the slopes of these lines, indicated by the arrows in the graph. In the race condition, unlike the base-

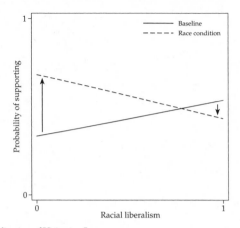

FIGURE 4.2 Racialization of Visitation Laws

line condition, racially liberal respondents were less supportive of visitation than were racial conservatives. For this issue, the treatment changed rather dramatically the basis for opinion and pushed racial conservatives to be much more supportive of visitation ($b_2 = -1.168$, one-sided $p = 0.036$).

The results for Social Security are displayed in figure 4.3. For this issue as well, the solid line indicates that baseline-condition respondents drew on their racial predispositions. Racial liberals were less likely to support privatization and more likely to support additional Social Security spending, compared with racial conservatives. This finding means that Social Security is racialized "naturally" to some extent among these participants.

These associations are altered substantially by the racial framing of the issue. For privatization, $b_2 = 0.836$ ($p = 0.094$), which means that the baseline effect of racial considerations has been nullified or even slightly counteracted by the race treatment. In the race condition, racial liberals are slightly more likely to favor privatization than are racial conservatives, as indicated by the slightly upward-sloping dashed line in the first panel of figure 4.3. In a similar way, the treatment also altered the racial basis for the opinion on increasing Social Security spending, completely nullifying the "natural" racialization so that racial predispositions are essentially unrelated to spending preferences ($b_2 = -1.196$, $p = 0.045$; $b_1 + b_2 = -0.038$). As with visitation, the impacts of the racial framing are quite large, as shown by the differences between the lines in the two panels of

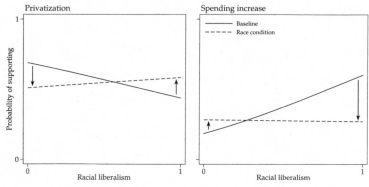

FIGURE 4.3 Racialization of Social Security

figure 4.3. For privatization, the effect is caused by changes at both ends of the racial liberalism scale: in the race condition liberals are more supportive of privatization and conservatives less supportive. For spending, the effect is driven largely by the racially liberal: they become much less supportive of spending for Social Security once it is linked with race.

For the economic issues, the results are less immediately clear. The minimum wage question is racialized as I expect: in the baseline condition it is moderately racialized, with racial liberals supporting an increase in the minimum wage. In the race condition it is much more strongly racialized ($b_2 = 1.231$; $p = 0.033$). The first panel in figure 4.4 shows this graphically. The baseline-condition participants racialize minimum wage moderately, whereas the much steeper race-condition line indicates that the racialized economic article led respondents to consider the minimum wage issue in even more racial terms.

On the jobs question, however, the b_2 coefficient is quite small, indicating that participants in the race and baseline conditions racialize it similarly. The reason for this result is that the jobs question is extremely racialized already in the baseline condition ($b_1 = 2.500$), indicating that racially conservative participants are far less supportive of government intervention to ensure jobs and a good standard of living. This baseline racialization creates a ceiling effect that limits the additional framing that might be possible in the race condition. The nonresult may not reflect a failure of the framing so much as the fact that there is simply little room for additional racialization, given the powerful racialization already present among those in the baseline condition.

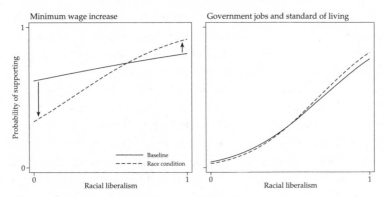

FIGURE 4.4 Racialization of Government Economic Role

This interpretation is supported by the results when participants are divided into groups that tend to racialize the jobs question less in the baseline condition. For example, women racialize the economic issue a bit less in the baseline condition (b_1 = 2.112) and are affected by the racial framing a bit more (b_2 = 0.581), although the framing effect is still not statistically significant. (Full results for these analyses appear in the Web appendix.) Even more striking are the differences between party identifiers. Republicans racialize less in the baseline condition (b_1 = 1.703) but are very influenced by the racial framing (b_2 = 2.865, one-sided p = 0.027), whereas Democrats racialize more in the baseline condition (b_1 = 2.841) and are relatively unaffected by the framing (b_2 = −0.651, n.s.). These result suggest that among groups of respondents who are less naturally inclined to racialize the jobs item (women and Republicans), the treatment elicits racial considerations. Among those respondents who strongly racialize the jobs item anyway, the treatment has little additional effect.

* * *

The jobs question aside, these results are consistent and strong, and because participants were randomly assigned to conditions, I can be confident that the differences between the conditions were caused by the treatments. Nevertheless, one could still question what the treatments really are—what schema they really tap. I argue that they evoke the race schema, but one might argue that the race treatments are in fact evoking ideological considerations.

There are several reasons to worry about this possibility. A close connection has existed between racial politics and partisan ideological conflict (Carmines and Stimson 1989; Edsall and Edsall 1992); debate over individual versus social locus of causality is an element of both racial and ideological disputes; and some analysts have argued that my measure of the racial schema (racial resentment) is connected closely with nonracial conservatism (e.g., Tetlock 1994; Sniderman and Piazza 1993).

To address this possibility, I explored whether the articles affected the relationship between opinion and ideological predispositions, in addition to or instead of affecting the relationship between opinion and racial predispositions. The results of this analysis, which appear in full in appendix 4, are clear. The racialization effects that I report above are unaffected by the inclusion of these control variables. To be sure, ideology is related to opinion for some issues and is engaged by some of the treatments as well. Nevertheless, the estimated degree of racialization is essentially the same across the various issues and control variables. These results make clear that the racializing frames really are tapping into racial predispositions.[15]

GENDER FINDINGS

Table 4.3 summarizes the basic results from the gendering analysis. As with table 4.2, it reports coefficients b_1 and b_2 from each model, the expected sign of b_2, and the one-sided p-value for b_2. All but one of the

TABLE 4.3   Experimental Gendering Results

	FAVOR VISITA- TION LAWS	PRIVATIZE SOCIAL SECURITY	GOV'T MANAGE SOC. SEC. ACCOUNTS	INCREASE SOCIAL SECURITY SPENDING	RAISE MINIMUM WAGE	GOV'T JOBS AND STD OF LIVING
Gender egalitarianism (b_1)	0.586	−0.576	−1.571	0.684	0.503	0.746
Gender egalitarianism × gender condition (b_2)	0.748	−1.644	1.823	0.769	0.366	−0.273
Hypothesized sign for b_2	+	−	+	+	+	+
One-sided p for b_2	0.245	0.067	0.053	0.264	0.374	0.401

Note: Entries are ordered probit coefficients. B_1 is the coefficient for the baseline condition; b_2 is the change in the impact of gender egalitarianism on opinion between gender and baseline conditions. Number of cases varies from 202 to 207; complete results are in the Web appendix.

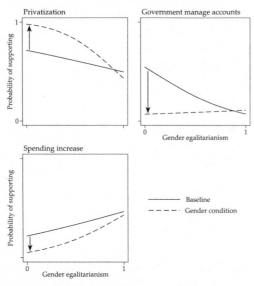

FIGURE 4.5 Gendering of Social Security

b_2 coefficients are again in the predicted direction, and most are substantively relatively large; nevertheless, the results are less clear-cut than those for racialization. Results are fairly clear for Social Security, more muddied for visitation, and downright opaque for the economic issue. At first glance, at least, the experimental gendering was less successful than the racialization.

The gendering results are strongest for Social Security. On privatization, baseline respondents associated gender considerations with opinion a bit, so gender egalitarians were somewhat less supportive of privatization than gender traditionalists. In the gender condition, on the other hand, when respondents saw the issue framed in symbolically gendered terms, the influence of gender considerations changed dramatically (b_2 = -1.644, one-sided p = 0.067). The first panel in figure 4.5 shows this graphically. The much steeper dashed line for the gender condition indicates that gender considerations play a much stronger role in privatization opinion in this condition; this effect is driven by gender traditionalists liking privatization more when they are induced to think about it in gendered terms.

Turning to the question of who should manage private accounts, we see that in the baseline condition gender egalitarians are much less support-

69

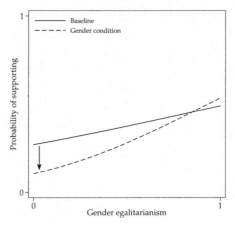

FIGURE 4.6 Gendering of Visitation Laws

ive of a government role. The gender framing eliminates this relationship entirely, as expected. The second panel in figure 4.5 shows that the gender treatment alters traditionalists' opinions dramatically, so they are no more likely than egalitarians to support government management ($b_2 = 1.823$, one-sided $p = 0.053$). Finally, the results for Social Security spending are consistent with the others, although smaller and less clear statistically. The item is gendered a bit in the baseline condition, with gender egalitarians more likely to support additional spending. The gender frame strengthens this gendering, as expected, although the framing effect is not statistically clear ($b_2 = 0.769$, n.s.). The somewhat stronger net gendering is shown by the steeper dashed line in the third panel of the figure.

The visitation framing was less successful. In the baseline condition visitation is perhaps slightly gendered ($b_1 = 0.586$, n.s.), and the gender treatment seems to increase this a bit, as expected, although the result does not approach statistical significance ($b_2 = 0.748$, one-sided $p = 0.245$). The net gendering in the gender condition is $b_1 + b_2 = 1.335$ (two-sided $p = 0.094$); this result is represented by the more steeply sloped line in figure 4.6.

One possible reason for this weak effect for the gender framing may be that the visitation issue is easy to associate with gender, even for some respondents in the baseline condition. Grandparent visitation involves family relationships; perhaps participants who are gender schematic (i.e., for whom the gender schema is chronically accessible) might view the issue through a gendered lens, regardless of which article they read. In other words, even without a gendered frame some respondents may understand this issue in ways that fit their gender schemas. This possibility makes it harder to perceive the effects of the gender article.[16] If this is the case, we would expect gender schematics to associate this issue with their gender predispositions, regardless of the article they read, because they are very inclined to draw on their gender schemas. Conversely, other respondents — who are not chronically prone to interpreting the social world through their gender schemas — should react to the gendering article as I expect.

It would be ideal at this point to use a separate measure of gender schematicity to separate cleanly the gender schematics from the nonschematics among study participants. Unfortunately, the study did not include any direct measures of gender (or race) schematicity. Still, I can make opportunistic use of one measure that was included in the study to shed some light on this possibility. One question asked whether respondents identify with feminists; this question lets me identify at least some likely gender schematics, because those who identify with feminists are likely to be gender schematic. Therefore, I examined the impact of gender framing separately among feminist identifiers and nonidentifiers. Clearly, this approach is not perfect: although feminist identifiers are probably relatively gender schematic, many gender schematics certainly do not identify with feminists. Nevertheless, it is a serviceable measure, as the results that follow indicate.

The results are consistent with this interpretation, as shown in figure 4.7. The left panel shows that this issue is strongly gendered by feminists, regardless of the article they read. The right panel shows that the gender framing had a substantial effect among nonfeminists. For nonfeminists exposed to the baseline condition, essentially no relationship exists between gender egalitarianism and opinion; among nonfeminists exposed to the gendered framing the relationship is much larger.[17] This analysis, although less than ideal, is consistent with the basic claim that the gender visitation treatment did induce group implication among a set of less-schematic respondents.[18]

Finally, the gender framing for the economic issues failed to influence the basis of opinion at all. Neither the minimum wage nor the government jobs and standard-of-living question is particularly gendered in the baseline condition, and neither is affected by the gender treatment (b_2 = 0.366 and −0.273 respectively). Figure 4.8 tells this story graphically: the relationship between gender egalitarianism and opinion is shallow for

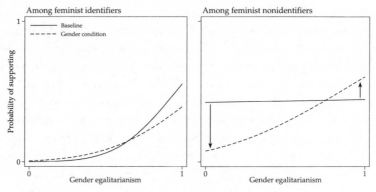

FIGURE 4.7 Gendering of Visitation Laws by Feminist Identification

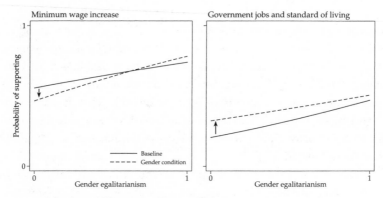

FIGURE 4.8 Gendering of Government Economic Role

both issues and is essentially identical across conditions.[19] Recall that the gendered framing for this issue was by far the most explicit. The treatment stated directly that one important justification for government economic intervention was to address gender inequality. This explicit argument did not lead respondents to evaluate the issue through their gender schemas. Rather, the most successful frames were more subtle and emphasized the symbolic fit with the schema.

Overall, then, the gendering experiment met with positive but mixed results. The Social Security treatment worked as I expected: the invocation of subtle and implicit gender implication led respondents to frame various aspects of the issue in gender terms. The visitation treatment presented a somewhat less clear, partially successful case. The results among all respondents were in the expected direction, but weakly so. Nonetheless, among nonfeminist respondents, who were less likely to gender the issue as a matter of course, the relatively subtle gender implication of the gender treatment did induce them to reframe the issue in terms of gender. Finally, the economic treatment, which invoked gender most explicitly, failed completely to influence participants' framing of the issue. This finding means that explicitly invoking gender in the treatment does not lead people to gender the issue, at least in this case. It seems that, as with racialization, the link with gender must be made symbolically and implicitly.

* * *

As with the racialization analysis, an additional concern is that the treatments evoke something other than the gender schema as I claim. The clearest possibility for the gender case is that the treatments might tap into a generalized distrust of authority and government, rather than gender in particular. The relationship between citizens and government can be understood in familial terms (Lakoff 1996), so perhaps the gender treatments simply tap into beliefs about the importance of limiting the scope and power of authority in political terms, rather than more-symbolic ideas about gender authority. This possibility is a particular concern for the Social Security issue, because the gender article for Social Security raises explicit concerns about "government bureaucrats" having too much power. To examine this possibility, I explored the effect of the gender treatments simultaneously on gender egalitarianism and support for limited government. The results of this analysis, which appear in appendix 4, indicate that the framed articles really are evoking the gender schema, not some broader concerns about the scope of government. Although endorsement of limited government is related to policy opinion for most of the issues in the baseline condition, the gender treatment had little or no effect on those relationships. Most important, the gendering effect of the treatments is about the same even when limited government is included in the model. These findings reassure us that the gender treatments for Social Security and visitation really do tap into gender schemas.[20]

THE IMPORTANCE OF STRUCTURAL FIT

Despite some nuances, these experimental results are strong, and they support the theoretical expectation that subtly crafted issue frames can

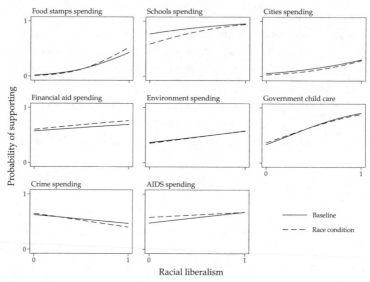

FIGURE 4.9 Racialization of Other Issues

induce group implication. Because the prime and the fit were confounded in the treatments, we have no direct way to assess the separate effects of each on the results.[21] Nevertheless, I can explore their separate effects indirectly.

If priming race schemas is enough to induce racial group implication, then the race treatments should racialize a wide range of issues in addition to the three discussed in the articles. And if priming gender is enough to induce gender group implication, then the gender treatments should associate gender ideology with a broad range of issues beyond those discussed in the articles. On the other hand, if structural fit is necessary for group implication, then the racialization and gendering results should be limited to the issues that were framed to fit the schemas by the articles. Other issues should *not* systematically become racialized in the race condition or gendered in the gender condition. To test this, I reran the basic analyses, substituting a range of other policy questions that appeared in the survey.

For racialization, these analyses make clear that the prime alone is not enough. Figure 4.9 shows the results of the now-familiar racialization analysis, conducted on a series of policies that were not discussed in the articles and that were not highly racialized in the baseline condition.[22]

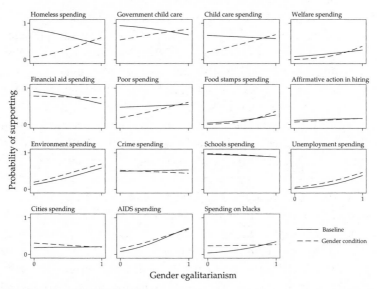

FIGURE 4.10 Gendering of Other Issues

(A table with the b_1 and b_2 coefficients, analogous to those in table 4.2, appears in appendix 5 as table A5.1.) The crucial concern is the effect of the treatments on opinion on these issues. If the prime alone is sufficient to racialize issues, we would expect big differences between the solid and dashed lines, in the positive direction. In fact, this is not the case at all. Although some issues are racialized to some extent in the baseline condition, as we might expect, the treatments had essentially no effects on their racialization. The differences between solid and dashed lines are small, in the wrong direction more than half the time, and not statistically significant. These results are clear evidence that the fit between issue and schema — as created by the frames in the articles — is necessary for racialization.

The results for gendering are slightly more mixed, although broadly supportive of the importance of fit for group implication. Figure 4.10 presents the relevant results. (Again, the coefficients appear in appendix 5 as table A5.2.) The pattern of results across the fifteen issues is not entirely clear. If simply bringing the gender schema to mind causes gender group implication, then we would expect the difference between baseline and gender conditions to be positive for these issues. For nine of the issues this was the case. For several of these nine, the treatment had important effects—important differences exist between the solid and dashed lines. For two of the issues—homeless spending and government child care—the impact of the treatment is statistically significant and in the direction we might expect, and in other cases the differences are moderately large, albeit not statistically significant. For six other issues the impact was negative, which is the opposite of what we would expect. So although priming the gender schema did not result in wholesale gendering of these policies, the evidence suggests some priming effect may be at work. The average b_2 coefficient across the fifteen issues is 0.530, compared with an average of -0.128 in the race analysis.

The issues that were most affected by the gender treatment can be considered to invoke elements of compassion (child care, the poor, financial aid) and so might be seen as "women's issues" by participants when gender schemas are cognitively accessible. This result might indicate that a range of social welfare issues are open to gendered interpretation, given mere availability of the gender schema. On the other hand, we should not make too much of these findings, as the effects are usually small and are not consistent across issues. For example, we might expect spending on schools, the unemployed, and AIDS to follow the same pattern; they do not. Nevertheless, it seems possible that gender is somewhat more susceptible than race to a simple priming effect, at least for some types of issues. The stronger results presented above for the experimental issues do suggest, however, that the *combination* of prime and fit carries the most impact.

INTERSECTIONALITY AND THE DISTINCTIVENESS OF RACE AND GENDER IMPLICATION

These additional analyses increase our confidence that the fit between frame and schema is necessary for group implication and that the frames really are evoking race and gender predispositions. One final question remains, then: whether race and gender predispositions themselves are completely distinct. So far we have treated race and gender predispositions independently: each is taken up one at a time. We have several reasons to suppose that they are more connected. First, group implication might evoke not separate race and gender schemas but rather some single, more general group schema. In this case, what I call "racial group implication" and "gender group implication" are psychologically exactly the same process in the sense that they evoke the same schema. Second, people might have separate race and gender schemas, but possibly they are so closely connected that evoking one inevitably activates the other as well. After all, race and gender are related in the simple empirical sense that individuals' views about race and about gender are correlated.

A more substantive concern is that race and gender are related structures of social stratification. Although each has distinct features, they also share a complex, interrelated history. Scholars of intersectionality argue that we cannot fully understand either in isolation because race and gender categories permeate each other. This argument means, for example, that the experience of race for African Americans is in important ways conditioned by the gender context; the experience of gender for whites is conditioned in important — if often overlooked — racial ways; and so on. Moreover, many powerful political images, such as the "welfare queen," invoke complexly intertwined elements of race and gender (e.g., Hancock 2004).

For all these reasons we might not find it meaningful to speak of race and gender implication as distinct processes. People's understanding of these two systems of social classification and hierarchy may be closely connected, either through their shared history or simply by both being examples of the general category of group relations. We can reasonably question, then, the degree to which the implication of one system influences the other in people's minds. That is, what effect, if any, does a racially charged discourse have on the relationship between people's gender predispositions and their policy opinions? Conversely, does a gender-implicated discourse affect the linkage between racial ideas and opinion?

These effects might work in one of two ways. On the one hand, schema theory suggests that schemas are relatively autonomous mental structures. Therefore, race and gender schemas should be distinct enough in people's minds that invoking one does not automatically invoke the other. On the other hand, race and gender may simply be specific examples of an overarching "group" schema. In this case, implicating one should implicate the other, at least to some extent. If so, then the claims I make about the distinctiveness of the two schemas may be overdrawn.

I can address this question by estimating the effect of each treatment on both race and gender predispositions at once. The basic strategy is to estimate one model for each issue that includes both race and gender predispositions, along with interaction terms between each predisposition and each group-implicated condition.[23] In this model, b_2 and b_5 estimate racialization and gendering, respectively. They are completely analogous to the b_2 coefficients from the separate racialization and gendering models estimated so far. The b_3 coefficient estimates the influence of the *gender* articles on *racial* predispositions — the degree to which the gender articles affect the link between racial predispositions and opinion. Analogously, the b_6 coefficient estimates the effect of the *race* articles on the relationship between *gender* predispositions and opinion.[24] These two coefficients — b_3 and b_6 — are the ones of interest in this analysis. If racialization and gendering are distinct processes, as I argue, then these coefficients should be essentially zero.

Unfortunately, the resulting model is extremely unstable, because the variables and interaction terms are highly correlated. The estimates of the basic gendering and racialization effects are consistent with those from the separate models, although more noisily estimated. The "cross-condition" estimates — b_3 and b_6 — bounce around from issue to issue, seemingly randomly. For some cases, the cross-condition coefficients are large and significant; in others, they are not. Moreover, the direction of these effects is inconsistent. Because there are only six dependent variables, it is impossible generalize about the nature of the cross-condition effects. The results could be driven by noise, or they could be driven by complex interactions between the specific issues and the specific frames.

It is possible, however, to step back from the blizzard of the issue-by-issue results to consider the shape of the snowdrifts. By creating a composite dependent variable from several of the specific policies, I can average out the idiosyncratic, issue-specific effects. To do this I averaged together three of the opinion variables: visitation, privatization of Social Security, and Social Security spending. For this combined variable my expectation is that the racialization effect of the race treatment will be negative and the gendering effect of the gender treatment will be positive. I expect that the race treatment will not have a gendering effect and that the gender treatment will not have a racializing effect.[25]

Table 4.4 shows the results of the analysis of this composite policy variable. The first two columns present separate analyses of racialization and of gendering for this variable. These results are completely analogous to the analyses presented so far. As we would expect, both racialization and gendering occur in the expected direction (as demonstrated by b_2 in the

TABLE 4.4   Comparison of Separate and Simultaneous Racialization and Gendering Analyses

	COMPOSITE POLICY OPINION		
	A	B	C
Racial liberalism (b_1)	1.142^{**}	—	1.022^{**}
Racial liberalism × race condition (b_2)	-1.577^{***}	—	-1.621^{**}
Racial liberalism × gender condition (b_3)	—	—	-0.043
Gender egalitarianism (b_4)	—	$1.002^{\wedge}$	0.469
Gender egalitarianism × gender condition (b_5)	—	$1.541^{\wedge}$	$1.668^{\wedge}$
Gender egalitarianism × race condition (b_6)	—	—	0.203
Race condition (b_7)	0.845^{**}	—	0.694
Gender condition (b_8)	—	$-1.442^{\wedge}$	-1.515^{*}
N	212	207	311
χ^2	8.100	14.178	24.978
Degrees of freedom	3	3	8

Note: Entries are ordered probit coefficients. Column A includes respondents in baseline and race conditions; B includes baseline and gender; C includes all conditions.
*** p < 0.01; ** p < 0.05; * p < 0.1; $^{\wedge}$ p < 0.2 two-sided.

first column and b_6 in the second). The third column of the table presents the simultaneous analysis. The first thing to notice is that the basic racialization and gendering results are entirely unaffected by the inclusion of the "cross" conditions. Racialization is -1.621 in the combined analysis, compared with -1.577 in the separate analysis. Gendering is 1.668 in the combined analysis, compared with 1.541 in the separate analysis.

The most interesting and important result is that the cross-condition coefficients are essentially zero. This result indicates that on average the racial treatments do not evoke gender predispositions, and on average the gender treatments do not evoke racial predispositions. Although the cross-condition coefficients bounce around from issue to issue, there is no systematic effect of racialized policy discourse on the gender schema and no systematic effect of gendered discourse on the racial schema. In other words, the schemas are cognitively distinct enough that discourse that fits one of them does not necessarily evoke the other. Of course, we can certainly imagine discourse that does evoke both schemas at once. Indeed, it seems likely that some of the language in the various articles in the experiment does just that, which explains why some issues do experience seemingly random cross-condition effects. The point here, however, is that racialized and gendered discourses do not inevitably and systematically evoke each other and that there are psychologically (and therefore politically) significant differences between the two schemas.

SUMMARY

This chapter has presented strong evidence for my model of group implication. In the racial realm, very subtle racial implication, with no explicit
mention of race and no plausible explicit link to race for participants,
was able to shift the basis of evaluation toward racial considerations. This
finding suggests that racial schemas are both close to the surface and positioned cognitively for easy assimilation to political matters. No doubt
America's long history of racial conflict and racialized political discourse
since the civil rights era — if not since the founding — make this so.

In the realm of gender, the results also support the theoretical model.
Again, quite subtle and implicit implication of gender affected the basis
for evaluation of two of the three issues. The pattern of success and failure
here is instructive. The most successful frame, on Social Security, was the
one with the most symbolic gender implication. The framing in this article
focused on the public-private aspect of the gender schema and referred
implicitly to the warm emotional connection within the private realm.
Visitation lay at a midpoint: the gender implication was somewhat more
explicit, mostly because the issue itself refers to family dynamics, which
may automatically evoke gender for some participants. The treatment
focused on the public-private distinction to some extent and on appropriate gender roles. Finally, the economic issue was explicitly framed in gender terms: the article referred directly to the effects of government policy
on women. It did not draw so much on the deeper structural aspects of
the gender schema; rather, it referred to women directly. Although I cannot draw firm general conclusions from these three frames alone, the pattern of results reinforces the point that symbolic, structural frames are
most effective at forging group implication. The economic treatment,
unlike the others, made an explicit claim about the domain that should
be used to evaluate the issue, rather than crafting a fit between the issue
and the domain — an explicit claim, it seems, that participants rejected or
found irrelevant. The more symbolic and structural frames for the other
issues were more effective.

Most important, these results matter. Although the treatments did
not persuade people in the aggregate, the results show that by reframing
the issues we can change the types of people who favor and oppose each
policy. This finding means that framing of the sort demonstrated here
can be useful to strategic politicians in the real world, beyond the labo-

ratory. Although I obviously cannot extrapolate my model coefficients directly to the general population, I can use my results to imagine the sorts of effects my findings imply. For example, the visitation issue does not polarize racial liberals and conservatives naturally, but with the right rhetoric, a liberal candidate might attract racial conservatives. With the wrong language, that candidate might drive racial conservatives away. Or a candidate could focus on visitation in an attempt to polarize the electorate on gender predispositions. Success would depend in large part on the nuances of the language used to discuss the issue.

This chapter has demonstrated group implication in the laboratory and has hinted at the political importance of the phenomenon. The next two chapters take up two cases of framing in American political discourse to demonstrate that both racial group implication and gender group implication have occurred in recent American politics, with important effects.

5

Racialization of Welfare and Social Security

The experiments reported in chapter 4 demonstrate that race and gender implication can occur when frames shape issues to be congruent with the structure of race or gender schemas. They provide strong evidence for the effects of group-implicating frames and the mechanisms by which they work. Nevertheless, experiments can say nothing about the prevalence of group implication in actual politics. I turn to that task in this chapter and the next, both of which take up analyses of actual discourse in recent American politics and of national opinion to explore the ways that this discourse has subtly associated issues with race or gender ideology. These analyses show that group implication occurs in American politics and demonstrate its political consequences.

In this chapter I take up welfare and Social Security. I show how the framing of these policies has structured them to fit racial schemas, albeit in very different ways from each other. Furthermore, I show that this racial framing has racialized public opinion on both policies. These associations between opinion and racial ideology are substantively large and politically important.

I begin this chapter by contrasting the analytical logic of the survey analyses with the experimentation in the previous chapter. Then I review the framing of welfare and Social Security over the past fifty years to show how it has structured those issues to fit the racial schema. As other analysts have documented, welfare discourse has associated the program with African Americans and with symbolically black attributes. I also show that the framing of Social Security shapes that program to fit the structure of the racial schema. Social Security, however, is racialized as the complementary mirror image of welfare. Just as welfare is associated with blackness, Social Security is associated with whiteness. That is, Social Security has been linked symbolically with the in-group and with hard work and legitimately earned rewards — values and attributes associated symbolically with whiteness in most (white) Americans' racial schemas.

Next, drawing on data from the American National Election Studies, I document the racialization of opinion among American whites from 1984 through 2000. Using a variety of measures of racial predispositions, I find that racially conservative whites are consistently less supportive of spending on welfare compared with racial liberals. Conversely, racially conservative whites are more supportive of Social Security spending compared with racial liberals. After exploring the extent of this racialization, I conclude the chapter by considering the broader significance of these findings.

This analysis of Social Security highlights its racialization, which is interesting and important in its own right. This study helps us to understand the program's enormous popularity and puts in a somewhat different light its purported universal quality. The analysis also puts in context the more commonly noted racialization of welfare and in so doing demonstrates the generality of the mechanism — group implication — that underlies both programs' racialization. Racialization — often studied in the context of welfare opinion — is more subtle and more pervasive in American politics than the welfare example alone might suggest.

FROM EXPERIMENT TO SURVEY

The experimental results reported in the previous chapter demonstrate that the right frame can engage people's race or gender schemas without mentioning race or gender explicitly. By randomly assigning the participants to conditions and by designing the frames to differ only in specific ways, I can be confident that the frames affected the basis of opinion formation.

This causal power comes with some costs, however. We cannot make inferences about two things from the experiment: first, we cannot generalize about the average levels of race or gender predispositions from the experiment to the general population. Second, the experiments tell us nothing about whether and how often these sorts of frames are actually deployed in political discourse. In combination, these limits mean we cannot make reliable inferences from experimental evidence alone about the extent of group implication in American politics.

The survey analyses presented in this chapter and the next address these shortcomings and allow me to demonstrate the substantive importance of group implication for modern American politics. Specifically, they demonstrate two points. First, they show that there are prominent frames in American political discourse that shape issues in ways that should fit race or gender schemas. In this chapter I analyze the framing of welfare and Social Security to show the ways that it structures those issues to be congruent with the racial schema. In the next chapter, I turn to the framing of health care reform in 1993–94 to show how it structured that issue to be congruent with the gender schema in ways that earlier and later framing did not.

Second, the survey analyses demonstrate that this framing affects public opinion in ways my theory predicts. In this chapter I demonstrate that white Americans draw on their racial predispositions in forming their opinions on Social Security and welfare. In the next chapter I show that Americans drew on their gender predispositions when thinking about health care reform in 1994 in ways that reflected the unique framing that year.

The survey analyses tell us much. They, too, have limits, however. No cross-sectional survey analysis can be definitive about causality. That is, we cannot be sure that the frames we observe are causing the opinion patterns we observe. Some other aspects of the political environment, besides the frames employed by political elites, could engage the race schema on welfare and Social Security (and the gender schema in 1994 on health care reform). And even if the frames do cause the patterns of opinion we observe, we can never be entirely sure that some other differences between citizens — other than their race or gender predispositions — explain their different opinions.

The analyses in this chapter and the next take steps to limit these dangers. By carefully describing the ways that my theory leads us to expect the framing of these issues to engage race or gender schemas, I increase our confidence that it really is the framing that causes the patterns of opinion. And by including control variables in the analysis, I minimize the risk that some other factor — other than race and gender predisposi-tions — is being engaged by those frames.

The survey analyses confirm two very important points. First, these sorts of frames *do* appear in real political discourse and not simply in articles crafted for a study. Second, group-implicating frames appear fre-quently and loudly enough that they affect people — even people who have not been asked to pay attention to those frames as part of a study. The inherent limits of nonexperimental cross-sectional analysis under-line the importance of pairing these chapters with experimental evidence that addresses those limits. It is the combination of results using both methods that lets us characterize both the psychological mechanisms and the political impact of group implication.

FRAMING POVERTY AND WELFARE

The racialization of media coverage of poverty and welfare programs has been extensively documented by historians and political scientists (Quadagno 1994; Bensonsmith 1999; Gamson and Lasch 1983; Fraser 1989; Huddy 2001; Cook 1992; Patterson 2000). The most recent and sustained political science account of welfare racialization comes from Martin Gilens, who traces both the racialization of welfare attitudes and the ways that media coverage and public discussion gave rise to it (1999). In this section I draw on elements of his account of the history of public discourse on poverty and welfare to set the stage for my public-opinion analysis later in the chapter.[1]

The Public Face of Poverty Becomes Black

Gilens argues that until the mid-1960s, the predominant image of pov-erty in America was white. The early "scientific" studies of poverty just after the turn of the century focused on the white poor, and this tendency strengthened during the Depression. Then in the 1940s and 1950s, pov-erty became less visible, as public attention turned to economic growth and to the cold war. In the early 1960s poverty was "rediscovered," spurred by John Kenneth Galbraith's *The Affluent Society* (1960) and Michael Har-rington's *The Other America* (1962). In part because of these books, the Kennedy administration began to focus some effort on poverty. Even at this point, however, the dominant image of poverty in America was of poor white Appalachians — not of black Americans in the urban North or the rural South.

Demographic and political trends were setting the stage for a major shift in perceptions of poverty. Beginning with the great migration in the 1920s, and again in the 1950s and 1960s, African Americans were moving north and into urban areas in large numbers. In 1920 blacks made up 2 percent of the northern population; by 1960 that proportion had grown to 7 percent overall and 12 percent in cities (Gilens 1999, 105). This move north meant that blacks were much more visible to nonsouthern whites. In addition, the racial composition of those receiving welfare was gradually changing.[2] The original welfare legislation gave states wide latitude to set eligibility requirements and standards; most southern states used this discretion to keep blacks off the roles or to set benefit levels very low. Through the 1960s and 1970s, however, the black proportion of welfare cases rose steadily, as court cases and legislative changes narrowed states' ability to exclude African Americans.

Both of these transitions were gradual, with roots beginning well before the mid-1960s. Nonetheless, they set the stage for events that transformed rather dramatically the face of poverty as perceived by the majority of white Americans. First, the civil rights movement shifted its focus from gaining basic civil rights, mostly in the South, to fighting for economic advancement in the North. This effort was exemplified most starkly by the protests led by Dr. Martin Luther King Jr. in Chicago against housing segregation in 1966. Also during this period, more-militant civil rights figures, such as Malcolm X and Stokely Carmichael, became more visible to white Americans. And most dramatic, the summer of 1964 saw the first uprisings against conditions in the northern urban ghettos, uprisings that would spread to other cities over the following years. These dramatic events precipitated major changes in media coverage and perceptions of poverty and welfare.

Media coverage of poverty followed these trends. Gilens shows that the raw number of poverty stories in national newsmagazines increased dramatically in the mid-1960s. After 1964 the percentage of black faces in the pictures of poor people accompanying those articles also increased dramatically, and the media picture of poverty has remained disproportionately black ever since. Most notable, the color of welfare in newsmagazine coverage depended significantly on the *type* of article. Articles that addressed new policy initiatives tended to have a neutral tone and to contain pictures of whites. On the other hand, articles critical of current policy were much more likely to picture blacks: "Media coverage from the early 1960s tended to use pictures of poor blacks to illustrate stories about waste, inefficiency, or abuse of welfare, and pictures of poor whites in stories with more neutral descriptions of antipoverty programs. This pattern is repeated in 1964 and 1965 as coverage of the War on Poverty becomes more critical and portrayals of the poor become 'more black'" (Gilens 1999, 177).

Moreover, this pattern of coverage was not unique to the War on Poverty era or limited merely to print media. Gilens conducted his content analysis of magazines through 1992 and found that they continued to overemphasize blacks among the poor — and especially among the "undeserving" poor — over the entire period. The face of poverty whitened somewhat during the recession of 1983–84, but blacks were overrepresented even then. In addition, Gilens's more-limited examination of television news suggests that the broadcast media followed a similar pattern of coverage over time.

Fit between Welfare and the Race Schema

The events of the mid-1960s and the patterns of media coverage from then onward drew attention to poor urban blacks, to be sure. As Kinder and Sanders argue (1996), however, the interaction of the conditions and events listed above did more than simply point out that poor urban blacks existed. Just at a time when many whites believed that the civil rights movement had achieved many of its goals in the South, such as voting rights and integration of public accommodations, the movement shifted to what seemed to some as new demands. And as this was happening, a more radical leadership cohort became visible in the movement. Finally, urban unrest also became visible at this time. Thus, many whites became aware of black poverty in a context that primed them to perceive blacks as ungrateful (for the advances they had won), lazy (for demanding economic advancement), and violent (for participating in civil unrest). In other words, these conditions and events highlighted and reinforced stereotypes about blacks just as their poverty became more visible as well.

This environment creates the perfect set of circumstances to link welfare with the racial schema. The fact that media coverage emphasized the black face of poverty would make the racial schema extremely accessible for perceiving poverty and poverty policy matters. At the same time, the events surrounding the civil rights movement and urban uprisings would have allowed for the creation of a structural fit between the poverty issue and the racial schema.

The new northern emphasis of the civil rights movement, along with a new focus on economic issues, would make the in-group/out-group distinction highly salient for all whites in a way that it may have been only for southerners in earlier years. This situation would also make the fact of vastly unequal outcomes crystal clear, if it was not already. The situational-individual evaluative dimension would be very salient, given the combination of unequal outcomes on the one hand and a more militant civil rights movement on the other. In this context, white Americans would find it very easy to understand black poverty — and poverty in general — in terms of the racial schema. The environment would present racial liberals with considerations and arguments that suggested that blacks still faced discrimination and systematic obstacles that were beyond their personal control. At the same time, racial conservatives would have plenty of evidence to fit with their predisposition to understand poverty as something brought on individuals by their own failings. Thus, by the 1970s at least, white opinion on welfare should be racialized. Moreover, it should be racialized not simply because white Americans came to see and believe that poor people are predominantly black but also because poor people and welfare recipients became associated with a set of characteristics — violence, laziness, and so on — that are *symbolically* black as well.

This association of welfare with blackness has been reinforced by frames deployed in later welfare debates. Ronald Reagan famously evoked the image of the "pink-Cadillac-driving welfare queen" who chose to have children in order to collect welfare rather than working for a living. Reagan drew on a long history of the image of the "welfare queen," which associated the prototypical welfare recipient with a range of negative black stereotypes, including laziness and dependency (Zucchino 1997, 64–65; see also Adair 2000; Hancock 2004).[3] Moreover, conservative political leaders and academic analysts have argued not just that welfare recipients are lazy and dependent but that the very design of welfare itself created perverse incentives that fostered those negative characteristics among recipients (e.g., Murray 1984). Thus, for example, in 1998 remarks to the Republican caucus, Newt Gingrich argued that welfare reform was "moving them into prosperity and giving them a chance to learn the work ethic and to learn how to manage their own budgets and to have a chance for their children to have a dramatically better future" (12).

FRAMING SOCIAL SECURITY

The racialization of welfare is a relatively well-known phenomenon. In what follows I suggest that Social Security has also been framed in ways that are structurally consistent with the race schema. Social Security represents an important complementary case to welfare for two reasons. First, the symbolic association of Social Security is with *whiteness,* the inverse of welfare's racialization. Second, although Social Security has been framed to fit the race schema, the program has not been explicitly associated with white recipients. Thus, any racialization of opinion on this program must be due to the structure of the frames and not simply a function of beliefs about the race of its beneficiaries. Although the racial framing of Social Security has not been documented, I will suggest that it is just as powerful as that of welfare, albeit in the opposite direction.

The initial design of Social Security policy did incorporate race indirectly. Various predominantly black categories of workers—most notably farm laborers—were excluded from Social Security to secure support from southern senators (on the history of Social Security, see Derthick 1979). Implementation has become less racialized over time as coverage has been expanded, however. Most important for my argument, the public discourse on Social Security has not been explicitly racial. In contrast to coverage of welfare or crime, the public is not receiving messages that suggest—explicitly at least—that Social Security disproportionately assists white Americans over other racial groups.[4] This condition may be partly due to the relative invisibility of whiteness for most white Americans; nevertheless, it means no explicit link exists between Social Security and race. Still, the ways that politicians and the media discuss Social Security align it *structurally* with the racial schema that I discuss above.

Policy makers have been centrally concerned with the public's image of Social Security since its inception. Martha Derthick argues that "one of the most conspicuous features of policymaking for Social Security is the preoccupation of policymakers with public psychology. They have been enormously concerned with the public's perceptions and subjective experience of the program" (1979, 183). In perhaps one of the earliest examples of "crafted talk" (Jacobs and Shapiro 2000) by leaders, those who designed and implemented Social Security chose their words carefully to help shape opinion in favor of the program. The framing choices they made—likely unintentionally—laid the groundwork for racialized public opinion.

The Social Insurance Frame

The creators of Social Security worked hard to frame it as an individual insurance program. According to Derthick, "'Insurance' was the central symbol of [official discourse on Social Security], and it was stressed precisely because it was expected to secure public acceptance. Because insurance implied a return for work and investment, it preserved the self-respect of the beneficiaries; because it implied a return in proportion to investment, it satisfied a widely held conception of fairness; and because it implied the existence of a contract, it appeared sound and certain" (1979, 198–99). All aspects of the program were — and generally still are — discussed in terms of this frame. Social Security taxes are called "contributions," there is talk of "old age insurance accounts" in Baltimore, and people are told that they are "paying for their own protection." Senator Goldwater stated in a congressional debate in 1972 that "Social Security payments are not gratuities from a benevolent central government. They are essentially a repayment of our own earnings" (cited in Tynes 1996, 191). This impression is further reinforced by the annual statements that the Social Security Administration began mailing to taxpayers in 1999, which have the look of a traditional retirement account report. In an entirely typical example, President Ford reinforced the link with work and individual contribution: "We must begin by insuring that the Social Security system is beyond challenge. [It is] a vital obligation each generation has to those who have worked hard and contributed to it all their lives" (United States Social Security Administration 2000, 16).

The contrast with other social welfare programs was explicit from the beginning, as is made clear by this passage from President Roosevelt's 1935 message to Congress: "Continued dependence on relief induces a spiritual and moral disintegration fundamentally destructive to the national fibre. To dole out relief in this way is to administer a narcotic, a subtle destroyer of the human spirit." Social insurance programs, on the other hand, "because they are based on regular contributions and on disbursements closely related to the amount contributed, derive their social legitimacy from the achievements of beneficiaries" (quoted in Schiltz 1970, 30). In 1998 Robert Ball, a former Social Security commissioner and longtime advocate of the program, summarized the link with work and the contrast with other programs: "It is an *earned* right, with eligibility for benefits and the benefit rate based on an individual's past earnings.

This principle sharply distinguishes Social Security from welfare and links the program, appropriately, to other earned rights such as wages, fringe benefits, and private pensions" (Ball and Bethell 1998, 60). This frame aligns Social Security with the racial schema in two ways. First, it associates Social Security with exactly the white-linked attributes of the racial schema, that is, work and just reward, and links the program with the sort of individual attribution favored by racial conservatives. Second, it sets up a sharp contrast with other social welfare programs, which tie benefits to need rather than to individual contributions and merit.

This symbolic contrast between Social Security and welfare mirrors the contrast between whiteness and blackness in the race schema, and the link with symbolically white attributes associates Social Security with the white in-group. The argument that Social Security represents insurance based on one's individual effort and commensurate with one's prior contributions maps precisely onto the conservative account of racial inequality. Other things being equal, then, this Social Security frame should attach Social Security recipients to the conservative end of the racial evaluative dimension, in an exact inversion of the connection between welfare recipients and the liberal end of the same dimension. This frame should resonate particularly for those who hold conservative racial beliefs, and it should attract them to Social Security. Racial liberals, on the other hand, will find Social Security somewhat less attractive than they otherwise might, because their racial schema attaches negative affect to the conservative constellation of beliefs.

The In-Group Linkage

Social Security is also associated rhetorically with in-groups, again precisely opposite the ways that welfare is linked with out-groups. This association reinforces the program's link with whiteness for white Americans. Because old age — unlike poverty — is something that everyone expects (and hopes) to experience, this in-group connection is easy to make. This universality of old age means that people are less likely to view the elderly as a "special interest"; they are the ultimate in-group, ourselves in a few years (e.g., Tynes 1996, 210).

Politicians and Social Security officials have a strong incentive to emphasize this in-group association. In a 1998 resource kit designed to help local Social Security offices develop information campaigns, for example, officials placed great emphasis on conveying the message that we all must pay attention to Social Security because it "affects everyone," not just the elderly (United States Social Security Administration 1998).

Political leaders also deploy this frame frequently. For example, after attempting to cut Social Security in 1981—an effort that was widely understood as hurting Republicans in the 1982 midterm elections, leading to the metaphor of Social Security as the "third rail" of American politics—Ronald Reagan moved quickly back to more-traditional rhetoric that implicitly distinguished Social Security from other social programs. At a January 1983 fund-raiser, for example, he referred to Social Security recipients in the first person for the first time, arguing that "[if Congress acts], all Americans can rest assured that the pensions of *our elderly,* both now and in the future, will be secure."[5] In addition, he began equating Social Security with the national good generally, as when he argued in his 1983 State of the Union address that the recent efforts to shore up Social Security "proved that, when it comes to the national welfare, Americans can still pull together for the common good." This remark is in stark contrast to his references to beneficiaries of other social programs in the same address. For example, on food stamp reform he said that "our standard here will be fairness, ensuring that the taxpayers' hard-earned dollars go only to the truly needy; that none of them are turned away, but that fraud and waste are stamped out." Throughout 1983 Reagan continued to refer to "our elderly," "our senior citizens," and the common good when discussing Social Security and to "those people" when discussing food stamps and welfare.

In the same 1998 speech on welfare that I cite above, Newt Gingrich demonstrated the in-group theme when he turned to Social Security. "Do we take seriously the responsibility to the baby boomers and their children to save Social Security in a way which is fair to every generation? That saves my mother and mother-in-law, that saves the baby boomers, and that is fair to younger Americans?" (2).

Social Security in Peril

The final important frame has been the vulnerability of Social Security. By the early 1970s, declining fertility rates and the ageing of the Baby Boom generation combined to jeopardize the long-run actuarial balance between payroll tax contributions to Social Security by current workers and the payment of benefits to current retirees. There has been a steady political discourse over the perilous condition of the program and the urgency of "saving Social Security," much of it sparked by regular reports on when the trust fund will run dry and much of it focusing on which political leaders can best be trusted to protect the program.[6]

There is considerable evidence that perceptions of threat lead people to exaggerate differences between in-group and out-group (Tajfel 1957, 1981) and increase the salience and impact of those predispositions on political attitudes and behavior (Lavine et al. 1999; Kinder and Sanders 1996; Stenner 2005; Feldman and Stenner 1997; Doty, Peterson, and Winter 1991; Sullivan, Piereson, and Marcus 1982). Thus, insofar as Social Security is a program that white Americans associate implicitly with their racial in-group, framing that emphasizes threat from bankruptcy may well increase the impact of their racial predispositions on their evaluation of Social Security. Although we might not expect this frame by itself to associate the program with race, we *should* expect it to increase the sense of threat felt by white Americans, insofar as they already associate Social Security with the in-group. That increased threat, in turn, should increase the salience of the racial schema for thinking about Social Security and thereby reinforce racial implication.

Thus, in its design and framing, Social Security is the symbolic complement to welfare. Just as welfare is associated with negative stereotypes of African Americans — in particular laziness — Social Security is associated with positive white stereotypes such as hard work. Moreover, the framing of both programs has implied that the fundamental design of each actually fosters those attributes in recipients. In a symbolic sense, at least, these frames suggest that welfare creates blackness and that Social Security creates whiteness.

EMPIRICAL EXPECTATIONS

I expect that white Americans' racial predispositions will influence their opinions on welfare and Social Security. Holding other relevant factors constant, racial conservatives should be less supportive of welfare spending, compared with racial liberals. For Social Security opinion, on the other hand, I expect that racial conservatives should be more supportive of spending compared with racial liberals, again holding all else constant. Moreover, because Social Security is associated with whiteness rather than blackness, I expect this racialization to operate in particular through feelings about the white in-group: I expect whites who feel warmer toward and closer to their own racial group to be more supportive of Social Security, again compared with those who feel cooler and less close. In contrast, welfare racialization should operate through feelings about the black out-group, with whites who feel cooler toward the black out-group being less supportive of welfare spending. Finally, I expect this racialization to be fairly constant over time, because the frames that racialize welfare and Social Security have themselves remained in consistent use over the past several decades.

I confine my expectations (and analysis) to whites for several reasons. First, nonwhites' racial schemas likely differ from whites', and so racialization would operate differently. More important, the frames that position Social Security as a program for the in-group and welfare as a program for the out-group do so in terms of an implicitly white in-group and black out-group. The "us" who deserve Social Security in return for our work are symbolically white, and the characteristics associated with Social Security recipients, such as hard work and self-reliance, are stereotypically associated with whiteness. The "them" who are on welfare are symbolically black, and the characteristics associated with welfare, such as laziness and perverse incentives, are stereotypically associated with blackness.

WELFARE AND SOCIAL SECURITY OPINION

My analyses make use of the excellent data available from the ANES because these data include consistent, parallel measures of Social Security and welfare opinion, plus measures of racial predispositions and important control variables in multiple studies over two decades.[7] I measure opinion on welfare and Social Security with the relevant items from the ANES spending battery, which asks respondents to indicate, for each of a series of programs, whether federal spending should be increased, kept the same, or decreased. In addition to appearing frequently, this item has the advantage of being quite general. Rather than asking about the details of program administration, viability, or particular reforms, this question taps people's general feelings about or their approval of Social Security at a fairly abstract level.[8]

Social Security is much more popular than welfare among white Americans. On a scale from zero to one, support for Social Security spending

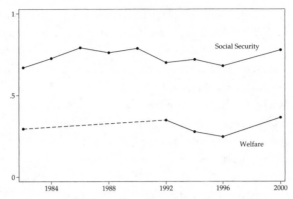

FIGURE 5.1 Mean Support for Welfare and Social Security Spending among Whites, 1982–2000. Variables are coded zero (decrease spending), 0.5 (keep the same), and one (increase). (Source: American National Election Studies.)

averages 0.74, or just about exactly midway between the "increase" and "keep it the same" responses; welfare averages 0.31, or just above the midpoint between "keep it the same" and "decrease." Figure 5.1 presents opinion on both issues over time. Over the past two decades, opinion on both has been relatively stable, although support increased somewhat in the mid-1980s and fell a bit in the late 1990s.

While relatively extreme, these levels of support are not unique. Compared with Social Security, white Americans are slightly more supportive of spending on crime control and on schools (overall means of 0.80 and 0.78, respectively). Support for welfare spending is only slightly lower than support for food stamps, which has a mean of 0.39 among whites.

Measurement of Racial Predispositions

Ideally, measures of racial predispositions would capture the structural features of whites' racial schemas. These measures would include the importance that whites place on the in-group/out-group distinction, the sorts of attributions they make for unequal outcomes, the degree of favoritism they display for the in-group over the out-group, and their attributions of stereotypical traits to the in-group and out-group.

In the analysis that follows, I make use of three different measures, each with advantages and disadvantages. The first set of measures is the so-called thermometer ratings of whites and of blacks. These ratings are drawn from a battery of questions in which respondents are asked to say how they feel about each of a large number of groups on a scale from zero, indicating a very negative or cold feeling, to one hundred, which would indicate a very warm or positive feeling (Weisberg and Miller 1980; see also Wilcox, Sigelman, and Cook 1989; Winter and Berinsky 1999). These measures have several advantages: first, ratings of both whites and blacks are available in most ANES studies since their inauguration in 1964, so they facilitate comparisons over time. Most important, they distinguish between the racial in-group and the out-group, so they allow me to assess the degree to which a policy is associated with one group or the other in addition to whether the policy is simply racialized. That is, because the frames depict Social Security as a policy that benefits and rewards the (implicitly white) in-group, I expect that racialization will take place particularly with regard to feelings about whites as a group as opposed to feelings about blacks. Conversely, welfare should be associated with feelings about blacks as a group, rather than with feelings about whites. In addition, the thermometer ratings are completely devoid of explicit policy content, so they likely tap relatively directly into feelings about the two racial groups themselves.

This generality also leads, however, to the primary weakness of the thermometers: they do not measure the structure of the race schema very specifically. In addition, the thermometer ratings are subject to social desirability and to response set, a particular concern for racial predispositions, which are subject to powerful egalitarian norms (Wilcox, Sigelman, and Cook 1989; Mendelberg 2001; Winter and Berinsky 1999). Therefore, I supplement the thermometer ratings with a pair of questions that appear periodically in the ANES that ask respondents to rate whites and blacks as hardworking, lazy, or somewhere in between.[9] As I discuss above, the stereotypes that whites are hardworking and blacks are lazy are important parts of the racial schema, and the framing of Social Security and welfare have emphasized the relationship of each program with work. Therefore, I would expect that respondents who endorse the stereotype of whites being particularly hardworking should be more supportive of Social Security, and respondents who endorse the stereotype that blacks are lazy to be less supportive of welfare.

Finally, in several studies the ANES includes racial resentment, a measure expressly designed to capture the complex ways that race has become enmeshed in modern political rhetoric (Kinder and Sanders 1996). The four items in the scale tap into the elements of the schema in relatively subtle ways, allowing respondents to indicate how they feel about the trade-offs between individual effort and the effects of discrimination and structural barriers.[10] Racial resentment measures whites' racial schemas with more subtlety and less social desirability bias than the other available items; it is also a multiple-item scale with proven validity and reliability. This scale's disadvantage is that it does not distinguish between the role played by in-group and out-group associations cementing racial implication of a policy. The items themselves focus on blacks in particular, although two of the items (the first and third) do draw a contrast between blacks and whites.

The race schema, however, does not consist of entirely independent beliefs and feelings about whites and about blacks. Rather, black and white are linked together and take meaning precisely through the contrast of superior and inferior groups. To say that "they" are violent and lazy is implicitly to suggest that "we" are peaceful and hardworking; insofar as welfare is a program associated with "them," then contrasting Social Security with welfare will implicitly associate it with "us." I therefore expect racial resentment—which measures in part the degree to which white Americans think of racial matters in terms of work, just reward, and the contrast between whites and blacks—to pick up the racialization of both welfare and Social Security as I describe it above. Neither racial resentment nor the stereotype measures are available in all years. Therefore, I use the thermometer ratings as my primary measure, supplemented with the others when they are available in order to ensure that the basic results are not driven by some quirk of the thermometer rating scale.

Control Variables

The model also includes a series of control variables. In cross-sectional survey analyses, we must worry that the effects of racial predispositions that we observe are in fact caused by some other factors that are correlated with racial predispositions, not by racial predispositions themselves. For example, racial conservatives tend to oppose an activist federal government in general, and racial liberals tend to support active government. If we do not hold constant the effect of limited-government preferences on Social Security opinion, then we will mistake the impact of those preferences as racial effects.[11]

Therefore, in addition to the racial predispositions measures of primary interest, I include in the models measures of a range of other predispositions that are likely correlated with racial ideology and that plausibly affect opinion on welfare and Social Security. First are measures of self-interest and group interest related to the programs, including social class (which is measured as income and education), age in years, being over age sixty-five, being retired, and being disabled. Second, I include measures of two important political principles or values: egalitarianism and support for limited government. Both of these values have played important roles in structuring American political discourse, and both have been linked with public opinion on a range of domestic policies (e.g., Feldman 1988; Feldman and Zaller 1992; Kinder and Sanders 1996). For egalitarianism I use the six-item scale developed by Feldman (1988). For limited government I construct a scale from two items that assess support for government effort in specific programmatic areas: the first asks respondents to indicate the degree to which the government should see to it that all Americans have a job and a good standard of living, and the second asks respondents to evaluate the trade-off between the government supplying more services versus cutting spending.[12] Third, I include measures of general political orientations, including partisan identification, liberal-conservative political ideology, and a measure of respondents' retrospective evaluations of the economy. Finally, I also include a set of indicators for demographic categories, including gender, living in the South, and marital status.[13]

I include these control variables primarily to ensure that I estimate correctly the impact of racial predispositions in each year, since racialization is the primary focus of this analysis. Some of these variables have interesting effects on opinion in their own right, however, so I will discuss these effects in the material that follows. All of the variables in the models are scaled to run from zero to one, with the liberal response coded as one for the nonindicator variables. I estimate the models using ordered probit because the welfare and Social Security spending questions have three ordered response categories (decrease, keep the same, and increase). The analysis includes presidential years from 1984 through 2000, plus 1994, because the ANES includes the complete set of control variables only for those years.

RESULTS: RACIALIZATION OF WELFARE AND SOCIAL SECURITY

Welfare

Table 5.1 gives the racialization results for welfare-spending attitudes. The first two rows of the table show the effect of racial predispositions on opinion, controlling for the other variables in the model. The basic racialization results are quite strong and in line with my expectations. For welfare spending the thermometer rating of blacks is substantially related to opinion (on average, b = 0.64 across the four years), and the coefficients achieve statistical significance in all years. The effect of the black thermometer rating on opinion is quite consistent over time, varying only slightly between 0.576 and 0.700.

The substantive impact of the black thermometer rating is substantial. Ordered probit coefficients do not translate transparently into substantive impacts, in part because the effect of each variable depends in part on the levels of the other independent variables in the model. Therefore, to give a substantive sense of the effect of the black thermometer rating, I use the model estimates to predict the welfare opinion of a range of hypothetical white ANES respondents. All are utterly average on all the control variables: in their support for egalitarianism, in their class loca-

TABLE 5.1   Racialization of Welfare among Whites, 1992–2000

| | WELFARE SPENDING | | | |
	1992	1994	1996	2000
Thermometer rating of whites	−0.142	0.078	−0.215	−0.676**
	(0.192)	(0.225)	(0.279)	(0.242)
Thermometer rating of blacks	0.583**	0.576**	0.684*	0.700**
	(0.191)	(0.203)	(0.285)	(0.236)
Egalitarianism	0.722**	0.858**	0.927**	0.967**
	(0.177)	(0.227)	(0.240)	(0.212)
Limited government	−1.576**	−1.570**	−2.126**	−1.247**
	(0.163)	(0.192)	(0.223)	(0.172)
N	1,609	1,300	1,190	1,052
χ^2 (26 degrees of freedom)	349.15	313.08	347.66	184.91

Source: American National Election Studies.
Note: Entries are ordered probit coefficients with standard errors in parentheses. Models also include the full set of control variables discussed in the text. Full results appear in the Web appendix.
** $p < 0.01$; * $p < 0.05$; ^ $p < 0.10$ two-sided.

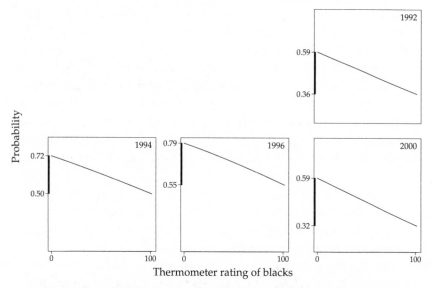

FIGURE 5.2 Impact of Racial Liberalism on Welfare Opinion among Whites, 1992–2000. Figure shows the predicted probability of favoring decreased welfare spending for otherwise average white respondents whose thermometer rating of blacks varies from zero to one hundred, on the basis of the model presented in table 5.1. Labeled points on the y-axis correspond to thermometer ratings of zero and one hundred; y-axis range runs from 0.2 to 0.8. (Source: American National Election Studies.)

tion, and the rest. They differ in one way, however: their placement of blacks on the thermometer ratings scale ranges from zero to one hundred. Using the estimates from the models presented in table 5.1, I calculate the probability that each of these hypothetical "average" white Americans supports cuts to spending on welfare. By plotting these probabilities, we get an indicator of the real-world impact of the black thermometer rating. Figure 5.2 presents the results of these calculations. Feelings about blacks as a group are strong predictors of opinion. In 1992, for example, the probability of supporting welfare spending cuts for an otherwise average white American is 0.59 if that person rates blacks at zero, versus 0.36 if he or she rates blacks at one hundred—a substantial difference of −0.23.

As expected, the effect of the *white* thermometer rating on welfare opinion is smaller and less consistent. For 1992 through 1996, the white thermometer rating is essentially unrelated to opinion—the coefficient is in the expected direction in two of the three years, but is quite small and statistically insignificant. This finding is consistent with the expectation that evaluations of welfare would operate largely though whites' views about the racial out-group. In 2000, however, the rating of whites is substantially related to opinion on welfare spending (b = −0.676), meaning that whites who feel warmly toward their own racial group are less supportive of welfare spending, above and beyond the effect of their feelings about blacks as a group. In 2000 this rating of whites has a large substantive impact: the analogous pair of average whites who rate *whites* at zero and one hundred favor decreased welfare spending with probabilities 0.24 and 0.48, respectively, a difference of 0.24. In other words, whites who feel very warmly toward whites as a group are much more likely to oppose welfare spending in 2000.

Several other results from the model are interesting in their own right. As we might expect, support for egalitarianism is strongly related to support for welfare spending (average b = 0.87; p < 0.01 in all four years), as is opposition to government action in general (average b = −1.63; p < 0.01 in all years).[13] Thus, those who support egalitarianism are more favorable toward welfare spending, and those who oppose government effort in general are less favorable toward welfare spending, compared with those who do not support those political principles.

The basic results, then, conform to expectations: welfare is racialized for white Americans. Moreover, it is racialized through evaluations of the black racial out-group consistently over the period for which we have measures of welfare opinion, as expected. Some evidence indicates that that may have changed somewhat in 2000 so that racialization also occurs in that year through evaluations of the white in-group.

Social Security

Table 5.2 presents the results of the parallel analysis of Social Security opinion. The first row of coefficients shows that white Americans who feel more warmly toward whites as a group are more supportive of Social Security spending, all other things held constant. The relationship is smaller in 1984 (b = 0.242) and does not achieve statistical significance; from 1988 onward the effect is both substantively large and statistically significant, averaging 0.59.

The substantive effect of the white thermometer ratings is demonstrated in figure 5.3, which presents the predicted probability favoring increased Social Security spending for otherwise average respondents whose ratings of *whites* range from zero to one hundred. In 1984 the

TABLE 5.2   Racialization of Social Security among Whites, 1984–2000

	SOCIAL SECURITY SPENDING					
	1984	1988	1992	1994	1996	2000
Thermometer rating of whites	0.242 (0.224)	0.564** (0.203)	0.596** (0.198)	0.482* (0.226)	0.573* (0.260)	0.710** (0.265)
Thermometer rating of blacks	0.004 (0.205)	−0.023 (0.202)	−0.396* (0.196)	0.095 (0.200)	−0.224 (0.261)	−0.752** (0.258)
Egalitarianism	0.424* (0.205)	0.268 (0.213)	0.430* (0.178)	0.248 (0.218)	0.015 (0.218)	0.768** (0.228)
Limited government	−1.048** (0.183)	−0.869** (0.192)	−0.992** (0.166)	−1.287** (0.195)	−1.701** (0.214)	−1.312** (0.193)
N	1,432	1,257	1,630	1,307	1,190	1,049
χ^2 (26 degrees of freedom)	240.45	181.05	295.75	299.74	276.37	205.49

Source: American National Election Studies.
Note: Entries are ordered probit coefficients with standard errors in parentheses. Models also include the full set of control variables discussed in the text. Full results appear in the Web appendix.
** $p < 0.01$; * $p < 0.05$; ^ $p < 0.10$ two-sided.

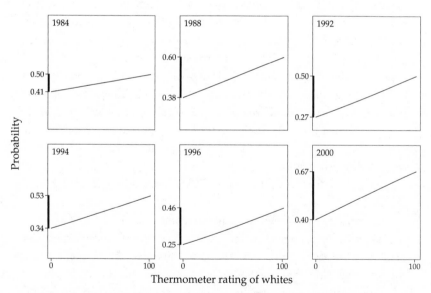

FIGURE 5.3 Impact of Racial Liberalism on Social Security Opinion among Whites, 1984–2000. Figure shows the predicted probability of favoring increased Social Security spending for otherwise average white respondents whose thermometer rating of whites varies from zero to one hundred, on the basis of the model presented in table 5.2. Labeled points on the y-axis correspond to thermometer ratings of zero and one hundred; y-axis range runs from 0.2 to 0.8. (Source: American National Election Studies.)

difference in probabilities between respondents who rate whites at zero and at one hundred is about 0.09 — a moderate but not trivial effect. From 1988 onward the racialization is substantial: the probability of favoring increased spending is between 0.19 and 0.27 higher among those who feel most warmly toward whites. Turning to the thermometer ratings of blacks, table 5.2 indicates that feeling warmly toward blacks, as measured by thermometer ratings, is associated with opposition to Social Security spending in four of the six years; as expected, the effect is substantively smaller and more variable and achieves statistical significance only twice.

The substantive impact of Social Security racialization is about the same as welfare's, although its roots differ. For welfare, feelings about blacks drive racialization. Across the four years, the average coefficient for the black thermometer rating 0.64. For Social Security, the racialization is of roughly similar magnitude, albeit largely through the thermometer rating of whites.

Some of the other results from the Social Security model are also interesting. First, support for egalitarianism is associated with favoring Social Security, but this association is relatively small and uneven from year to year and hovers on the edge of statistical significance. This finding contrasts with welfare, support for which is strongly and consistently associated with egalitarianism. This result makes sense in terms of the different framing of the two programs: Social Security is earned, whereas welfare is a matter of need. It makes sense, then, that feelings about inequality are more strongly tied to welfare opinion. Second, opposition to expansive government action in the social realm is strongly and consistently associated with opposition to Social Security spending in particular. Again, this finding is as we would expect — insofar as people support government activism in general, that support extends to Social Security spending (average $b = -1.20$).

The measures of self-interest and group interest are associated weakly, if at all, with Social Security opinion. Retirees are no more supportive of Social Security spending, and those over age sixty-five are actually *less* supportive. Although this result might seem counterintuitive, it is in fact consistent with prior research.[14] Similarly, social class location is only mildly related to opinion. In all, these results conform to the typical pattern of weak linkages between self-interest and public opinion (Bobo and Kluegel 1993; Sears et al. 1980; Green and Cowden 1992; Sears, Hensler, and Speer 1979; McConahay 1982; Sen 1990).[15]

TABLE 5.3   Racialization of Welfare and Social Security among Whites
(Stereotype Measures), 1992–2000

	1992	1996	2000
	Welfare Spending		
Whites hardworking	−0.292^	−0.280	−0.151
	(0.164)	(0.220)	(0.188)
Blacks hardworking	0.710**	0.566**	0.466*
	(0.159)	(0.211)	(0.192)
	Social Security Spending		
Whites hardworking	0.324^	0.449*	0.918**
	(0.168)	(0.208)	(0.210)
Blacks hardworking	−0.346*	−0.335^	−0.335
	(0.163)	(0.196)	(0.217)

Source: American National Election Studies.
Note: Entries are probit coefficients with standard errors in parentheses. Models also include the full
set of control variables discussed in the text. Number of cases varies from 1,099 to 1,613; full results
appear in the Web appendix.
** p < 0.01; * p < 0.05; ^ p < 0.10 two-sided.

Overall, then, these results suggest that public opinion on Social Security spending is indeed racialized in the ways I expected. The association between feelings about whites and Social Security opinion is strong and consistent. This finding is strong evidence of racialization across independent samples of white Americans spanning different political contexts over two decades. This racialization is clear and strong from 1988 through 2000; it is somewhat weaker and not statistically significant in 1984.

Other Measures of the Racial Schema

Next, I turn to the other measures of the racial schema. Table 5.3 presents the results of analyses that substitute the stereotype measures for the thermometer ratings in 1992, 1996, and 2000 for both welfare and Social Security. These results confirm the findings so far: white Americans racialize welfare most directly in terms of their feelings about the black out-group, and they racialize Social Security in terms of their in-group feelings. Those who feel that blacks are particularly hardworking are more favorable toward welfare spending, and those who feel that whites are hardworking are more supportive of Social Security spending. The substantive sizes of these associations are large and roughly comparable across the two policies. The other effects are in the direction we might

TABLE 5.4   Racialization of Welfare and Social Security among Whites (Racial Resentment), 1988–2000

	1988	1992	1994	2000
		Welfare Spending		
Thermometer rating of whites	—	0.000	0.202	−0.460^
		(0.195)	(0.228)	(0.247)
Thermometer rating of blacks	—	0.317	0.437*	0.433^
		(0.198)	(0.207)	(0.243)
Racial resentment	—	−0.837**	−0.784**	−0.941**
		(0.159)	(0.194)	(0.192)
		Social Security Spending		
Thermometer rating of whites	0.493*	0.488*	0.406^	0.549*
	(0.207)	(0.200)	(0.229)	(0.269)
Thermometer rating of blacks	0.066	−0.187	0.173	−0.560*
	(0.208)	(0.203)	(0.203)	(0.265)
Racial resentment	0.355^	0.685**	0.467*	0.695**
	(0.197)	(0.164)	(0.195)	(0.209)

Source: American National Election Studies.
Note: Entries are ordered probit coefficients with standard errors in parentheses. Models also include the full set of control variables discussed in the text. Number of cases varies from 1,047 to 1,629; full results appear in the Web appendix.
** $p < 0.01$; * $p < 0.05$; ^ $p < 0.10$ two-sided.

expect, and, also as expected, they are smaller. Stereotyping *blacks* as hardworking is somewhat associated with less support for Social Security, and stereotyping *whites* as hardworking is somewhat associated with less support for welfare spending.

These results provide additional confidence in the results presented so far. This measure is both more specific and more precisely tied to a central aspect of the framing of the two programs. Respondents who feel that their racial group is particularly hardworking support more spending on Social Security—a program that is framed as a just reward for hard work. Conversely, respondents who feel that the blacks are lazy (i.e., not hardworking) oppose more spending on welfare, a program framed in part as a handout to blacks.

Table 5.4 shows the relevant results from a model that includes racial resentment as well as the thermometer rating measures in 1988, 1992, 1994, and 2000. As expected, racial resentment is a powerful predictor of both welfare and Social Security opinion among white Americans, in opposite directions. Racially resentful whites like Social Security more, and welfare less, compared with nonresentful whites. Across the four years, the ordered probit coefficient in the Social Security model averages 0.55, with somewhat larger estimated associations in 1992 and 2000; the average coefficient in the welfare model is −0.85. These results provide further strong support for the hypothesis of racialization, making use of an established, reliable, and valid measure of racial predispositions.

Moreover, even with the inclusion of racial resentment, the association of opinion with thermometer ratings is robust. In the Social Security model, the estimated coefficient on the white thermometer rating is somewhat smaller (averaging 0.48 across these years, compared with 0.59 over the same years in the model without racial resentment). The estimated effect of the black thermometer rating is even noisier in this specification than in the basic model; the coefficient has the "wrong" sign in two of the four years. Similarly, in the welfare model the coefficient on the black thermometer rating averages 0.40 across the three years. These effects are not surprising; although all three measures tap aspects of the racial schema, racial resentment is presumably the most reliable measure.[16] These results confirm that, even above and beyond the effect of racial resentment, feelings about the white in-group are strongly related to opinion on Social Security, and feelings about blacks are related to opinion on welfare.[17]

Other Domestic Spending Programs

Finally, it is instructive to compare the results so far with analogous analyses of other programs that I do not expect to be racialized. This analysis will help to confirm that the results so far do not reflect either a general racialization of social policy or some fluke of question wording in the spending battery. To this end, table 5.5 presents the results for a series of social welfare spending items that have not been traditionally framed in racialized ways and that therefore would not be expected to contain racialized opinion. I ran models for six policies that appeared in at least three of the six ANES studies: spending on schools, child care, the poor, the unemployed, the homeless, and college financial aid. For each policy I ran the same ordered probit model, separately for each study year. The table displays the coefficients on the two racial thermometer rating measures from each model.[18]

Opinion on these policies is not consistently racialized. Certain policies were somewhat racialized in a particular year but none steadily through time. These results are consistent with the claim that *all* social welfare

TABLE 5.5   Racialization of Social Welfare Spending Preferences among Whites, 1984–2000

	1984	1988	1992	1994	1996	2000
			Schools Spending			
Thermometer rating of whites	0.283	0.456*	−0.027	0.227	0.485^	−0.037
Thermometer rating of blacks	0.260	−0.471*	0.070	0.181	−0.073	−0.161
			Child Care Spending			
Thermometer rating of whites	—	0.229	0.229	0.710**	0.757**	0.173
Thermometer rating of blacks	—	−0.139	0.000	−0.040	−0.139	−0.135
			Spending on the Poor			
Thermometer rating of whites	—	—	0.259	—	0.130	0.241
Thermometer rating of blacks	—	—	0.612**	—	0.377	0.103
			Spending on Unemployed			
Thermometer rating of whites	0.255	0.109	0.145	—	—	—
Thermometer rating of blacks	0.226	0.286	0.465*	—	—	—
			Homeless Spending			
Thermometer rating of whites	—	0.162	0.339	—	0.541*	—
Thermometer rating of blacks	—	0.623**	0.231	—	0.176	—
			Financial Aid Spending			
Thermometer rating of whites	—	0.149	0.500*	—	0.336	—
Thermometer rating of blacks	—	0.318^	0.153	—	−0.247	—

Source: American National Election Studies.
Note: Entries are ordered probit coefficients. Models also include the full set of control variables discussed in the text. N varies from 1,045 to 1,634. Full results appear in the Web appendix.
** $p < 0.01$; * $p < 0.05$; ^ $p < 0.10$ two-sided.

policy discourse invokes race implicitly to some extent (e.g., Edsall and Edsall 1992). Perhaps certain policies in certain years were framed in ways that — relatively idiosyncratically and temporarily — lit up racial considerations.[19] Nevertheless, no general pattern of racialization exists, either by policy or by year. This finding indicates that the extremely consistent results for Social Security (and welfare) reflect racialization of those policies in particular, rather than a racialization of the social policy generally or question wording or ordering effects.

Gendering of Social Security and Welfare

All these results demonstrate that both welfare and Social Security are racialized in the ways their framing would lead us to expect. An interesting question, though, is whether they are gendered as well.

We might expect that they would be for several reasons. First, poverty itself is gendered, as is policy making on welfare and Social Security. Women (and children) are more likely than men to be poor. Moreover, the New Deal social welfare system was premised on traditional gender relations. Social Security and unemployment insurance were built on the assumption that male workers and their families are the beneficiaries (Mettler 1998), and welfare grew out of programs for widows and orphans (Fraser 1989; Skocpol 1992). Insofar as people are aware of these gender connections, we might expect their gender predispositions to influence their welfare attitudes. Moreover, the framing of welfare has highlighted gender as well as race — in particular through the image of the "welfare queen" (Hancock 2004; Zucchino 1997). Although most research on welfare attitudes has focused on race, some evidence suggests that gender stereotypes are also linked with welfare opinion (e.g., Soss and LeClair 2004). Finally, race and gender are both group-based systems of social stratification. I have argued that they have important structural and ideological differences, but it is certainly possible that racial implication — which works through the racial schema — may also trigger the gender schema if the two schemas are cognitively linked. Although there was no evidence of this cognitive linkage in the experiments reported in the previous chapter, the evidence may be different for the American public as a whole.

On the other hand, we have seen that the framing of both issues does fit the race schema. Because the race and gender schemas have different structures, we should not necessarily expect that framing to fit the gender schema as well. Moreover, in contrast with welfare, Social Security's framing has not drawn on evocative gender images such as the welfare queen.

The results, presented in table 5.6, suggest that welfare may be slightly gendered, but to a much lesser extent than it is racialized.[20] The gendering is much smaller than the estimated racialization, varies somewhat from year to year, and hovers on the edge of statistical significance. Nevertheless, those whites who favor more egalitarian gender roles are somewhat more supportive of spending on welfare than similar whites who favor traditional gender roles.

We find even less evidence of gendering for Social Security. Gender egalitarianism is all but unrelated to Social Security opinion from 1984 through 1996. The ordered probit coefficient averages 0.19 in those years and never approaches statistical significance. The only possible exception is 2000, when Social Security opinion is substantially associated with gender egalitarianism. The estimated coefficient in that year is 0.82,

TABLE 5.6   Gendering and Racialization of Welfare and Social Security among Whites, 1988–2000

	1984	1988	1992	1994	1996	2000
			Welfare Spending			
Thermometer rating of whites	—	—	−0.217	0.035	−0.378	−0.764**
			(0.197)	(0.233)	(0.288)	(0.255)
Thermometer rating of blacks	—	—	0.611**	0.514*	0.735*	0.730**
			(0.196)	(0.212)	(0.292)	(0.249)
Gender egalitarianism	—	—	0.362*	0.335^	0.414^	0.253
			(0.182)	(0.198)	(0.246)	(0.253)
			Social Security Spending			
Thermometer rating of whites	0.264	0.606**	0.607**	0.416^	0.576*	0.661*
	(0.236)	(0.208)	(0.202)	(0.234)	(0.264)	(0.275)
Thermometer rating of blacks	0.013	−0.005	−0.493*	0.188	−0.260	−0.763**
	(0.221)	(0.210)	(0.201)	(0.207)	(0.263)	(0.268)
Gender egalitarianism	0.145	0.181	0.296	−0.033	0.352^	0.822**
	(0.187)	(0.191)	(0.184)	(0.191)	(0.213)	(0.269)

Source: American National Election Studies.
Note: Entries are ordered probit coefficients with standard errors in parentheses. Models also include the full set of control variables discussed in the text. Number of cases varies from 982 to 1,584; full results appear in the Web appendix.
** $p < 0.01$; * $p < 0.05$; ^ $p < 0.10$ two-sided.

indicating that gender egalitarians are much more supportive than traditionalists of Social Security spending. It is not clear from the data available whether this result represents a true shift in the implication of Social Security or whether it is simply a fluke in that one year.

The overall picture is consistent with the experimental findings. Frames that induce racial implication do not automatically engage the gender schema as well. This finding reconfirms the distinction between the two processes and indirectly reinforces the point that group implication occurs when frames fit the specific structure of a particular schema.

SUBGROUP ANALYSES

Because the racialization of both welfare and Social Security has its roots in elite political rhetoric, we might expect different citizens to react differently to that framing. Specifically, we might expect those who are more attentive to politics in general to be more likely to have received and absorbed that framing, and we might expect citizens' political predispositions to moderate their reactions to it (e.g., Zaller 1992; Converse 1990). In this final analysis section I examine differences in welfare and Social Security racialization along two dimensions: partisanship and political engagement.

Partisanship

Debate over welfare has been highly partisan and has formed an important part of the political landscape during the New Deal and post–New Deal party systems. Therefore, we might expect people who identify with one or the other of the major parties to differ in their understandings of welfare. Nevertheless, although the parties generally disagree on the correct welfare policies, there is little evidence that they differ in the frames they bring to the issue. It is quite possible, then, that Democratic and Republican citizens both racialize the issue, while disagreeing on the correct policy course. We shall see.

Social Security has also been an extremely partisan issue at various times throughout its history and has been especially so in the period since 1980. When Social Security was founded, Republicans opposed it along with much of the New Deal. This partisan conflict moderated during the subsequent period of program expansion. In 1981 it again became sharply associated with the political parties, as Ronald Reagan proposed broad changes and cuts to the program. Social Security played an important role in the 1982 campaign, and the issue has reappeared consistently on the partisan agenda and as part of presidential campaigns since. During the 1980s and early 1990s most of the contention has been over who might best protect Social Security, rather than over the merits of the program itself. This dynamic is a legacy of the poor reputation that Republicans have on Social Security since Reagan. More recently, proposals for more drastic reforms and restructuring have been on the table, with attendant partisan differences.

News coverage has reflected the important role of the parties. In their analysis of media coverage, for example, Jacobs and Shapiro find that the large majority of Associated Press stories on Social Security from 1977 to 1994 draw on party officials as sources (1995, table 9). The public also understands the issue in terms of partisanship. In the 1988 and 1990 ANES studies, for example, about 40 percent of white Americans believed that Republicans were more likely to cut Social Security, whereas only 6 percent believed that Democrats were more likely to do so. Along similar

TABLE 5.7   Racialization of Welfare and Social Security among Whites by Partisanship

	DEMOCRATS	INDEPENDENTS	REPUBLICANS
	Welfare Spending		
Thermometer rating of whites	−0.060	−0.113	−0.535*
	(0.196)	(0.183)	(0.216)
Thermometer rating of blacks	0.412*	0.634**	0.804**
	(0.178)	(0.191)	(0.204)
	Social Security Spending		
Thermometer rating of whites	0.389*	0.391**	0.627**
	(0.165)	(0.148)	(0.159)
Thermometer rating of blacks	−0.243	0.041	−0.240
	(0.155)	(0.147)	(0.149)

Source: American National Election Studies.
Note: Models are pooled across years (1984–2000 for Social Security, 1992–2000 for welfare) and run separately by partisan identification. Entries are ordered probit coefficients with standard error in parentheses. Models also include the full set of control variables discussed in the text plus dummy variables for each study year. Number of cases varies from 2,473 to 2,869; full results appear in the Web appendix.
** p < 0.01; * p < 0.05; ^ p < 0.10 two-sided.

lines, in his work on partisan issue ownership, Petrocik finds that Social Security is perceived as a Democratic issue (1996).

It is not clear whether this situation should translate into differences in racialization, however. There is no evidence that Democratic and Republican elites frame Social Security differently. They may differ in emphasis, but neither frames the issue in a way that seriously contests the racial structure of the dominant frames. Most mainstream elites emphasize elements of hard work, deservingness, and the rest when discussing Social Security, although they may advocate different policies for saving it. Given this fact and given that Social Security has been discussed in racialized terms since the 1930s, I do not expect large partisan differences. To find out, I pooled the available years of data and reran the basic racialization model separately by partisan identification.[21]

The findings, presented in table 5.7, show that Republican identifiers are somewhat more inclined than Democrats to racialize both welfare and Social Security, with independents falling somewhere in between. For the welfare model, the coefficient on the thermometer rating of blacks is almost twice as large among Republicans as among Democrats, although the difference is not statistically significant (p = 0.16, two-sided); Republicans are also the only partisan group to associate welfare with the white thermometer score as well. For the Social Security model, the coefficient on the white thermometer rating is about 50 percent larger among Republicans than Democrats, although again that difference is not significant (p = 0.35, two-sided). Despite these differences, the evidence clearly shows that partisans of all stripes racialize both programs, albeit with some indication that Republicans do so a bit more than other partisans.

Political Engagement

The second potential moderating division is political engagement. Citizens vary widely in their interest in and attention to politics. This variation influences who is most affected by elite frames in two ways. First, those who are more engaged are more likely to receive and absorb elite political rhetoric and therefore be open to influence. Second, however, the better engaged are more able to recognize whether rhetoric they receive comes from political elites they disagree with and reject it (e.g., Zaller 1992).

For racial group implication of welfare and Social Security, I expect most of the action to occur at the first, reception, stage, rather than at the second, acceptance/rejection, stage. There is little reason to expect citizens to reject the racializing rhetoric due to its racial content, because these frames — especially those for Social Security — are so subtle that even highly engaged citizens are unlikely to recognize their racial nature.

Therefore, I expect the most engaged citizens to racialize welfare and Social Security the most, because they will have received these frames most consistently by virtue of their attention to matters political. Given the prevalence of these frames over several decades, however, I am less certain about the degree of drop-off to expect among the less engaged. Perhaps the racialization of these policies has been so thorough that less-engaged citizens have picked it up as well. We shall see.

To examine this situation, I pooled the available years of ANES data, and I ran regression models separately for the top, middle, and bottom thirds of the sample in terms of level of political engagement.[22] The ordered probit results are displayed in table 5.8. For welfare, there is striking consistency in racialization across information levels. Comparing the least and most informed, we find that the impact of ratings of blacks on welfare attitudes is essentially indistinguishable. In the case of Social Security, on the other hand, those who are most informed about politics racialized

TABLE 5.8 Racialization of Welfare and Social Security among Whites by Political Engagement

	LOW ENGAGEMENT	MIDDLE ENGAGEMENT	HIGH ENGAGEMENT
	Welfare Spending		
Thermometer rating of whites	−0.130	−0.141	−0.629**
	(0.173)	(0.198)	(0.235)
Thermometer rating of blacks	0.629**	0.672**	0.767**
	(0.167)	(0.191)	(0.229)
	Social Security Spending		
Thermometer rating of whites	0.323*	0.439**	0.621**
	(0.150)	(0.155)	(0.168)
Thermometer rating of blacks	0.067	−0.321*	−0.100
	(0.145)	(0.147)	(0.161)

Source: American National Election Studies.
Note: Models are pooled across years (1984–2000 for Social Security, 1992–2000 for welfare) and run separately by political information. Entries are ordered probit coefficients with standard errors in parentheses. Models also include the full set of control variables discussed in the text plus dummy variables for each study year. Number of cases varies from 2,578 to 2,665; full results appear in the Web appendix.
** $p < 0.01$; * $p < 0.05$; ^ $p < 0.10$ two-sided.

Social Security greatly in terms of white evaluations (b = 0.621, p < 0.01 among the top third in information), and racialization decreases steadily as information decreases (b = 0.323, p < 0.05 among the least informed), although the differences across levels are not statistically significant (p = 0.25). The least informed racialized Social Security to some extent, to be sure, but racialization is more than twice as strong among the most informed, with middle-information respondents falling between the other two groups. Thus, white Americans of all engagement levels do racialize Social Security, but the most engaged, who are most attuned to the framing in elite discourse, do so the most.

SUMMARY AND THE NET IMPACT OF RACIALIZATION

In this chapter I applied the theoretical argument from earlier chapters to racialization in recent American politics. The chapter discussed the ways that the framing of welfare and Social Security should resonate with racial schemas among the American public and then demonstrated that public opinion does indeed reflect just the sort of racialization this leads us to expect. I found that white Americans' feelings toward blacks are substantially related to their opinions on welfare. Although this demonstration is not entirely surprising in light of past work on welfare opinion, it has served as an initial demonstration of group implication in action. In addition, and perhaps more surprising, white Americans' racial predispositions are also associated with their opinion on Social Security. This racialization is driven through whites' feelings about their own racial group, as we might expect, given the way the frames fit the racial schema. The substantive impact of racial predispositions on Social Security spending opinion is about the same as their impact on welfare spending opinion, although the direction of the effect is opposite and the specific predispositions involved are different. Just as our understanding of in-group and out-group — of whites and blacks — takes its meaning in important ways from the contrast between the groups, so the framing of welfare and Social Security has created symbolic meanings for those programs that draw in contrasting ways on those interlocked racial identities.

*   *   *

It matters, of course, that opinion on both welfare and Social Security is driven by racial considerations. Another interesting question, though, is what net impact this racialization has on the distribution of support for these policies. In other words, what might opinion on welfare and Social Security look like in a world without racial group implication?

We obviously have no way to know for sure, because a political world without frames that associate these two policies with racial considerations would be very different in all sorts of ways, many of which would also affect opinion. Nevertheless, we can gain a useful perspective on the political importance of racial group implication by considering, however hypothetically, what opinion might look like without it. Of course, the net effect of group implication will depend on the distribution of predispositions among the public and on the relative positive or negative impact of the frame. That is, the net impact will depend on who is affected most by the frame, compared with the hypothetical world without the group-implicating frames. Thus, a particular set of frames could induce "positive" racial implication by increasing support for a policy among racial liberals, by increasing *opposition* among racial conservatives, or by some combination — with very different effects in each case on overall opinion. Nevertheless, we can make some plausible assumptions about the direction of these effects. We can reasonably assume that the net effect of welfare racialization is to push racially conservative whites further against the program than they might otherwise be; it is also plausible to assume that the racialization of Social Security pushes racially conservative whites to be more in favor of that program (rather, that is, than moving racial liberals toward welfare and away from Social Security). With these entirely hypothetical — but perhaps reasonable — assumptions in hand, we can use the results of the statistical models presented above to simulate what opinion might look like, absent racial group implication.[23]

For welfare I use the results of the models presented in table 5.1 (and in figure 5.2) to simulate the distribution of welfare opinion in each year if everyone were as favorable toward welfare as an otherwise equivalent person who rated blacks at one hundred on the thermometer rating scale. That is, I assume the effect of racialization is to decrease support for welfare and in particular to depress support among racial conservatives.[24] For Social Security, I use the results of the models presented in table 5.2 (and figure 5.3) to simulate opinion in each year, on the assumption that everyone rates Social Security as an otherwise equivalent person who rates whites at zero on the thermometer rating scale. This supposition corresponds to the assumption that the racial framing of Social Security increases support among racial conservatives.

Figure 5.4 compares the results of these simulations with the actual distribution of welfare and Social Security opinion from 1984 through 2000. The solid lines represent the actual average opinion in each year, and the dashed lines represent what opinion would be under the assumptions of the simulation. The results suggest that racial group implication has a large impact on opinion for both policies and that it therefore contributes substantially to the enormous gap in support between them. In 1996, for example, Social Security opinion averaged 0.67 on the zero-to-one scale and welfare averaged 0.23 — a gap of 0.44. In the simulated world that gap is reduced by about a third, to 0.29.[25] Across the four years for which we have both welfare and Social Security data, the gap between the two programs is reduced substantially, by something between a quarter and a half.

Of course, these simulations are speculative, and different assumptions would lead to different estimates of the impact of group implication. Nevertheless, the overwhelmingly negative portrayals of welfare and the extremely positive portrayals of Social Security suggest that these assumptions may not, in fact, be all that unreasonable.

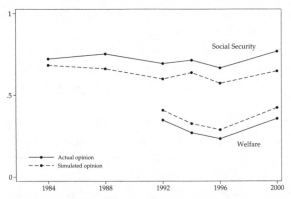

FIGURE 5.4 Actual and Simulated Welfare and Social Security Opinion among Whites, 1984–2000. Figure shows simulated and actual mean opinion. Simulation based on the models presented in tables 5.1 and 5.2. Simulation of welfare opinion calculated by setting each respondent's rating of blacks at one hundred, and simulation of Social Security opinion calculated by setting each respondent's rating of whites at zero. (Source: American National Election Studies.)

If Social Security were not associated with whiteness, we might expect its politics to look different in other ways as well. The popularity of Social Security is often attributed in part to its universality—to the fact that it benefits (almost) everyone and in particular that it is one of relatively few programs that people perceive as benefiting the middle class. My results do nothing to undermine this basic account, although they do suggest some modifications to our understanding of it. Although Social Security may be universal in its benefits, its framing is decidedly not universal in important ways. The framing of Social Security symbolically excludes some groups, as surely as the framing of welfare excludes others. That those included under Social Security's symbolic umbrella are the racial majority in America obfuscates that exclusion, especially for white Americans. But it does not eliminate it.

Various scholars of whiteness have analyzed the ways that their race confers both material and psychic advantages on white Americans (Lipsitz 2006; Roediger 1999; Harris 1995). For white Americans, Social Security may not be simply another (popular) program; rather it is part of what it means, symbolically, to be white in America. Insofar as Social Security is part of the birthright of whiteness, attempts to cut it or take it away can be expected to provoke the strong emotional reactions that social identity theory predicts for any perceived threat to a valued in-group. It is likely this phenomenon that helped spark the firestorm over President Reagan's attempts to cut Social Security in 1982, leading to the characterization of Social Security as the third rail of American politics. And this association with whiteness likely makes Social Security more popular among white Americans than a universal program would otherwise be; after all, Social Security is not for "everyone"—in important ways for white Americans, it is for "us."

Social Security's racialization may play an important role in shifting partisan coalitions as well. The association of welfare and other "big government" programs with blacks is one of the bases for Republican appeals to "Reagan Democrats"—the blue-collar, socially and racially conservative voters who formed a central part of the New Deal Democratic coalition. Social Security has traditionally been associated with the Democratic Party (Petrocik 1996), which means that the mirror-image racialization of Social Security should increase somewhat the appeal of the Democratic Party among some of these same voters. Symbolically, support for and protection of Social Security may serve to ally the Democratic Party with the white in-group for some racially conservative whites and, in so doing, counteract some of the draw of the Republican Party. In this light, Democrats' strategy of positioning themselves as protectors of Social Security seems wise, at least as a way to limit the loss of "Reagan Democrats."

* * *

These survey-based results dovetail nicely with the experimental results discussed in the prior chapter. The experiment demonstrated that racial implication of ostensibly nonracial social policy is possible and that it can be created by rather subtle rhetoric that evokes a relevant schema implicitly. These results show that racialization really does occur in the real world for issues that we might not expect. Social Security rhetoric has been structured in ways that fit the racial schema, but that rhetoric has generally not mentioned race explicitly. Nevertheless, public opinion on Social Security reflects this implicit racialization. This demonstration is important theoretically because it shows that racial group implication extends beyond the laboratory. It also matters politically because it shows that racial group implication is a phenomenon with an important impact on American politics and with important implications for how we understand the intersection of race and politics. In the next chapter, I turn to gender implication and to health care reform.

6

Gendering of Health Care Reform

In this chapter I turn to health care reform, and I move from a focus on racialization to a focus on gendering. I will demonstrate the ways that the 1993–94 debate on health care reform induced gender implication. The health care case serves three purposes. First, this case is another demonstration of group implication in action that shows its broad extent in American politics. Second, by demonstrating gender group implication, the case shows that the subtle association of opinion with feelings about groups is not limited to race. And third, the case provides unique analytic leverage to demonstrate that elite framing causes group implication, because it shows how a change in elite frames led to a change in mass opinion.

Before 1993, mass opinion on health care reform was not linked with gender ideology. The politics and rhetoric deployed during 1993–94 changed this by linking health care with gender in new ways. These linkages were subtle and symbolic, and they unconsciously associated people's feelings about gender relations with their thinking about health care reform. After reform efforts died, these linkages faded among the public. The analysis of Social Security in the last chapter showed the symbolic nature of group implication and demonstrated a case of stable racialization over a relatively long period. In contrast, health care reform serves as a convenient quasi experiment (Campbell and Stanley 1963) and lets us observe a case where a shift in framing — in the context of very salient policy debate — induced group implication.

I begin the chapter by sketching an account of the Clinton administration's 1993–94 health care reform effort, with a focus on the frames deployed by supporters and opponents of reform. In this discussion I demonstrate how these frames were consistent with gender implication. Then I use survey data from the American National Election Studies to demonstrate that public opinion did become gender implicated in response to these frames. Finally, I conclude with some observations about the significance of the findings for health care reform specifically as well as for our understanding of the role of gender implication in political cognition and politics.

FRAMING HEALTH CARE REFORM

After making comprehensive national health care reform a major campaign issue in 1992, the Clinton administration put together a large task force to construct and promote a plan for health care reform. Led by Hillary Rodham Clinton, the task force put together a complex and comprehensive plan, which sought to guarantee universal coverage and contain costs. In September 1993 the White House launched the Health Security Act proposal; after a year of intense debate, comprehensive health care reform was essentially politically dead.

Rather than work closely with cabinet officials, interest groups, and Congress, the administration developed the policy in relative isolation and then tried to sell the plan to the public to create pressure for passage.[1] In response to the administration's "public opinion" strategy, a wide range of players who had been closed out of the policy development process also tried to shape opinion, including various interest groups, Democrats and Republicans in Congress, and others. All sides of the debate focused on crafting and disseminating appeals to the public. These efforts meant that the public was awash in communications campaigns relating to health care reform, which created good conditions for changes in framing to influence the structure of public opinion. In the sections that follow, I note the gendered character of health care policy and then review the frames that both sides deployed during 1993–94, focusing on the ways that these frames — unlike those that came earlier — should have engaged the public's gender schemas.

Health Care as a Gendered Policy Domain

The entire American social welfare system is built on gendered assumptions about the roles of service providers and recipients (Sapiro 1986); in the medical realm this gendering is reinforced by the fact that women and men have different medical needs — some due to biological difference and many more due to the effects of gendered differences in socialization, insurance coverage, poverty, and other social and economic resources (e.g., Tolleson Rinehart and Josephson 2005). Health care is also gendered symbolically. Linda Gordon argues that "in establishing themselves as professionals with cooptive authority to admit or exclude others, doctors made particular use of their power over women" (1990, 157).[2] This symbolic gendering continues today. As Mary Ellen Guy describes: "Gender power relations in medicine are an exaggeration of [gendered] power relations embedded in the political culture. Patients spend more time with nurses but pay physicians. . . . Most reimbursement schedules are predicated on whether the physician orders the services of the ancillary professional" (1995, 243).[3] This symbolic gendering extends, finally, to the doctor-patient relationship itself, as doctors maintain a sort of paternalistic control as the only professional in the system qualified to assess the patient's best interest.

None of this guarantees that health care opinion will be gender implicated among the public without frames that engage the gender schema. As we shall see, though, the gendered character of health care policy and delivery provides fertile ground for these sorts of frames.

Health Care during the 1992 Campaign

During the 1992 presidential campaign Bill Clinton emphasized universal health coverage and cost limitations. The George H. W. Bush campaign stressed free-market approaches, including tax incentives to expand coverage and efficiency measures to cut costs. In his July 3, 1992, weekly radio address, President Bush said, "We would lower costs for patients and providers alike by keeping high taxes, costly litigation, and big bureaucracies off their backs. . . . The biggest story of our time is the failure of socialism and all its empty promises, including nationalized health care and government price-setting" (1993, 1077–78).

Others have shown that Clinton's emphasis on costs and universal coverage evoked considerations of equality among the public (Koch 1998; Jacobs and Shapiro 2000); we would also expect that the Republican framing would evoke concerns about the scope of government. In short, during 1992 health care was framed in terms of the traditional post–New Deal partisan alignment, with Democrats calling for greater government effort to promote equality and Republicans championing a more limited government role.

The Clinton Administration's "Health Security" Frame

This framing changed in 1993. The administration feared that discussing cost controls would frighten middle-class voters who had health coverage and that emphasizing universal coverage would draw attention to the poor (Skocpol 1997, 117–20). Therefore, members of the administration focused on two different themes: security and personal impact. Their consulting team advised that in discussing the plan, *"the dominant goal should be health security. . . .* There is also an emotion in security (lacking in cost) that empowers our rationale for bold change." They advised that discussion of the plan should focus on "personal, human impact" and on "you and your family" (quoted in Skocpol 1997, 117). Thus, "security" was the first of five principles that President Clinton articulated in his September 1993 speech that launched reform, and that speech included frequent references to the health care woes of ordinary families.

Opponents' Frames: Big Government and Private Decision Making

Opponents focused on two frames: that the plan would create giant new government bureaucracies and that it would project the government into the private realm of health care provision. Opponents believed that "support for Clinton's plan could be eroded by accentuating and arousing Americans' dread of government and the personal costs of health reform" (Jacobs and Shapiro 2000, 130). For example, Representative Dick Armey suggested in an October 1993 letter to the *Wall Street Journal* that the "Clinton health plan would create 59 new federal programs or bureaucracies, expand 20 others, [and] impose 79 new federal mandates. . . . The Clinton plan is a bureaucratic nightmare that will ultimately result in higher taxes, reduced efficiency, restricted choice, longer lines, and a much, much bigger federal government" (quoted in Skocpol 1997, 144–45).

Opponents coupled these standard invocations of bureaucracy run amok with claims that those bureaucrats would intrude in the private health care realm. Images of intrusion built on existing images of health care provision; the implicitly private "doctor-patient relationship" has been an icon of health care discussion since the American Medical Association worked to kill "socialized" health care in the 1930s (e.g., Patel and Rushefsky 1995, 21–22). More recently, in the aftermath of the failure of Clinton's plan, the American Medical Association described that relationship this way: "The patient-physician relationship must ultimately be one of trust, but all too often trusting relationships are disrupted not because of dissatisfaction between patient and physician but because of choices made by the patient's employer, a health insurance plan, or both" (Dickey and McMenamin 1999).

Jamieson and Capella (1994) found that bureaucratic control and diminished doctor choice were two of the major themes that appeared in commercials that opposed reform. The most famous example was a series of "Harry and Louise" advertisements, which portrayed a fictitious forty-something couple discussing their concerns about the administration's plans. One major theme was the impending intrusion of the federal government into a traditionally private domain: "'There's got to be a better way,' Harry and Louise opined for the cameras, as they discovered the horrible possibilities of bureaucrats choosing their health care plan" (Skocpol 1997, 137). Although they received only moderate airplay, these advertisements' influence was magnified by extensive media coverage.

Conservative activists also saw the debate as an opportunity to mobilize opinion against Democratic social programs more generally. Republican operative William Kristol warned in 1994 that the administration plan would "relegitimize middle class dependence for 'security' on government spending." He argued that Republicans should oppose *any* reform and should advance a broader antigovernment agenda (Skocpol 1997, 145). Kristol advocated exploiting this opportunity by focusing on personal fears and the intrusion of the government into the private sphere.

Skocpol shows how this strategy turned into a veritable blizzard of media coverage and grassroots mobilization against the plan. For example, in December 1994 the conservative Heritage Foundation's *Policy Review* warned that "we [will be] forced to purchase health care insurance through our regional alliances" and that "a basic concern is whether [patients] will be able to keep their own doctors under the Clinton plan."

This emphasis on large government bureaucracy and private intrusion spread to the popular media. For example, a March 1994 *Reader's Digest* article emphasized that "they are taking away our choice of doctor" (both quotations cited in Skocpol 1996, 147–49). Other interest groups also employed these two frames. On their Web site, Patient Advocacy, a Washington, D.C., group, put it this way: "What qualifies a bureaucrat — whether it be a federal one or a private sector one — to make medical decisions? These decisions should be left to the patient and his or her doctor" (1994).

Of course, criticism of government bureaucracy was nothing new. As I discuss above, the Bush campaign employed this frame in discussing health care in 1992, and as Skocpol notes, "1994 is hardly the first time that political conservatives and business groups have used lurid antistatist rhetoric to attack Democratic-sponsored Social Security initiatives" (1997, 164). What was new to the health care debate was the way this frame was combined with the focus on personal, private-realm interference. Health care was gender implicated by the prospect of vigorous government effort to meddle with private health decisions and disrupt established power relationships within health provision.

Hillary Rodham Clinton as a Gendered Image

Hillary Rodham Clinton's close association with reform further reinforced the gendering effect of these frames. Of course, because she is a woman her prominent participation would have raised the salience of the gender schema among the public (Glick and Fiske 2001). More important, as head of the administration's task force Clinton "violate[d] the traditional separation of the masculine sphere and the feminine domestic sphere that ha[d] previously defined the role of First Lady" (Burrell 1997, 18). Consequently, she became the focus of public debate on changing gender roles in 1993 and 1994. Moreover, her role put a woman in charge of reforming the traditionally male-controlled health care industry (Burrell 1997; Burden and Mughan 1999). As Skocpol argues, "Hillary Rodham Clinton could easily appear 'too strong' in relation to a husband many thought was 'too weak.' She also symbolized the increasing presence and assertiveness of career women, whom many people — including men in elite, professional positions — secretly or not so secretly fear and hate. . . . Cartoonists and talk radio hosts could ridicule the Clinton plan for its alleged governmental overweeningness — and in the process subliminally remind people how much they resent strong women" (1997, 152–53). Her association thus served to reinforce the gender implication inherent in the issue rhetoric over reform.

EMPIRICAL EXPECTATIONS

My expectation is that the frames deployed during the reform debate influenced opinion on health care reform. Specifically, I anticipate that the reform debate made Americans much more likely to evaluate health care reform through a gender schema, which means that health care opinion should have become more strongly associated with gender ideology in 1994. Compared with other years, in 1994 I expect Americans who hold traditional gender views to oppose reform more (or support it less) than otherwise similar gender egalitarians. In addition, I expect these patterns of gender implication will operate similarly among men and women. Although men and women may differ in their average position on the evaluative dimension of the gender schema, both men and women should apply the gender schema to their evaluation of health care reform in 1994.

HEALTH CARE OPINION

The ANES includes a question about respondents' support for a government insurance plan to address rising health costs.[4] This general measure has several advantages, compared with questions that focus specifically on the Clinton plan. First, because I seek to compare gender implication over time, I need a consistent measure, rather than one tailored specifically to any particular year. Second, this measure represents a somewhat conservative test of gender implication. If the 1993–94 debates gendered opinion on the administration's plan and nothing else, that would not say much for the scope of gender implication generally. I am interested precisely in whether a wide-ranging and symbolically rich debate had effects on opinion within the domain of government action and health care more generally. Finally, there is precedent for the use of this standard ANES measure in analyses of the effects of health care reform on opinion (Koch 1998).

I have recoded the seven-point ANES measure to run from zero (most

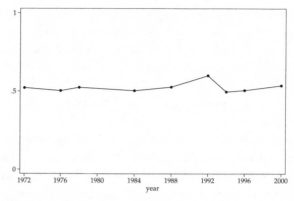

FIGURE 6.1 Mean Support for Government Health Insurance, 1972–2000. (Source: American National Election Studies.)

opposed to government involvement) to one (most in favor of involvement). This measure has an overall mean between the years 1972 and 2000 of 0.53 and a standard deviation of 0.36. As figure 6.1 demonstrates, support was fairly stable through the 1970s and early 1980s. Americans became somewhat more favorable toward a government role in health care in the late 1980s and quite a bit more favorable in 1992, likely as a result of the emphasis on health care during the campaign. Support dropped to its lowest point in 1994 — probably as a reaction to the reform debate — and has been rising moderately since.

Gender Predispositions

Unfortunately, compared with racial ideology, the ANES instrumentation on gender predispositions is far less rich and consistent over time. In particular, no multiple-item scale of gender predispositions appears in all the necessary studies for this analysis. Nevertheless, there are two ANES measures that capture elements of the gender schema. The first is the women's equal-role item, which asks whether women's place is in the home or whether they should be equal with men in "business, industry, and government."[5] This item is ideal in that it addresses the intersection of gender and social roles and duties and focuses on what roles men and women *should* have in society. It captures the public-private distinction, it focuses on the cognitive, and it avoids gender identity and the details of current political conflict over gender. The disadvantages with this measure are that it is a single item and that it is somewhat skewed toward the egalitarian response.

The second measure comes from the thermometer rating battery, in which respondents were asked to rate their feelings about the women's movement and feminists on a scale of zero to one hundred. These groups are both closely associated with efforts to make gender arrangements more egalitarian, and so people's positive or negative evaluations of them should relate closely to their own beliefs about proper gender arrangements (Huddy, Neely, and LaFay 2000). My strategy was to build a single composite measure by averaging the equal-role item and whichever thermometer score is available in a given year. Although I would prefer a longer battery of gender ideology questions crafted to measure the gender schema with more nuance, this composite measure serves my purposes.[6]

Control Variables

I include the same set of control variables in this model as appeared in the welfare and Social Security models in chapter 5, and I do so for the same reason: to control for other factors that both affect opinion and are correlated with gender ideology. These variables include the principles of egalitarianism and limited government; partisan and ideological predispositions; and income, education, gender, age, retirement status, disability status, and marital status. In addition, because this analysis is not limited to whites, I included an indicator variable for black respondents.

I ran a series of regressions, one per year, of support for government health insurance on gender ideology and the control variables.[7] I ran this model for presidential years from 1988 through 2000, and for 1994, providing two years on either side of the crucial 1994 study for comparison.

RESULTS: GENDERING OF HEALTH CARE OPINION

Table 6.1 presents the results from this model. The first row gives the effect of gender ideology on health care opinion in each year. In years other than 1994, health care opinion is slightly gender implicated. The coefficients vary around an average of 0.065 and hover on the edge of statistical significance. This is a small effect — compared with gender tra-

TABLE 6.1   Gendering of Health Care Opinion, 1988–2000

| | GOVERNMENT HEALTH PLAN | | | | |
	1988	1992	1994	1996	2000
Gender egalitarianism	0.044	0.094*	0.175**	0.099*	0.022
	(0.043)	(0.040)	(0.040)	(0.043)	(0.060)
Limited government	−0.527**	−0.404**	−0.482**	−0.476**	−0.409**
	(0.044)	(0.036)	(0.040)	(0.043)	(0.044)
Egalitarianism	0.035	0.150**	0.121*	0.050	0.244**
	(0.050)	(0.040)	(0.047)	(0.045)	(0.055)
Democrat	0.008	0.024	0.023	0.035^	0.010
	(0.021)	(0.017)	(0.019)	(0.019)	(0.024)
Republican	−0.076**	−0.053**	−0.107**	−0.079**	−0.080**
	(0.022)	(0.018)	(0.019)	(0.021)	(0.027)
N	1,216	1,683	1,403	1,234	1,151
R-squared	0.23	0.25	0.35	0.30	0.29
Standard error of regression	0.29	0.28	0.27	0.26	0.32

Source: American National Election Studies.
Note: Entries are OLS regression coefficients with standard errors in parentheses. Models also include the full set of control variables discussed in the text. Full results appear in the Web appendix.
** $p < 0.01$; * $p < 0.05$; ^ $p < 0.10$ two-sided.

ditionalists, the most egalitarian respondents are 0.065 more supportive of government health care, which is less than half of the distance between two points on the seven-point scale.

The impact of gender ideology on health care opinion is almost three times larger in 1994 ($b = 0.175$, $p < 0.01$) than in earlier years. Now the most gender-egalitarian respondents support government health care by just over one point on the seven-point scale, compared with the most traditionalist respondents. This finding supports the hypothesis that the frames deployed in the debate associated gender ideology with health care opinion in 1994. These results are illustrated in figure 6.2, which depicts graphically how health care opinion varies with gender ideology for a hypothetical respondent who is average on all the control variables. Thus, for example, in 1988 we predict that an otherwise typical respondent who falls at the most gender-traditionalist end of the gender ideology scale would fall at the middle (0.50) on the health care question. In comparison, a gender egalitarian who was otherwise identical would fall at 0.54, a difference of only 0.04. In contrast, in 1994 those two respondents would differ by 0.18 on the zero-to-one health care scale.

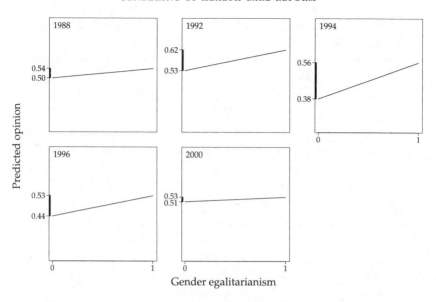

FIGURE 6.2 Impact of Gender Egalitarianism on Health Care Opinion, 1988–2000. Figure shows the predicted opinion for otherwise average respondents whose gender egalitarianism varies from zero to one, on the basis of the models in table 6.1. Labeled points on the y-axis correspond to gender egalitarianism scores of zero and one; y-axis runs from 0.25 to 0.75. (Source: American National Election Studies.)

Interestingly, although support for limited government is substantially related to health care opinion, the impact of limited government is *not* noticeably larger in 1994 (−0.482 in 1994, compared with an average of −0.45 in the other years). Despite opponents' emphasis on the specter of government bureaucracy, citizens' feelings about the appropriate size and scope of the federal role played no stronger a role in 1994 than they played throughout the late 1980s and 1990s. This finding provides additional indirect evidence that the frames deployed in 1993–94 did not resonate particularly with fear of the federal government in the abstract. Rather, this rhetoric — combined with claims that the plan would interfere in the private realm of health care and family — resonated with the gender schema and thereby increased the association between gender ideology and opinion.

Several other results are interesting. Controlling for the other factors in the model, partisan differences sharpened slightly in 1994, as we might expect given the partisan nature of the debate and of the 1994 congressional campaigns. Republican identifiers were 0.107 more conservative on health care in 1994, compared with independents. In 1988 and 1992, on the other hand, they were only 0.065 more conservative on average. This partisan difference faded slowly after 1994, with the estimated coefficient back to −0.08 after 1994.

The results for egalitarianism parallel those of Koch (1998): it is strongly associated with opinion in 1992, probably as a result of the egalitarian frames deployed during the campaign. When the debate shifted in 1994 away from egalitarian frames, Americans became less likely to view health care through an egalitarian lens.

One last finding bears mention. There is a small gender gap in health care opinion: across the five years in my analysis, women are about 0.05 more supportive of a government role, and this gap was slightly larger in 1994 (0.07). Nevertheless, once all the other factors in the models are taken into account, the gender gap disappears completely. Thus, the relatively modest gender gap on health care operates through the various other predispositions included in the model.

Feelings toward Hillary Rodham Clinton

I suggest above that Hillary Clinton's role in health care reform should have operated symbiotically with the gendering rhetoric to solidify the gender implication of health care. Another possibility is that the apparent increase in gendering merely reflects the association of Hillary Rodham Clinton, who is herself gendered, with health care policy. To assess this possibility, I ran a model of health care opinion that adds the thermometer score rating of Hillary Rodham Clinton in the years following 1992, when it is available. Table 6.2 presents the coefficients of interest from this model.[8]

These results confirm that feelings about health care did become associated with feelings about Clinton in 1994. In 1992 one's rating of Hillary Clinton is barely related to health care opinion ($b = 0.049$, $p > 0.10$); by 1994, that rating is substantially related to opinion ($b = 0.116$, $p < 0.01$). The association begins to fade in 1996 ($b = 0.086$, $p < 0.05$) and falls further in 2000. Including Hillary Clinton ratings reduces the estimates of gender implication by about a quarter from 1992 through 1996 but, if anything, sharpens the central finding that gender implication was stronger in 1994 than in other years. Health care was gender implicated in 1994

TABLE 6.2   Health Care Opinion Model with Hillary Rodham Clinton Rating, 1992–2000

| | GOVERNMENT HEALTH PLAN | | | |
	1992	1994	1996	2000
Gender egalitarianism	0.066	0.140**	0.083^	0.015
	(0.042)	(0.040)	(0.045)	(0.062)
HR Clinton thermometer rating	0.049	0.116**	0.086*	0.055
	(0.036)	(0.032)	(0.035)	(0.040)
N	1,586	1,396	1,220	1,141
R-squared	0.26	0.35	0.30	0.29
Standard error of regression	0.27	0.27	0.26	0.32

Source: American National Election Studies.
Note: Entries are OLS regression coefficients with standard errors in parentheses. Models include full set of control variables; results appear in the Web appendix.
** $p < 0.01$; * $p < 0.05$; ^ $p < 0.10$ two-sided.

both directly and by its association with a prominent and highly gendered First Lady.

Racialization of Health Care?

Another interesting question is the role that *racial* predispositions play in health care opinion. I have no theoretical reason to expect health care opinion to be racialized in general. The rhetoric surrounding health care has generally focused on health care as a right for all Americans rather than as a program for certain populations; this language should frame it in terms of egalitarianism perhaps, but probably not in terms of race.[9] Because the race and gender schemas have different structures, I expect the gender-implicating frames in 1994 *not* to induce racial implication as well. Moreover, the Clinton administration was very careful to craft language that implied that all Americans (including the "middle class") would benefit from the reforms. Again, this sort of language should militate against racialization, which my theory suggests should require the suggestion of in-group and out-group.

Of course, Social Security is framed as a universal program as well, yet that program *is* racialized. On the basis of the structure of the racial schema, I argue that the racial implication of Social Security requires not simply a reference to "all Americans" (which many white Americans no doubt understand to mean themselves) but also the invocation of

TABLE 6.3   Gendering and Racialization of Health Care Opinion

	GOVERNMENT HEALTH PLAN				
	1988	1992	1994	1996	2000
Gender egalitarianism	0.047	0.110**	0.181**	0.101*	0.012
	(0.044)	(0.040)	(0.040)	(0.045)	(0.063)
Thermometer rating of whites	−0.111*	−0.047	−0.096*	0.061	0.087
	(0.048)	(0.043)	(0.048)	(0.055)	(0.064)
Thermometer rating of blacks	−0.001	−0.052	−0.011	−0.135*	−0.072
	(0.050)	(0.045)	(0.043)	(0.055)	(0.062)
N	1,185	1,645	1,355	1,199	1,099
R-squared	0.23	0.25	0.35	0.30	0.29
Standard error of regression	0.29	0.28	0.27	0.26	0.32

Source: American National Election Studies.
Note: Entries are OLS regression coefficients with standard errors in parentheses. Models also include the full set of control variables discussed in the text. Full results appear in the Web appendix.
** $p < 0.01$; * $p < 0.05$; ^ $p < 0.10$ two-sided.

symbolically white attributes such as hard work and individual responsibility. So health care gives us a chance to examine this claim with some evidence. Both health care and Social Security are discussed in universal terms. But Social Security is framed as a reward for those who fit the (symbolically white) criteria; health care is framed as a basic human right.

To examine the role of racial predispositions, I ran a model of health care opinion that added two measures of racial predispositions: respondents' thermometer ratings of whites and of blacks.[10] Including measures of racial predispositions does nothing to our estimate of gendering, as indicated by the results in table 6.3. These results mean, first, that the estimates of gender implication are not racialization in disguise. Second, health care opinion is not racialized. The relationship between the thermometer ratings and opinion varies a bit from year to year—those who feel warmly toward whites in 1988 are somewhat less supportive of government health care, and those who feel warmly toward blacks in 1996 are somewhat less supportive in 1996. Nevertheless, health care opinion is not connected with racial considerations in any consistent way. And most important, the gender implication of 1994 does not seem to have caused any spillover into racialization in that year; this result reconfirms that racialization and gendering are indeed distinct processes.

TABLE 6.4   Gendering of Health Care Opinion by Gender

| | GOVERNMENT HEALTH PLAN | | | | |
	1988	1992	1994	1996	2000
Among women	0.085	0.104^	0.192**	0.139*	−0.010
	(0.057)	(0.053)	(0.056)	(0.060)	(0.086)
Among men	−0.009	0.086	0.157**	0.045	0.061
	(0.068)	(0.060)	(0.057)	(0.065)	(0.085)

Source: American National Election Studies.
Note: Entries are OLS regression coefficients with standard errors in parentheses. Models also include the full set of control variables discussed in the text. Number of cases varies from 514 to 869; full results appear in the Web appendix.
** $p < 0.01$; * $p < 0.05$; ^ $p < 0.10$ two-sided.

SUBGROUP ANALYSES

As with the analyses of welfare and Social Security in chapter 5, it is instructive to consider how the group implication of health care varies among subgroups of the American population. Therefore, in this section I consider three lines of division among the public: gender, partisanship, and political engagement.

Gender

The results above show that women's and men's opinions differ little from each other once we take account of gender predispositions and the other independent variables. I also expect that group implication should work the same way. To explore this I ran the gendering analysis separately among men and women; the relevant results are presented in table 6.4. Women may be slightly more prone to perceive health care through the gender schema in the years other than 1994 (the average coefficient is 0.08 among women and 0.05 among men in these years). Most important, women and men reacted identically to the gendering rhetoric during the reform debate. In 1994, the effect of gender ideology on health care opinion is 0.192 among women and 0.157 among men. This finding means that both had their gender schemas engaged to a very similar extent in 1994. This gendering persisted somewhat among women in 1996 ($b = 0.139$, $p < 0.05$) but not men ($b = 0.045$, n.s.). By 2000, gendering had faded essentially to zero for both. This analysis confirms the basic expectation that men and women would react to the gendering rhetoric in similar ways.

TABLE 6.5   Gendering of Health Care Opinion by Partisanship

| | GOVERNMENT HEALTH PLAN | | | | |
	1988	1992	1994	1996	2000
Among Democrats	0.065	0.022	0.226**	0.077	0.060
	(0.071)	(0.071)	(0.077)	(0.082)	(0.122)
Among independents	−0.025	0.122*	0.211**	0.130	−0.085
	(0.077)	(0.061)	(0.074)	(0.083)	(0.097)
Among Republicans	0.088	0.159*	0.079	0.067	0.108
	(0.078)	(0.080)	(0.059)	(0.064)	(0.104)

Source: American National Election Studies.
Note: Entries are OLS regression coefficients with standard errors in parentheses. Models also include the full set of control variables discussed in the text. Number of cases varies from 316 to 644; full results appear in the Web appendix.
** $p < 0.01$; * $p < 0.05$; ^ $p < 0.10$ two-sided.

Partisanship

We might also expect citizens' partisan attachments to have conditioned their reactions to the very partisan health care debate. To assess this possibility, I ran the basic model separately among identifiers of the two major parties and among independents. Table 6.5 presents the relevant results.

Here we do find some variation. Democrats and independents followed the pattern observed so far: they gender health care quite substantially in 1994 (b = 0.226 and 0.211, respectively) and much less both before and after (average b = 0.056 and 0.036). In contrast, Republicans seem entirely unaffected by the gendering discourse of 1993–94: in 1994 they gendered health care a bit less, if anything, than in other years (b = 0.079 in 1994, compared with an average of 0.106 in the other years). It is not entirely clear why this would be the case for Republicans, but it does suggest that the gendered frames employed by opponents were effective in broadening opposition to the Clinton plan by appealing in particular to gender-traditionalist Democrats and independents.

Political Engagement

Finally, we know that citizens vary greatly in the attention they pay to politics and in their exposure to political discourse (e.g., Converse 1972; Zaller 1992). If changes in political discourse truly caused the effects I observed above, then those effects should be strongest among respon-

TABLE 6.6   Gendering of Health Care Opinion by Respondent Engagement

| | GOVERNMENT HEALTH PLAN | | | | |
	1988	1992	1994	1996	2000
Among most engaged	0.090	0.117^	0.189**	0.164*	0.057
	(0.063)	(0.064)	(0.056)	(0.064)	(0.115)
Among mid-level engaged	0.030	0.017	0.272**	0.064	0.086
	(0.085)	(0.069)	(0.070)	(0.074)	(0.108)
Among least engaged	−0.013	0.118	−0.007	0.021	−0.048
	(0.092)	(0.076)	(0.090)	(0.100)	(0.098)

Source: American National Election Studies.
Note: Entries are OLS regression coefficients with standard errors in parentheses. Models also include the full set of control variables discussed in the text. Number of cases varies from 294 to 627; full results appear in the Web appendix.
** $p < 0.01$; * $p < 0.05$; ^ $p < 0.10$ two-sided.

dents most exposed to the discourse. Insofar as the gendered discourse was subliminal, and people were not aware of the gender implication, I expect that gendering should increase with the reception of gendering messages, which should itself increase with political engagement. And as with Social Security and welfare racialization, I do not expect even the most engaged citizens to recognize — and possibly reject — the gendered nature of the frames. Table 6.6 presents the results of the health care opinion model, run separately for respondents in the top, middle, and bottom third of political information.

As expected, political engagement sharply conditions the results. The least engaged respondents reacted not at all to the gendering rhetoric. It would seem that the relatively subtle nature of the gender implication passed them by in 1994. Middle- and high-information respondents, on the other hand, reacted sharply to the gendering rhetoric of 1993–94. Before the reform debate, mid-information respondents did not gender health care (b averaged 0.02 in 1988 and 1992, n.s. both years). In 1994 the impact of gender ideology is much stronger (b = 0.272, p < 0.01), and it drops precipitously in 1996 (average b = 0.08 in 1996 and 2000).

Highly engaged respondents also gendered health care much more in 1994 (b = 0.189, p < 0.01) than in 1988 and 1992 (average b = 0.10). Among this well-informed group, however, the effect persisted through 1996 (b = 0.164, p < 0.01) before fading by 2000. Thus, those who pay at least moderate attention to politics picked up on the gendering rhetoric, and the best-informed remembered it for some time.[11] The fact that political engagement conditions gendering so sharply serves as additional confirmation that this gendering was driven by the political discourse, insofar as only those who were reasonably engaged in politics were affected by it.

SUMMARY AND THE NET IMPACT OF GENDERING

Clearly, we can find many deep roots of the failure of health care reform in 1994. The American political system makes major policy innovation difficult to achieve under the best conditions, and health reform has failed repeatedly during the twentieth century. Many factors having nothing to do with public opinion contributed to the failure in this instance (e.g., Hacker 1997). Nevertheless, the administration's choice of a public-opinion strategy does raise the question of what impact, if any, the gender implication of opinion had on the overall fate of the reform effort and whether there might have been ways the administration could have countered the gender implication.

First, because gender implication implies polarization on gender ideology, it is theoretically possible that gender implication *increased* support for reform by increasing the support of gender egalitarians over what it otherwise would have been. Because gendering frames came primarily from reform opponents, however, it is reasonable to assume that the net effect of gender implication was to depress opinion by reducing the support of gender traditionalists below what it would have otherwise been. We can see this in figure 6.2 by comparing the 1992 and 1994 panels. The entire line is lower in 1994, but support among gender traditionalists (at the left end of the line) fell much more than it fell among gender egalitarians (at the right end). Specifically, support among traditionalists fell by 0.147 (from 0.531 to 0.384), whereas support among egalitarians fell 0.067 (from 0.625 to 0.558). The debate over reform decreased enthusiasm for a government role in health care across the board, but the drop was more than twice as large among gender traditionalists.

An instructive exercise is to imagine that support among gender traditionalists had not declined any more precipitously than among egalitarians—that support declined by 0.067 across the board. In this scenario, the left-hand end of the line in the 1994 pane of figure 6.2 would be rotated upward until it paralleled the 1992 line, albeit at a lower level. In this case, the overall average opinion in 1994 would have been 0.533 on the zero-to-one scale — just above its level in 1988.[12] This number is not over-whelmingly higher, but still represents a significant difference politically. Clearly this difference alone would not have turned the tide of opposition to the administration plan, but it does suggest that gender implication added an additional nail to the coffin.[13]

If we grant for a moment that the gendering frames depressed net opinion and thereby hurt reform, how might the administration have countered or avoided the gender implication? Unless the plan itself had been radically different, the administration could probably not avoid anti-government frames from opponents. Nevertheless, if the Clinton team had managed to keep that aspect of the debate focused on who should be responsible for paying rather than who would be responsible for deci-sion making, then the specifically gendered impact of opposition frames might have been muted. Schlesinger finds that Americans are much more supportive of government financing of health care compared with govern-ment influence on the content of health care provision (2004); perhaps if the administration had not opened the door by focusing on personal benefits, then opponents would have been prevented from deploying the potent *combination* of limited government and private-sphere interfer-ence frames — or perhaps not. In any case it seems likely that a traditional debate over the relative efficiency of government versus private-sector provision and over the need for a systemic approach to universal coverage would have been better for reform advocates.

On a broader scale, the results presented in table 6.5 indicate that the impact of gendering was strongest among Democrats and independents, which suggests the gendering frames were particularly effective at decreas-ing support among these groups. Thus, the gendered frames may have been particularly effective for opponents of reform insofar as they sepa-rated gender-traditionalist Democrats (and independents) from the rest of the Democratic coalition. In this sense, gender implication may have served an analogous role to the implicitly racialized rhetoric deployed by Republicans to attract support from racially conservative Reagan Demo-crats in the 1980s (Edsall and Edsall 1992; Kinder and Sanders 1996).

Gender issues have come on and off the political agenda over the years, but, in contrast with matters of race, gender issues have not served as a fundamental basis of partisan alignment.[14] This difference likely means that elite debate does not invoke gender frames as frequently as racial frames and that the public is therefore less well trained to view political issues through the "lens of gender."[15] Nevertheless, the current analysis shows that gender can serve as an organizing principle for a political issue under the right circumstances. We can imagine gender implication happening for other issues, that is, when political elites choose frames that trade on gender schemas among the mass public and convey those frames loudly enough. We would not expect these sorts of frames to appear often, however, because gender is not central to the mainstream partisan alignment. Precisely for this reason, though, gendering can be a useful strategy for fracturing an existing coalition (e.g., Riker 1986). Just as the gendered frames moved gender-traditional Democrats and independents against health care reform, we might expect there to be other issues where Republicans can use gendered frames in this way. In fact, Republicans' ability to attract gender-traditionalist Democrats and independents with implicitly gendered political rhetoric is a pattern we may be seeing continued today with the explicit emphasis on so-called cultural issues, many of which involve matters of gender ideology at their heart.

More broadly, this chapter demonstrates that gender can matter for public opinion in ways that go beyond our current approaches. Virginia Sapiro lays out a typology of three ways that public policies may be gendered: because they are "manifestly about gender," because men and women have "different experiences, needs, or problems" relating to the policy, or because policies inadvertently affect men and women differently. She points out, though, that there is no necessary correspondence between the gendered content of policies and the public's perception of those policies in gendered terms and suggests that more research is needed to examine "the conditions under which culturally derived stereotypes and frames are activated" (2003, 619–20). This chapter represents an example of how this investigation can take place for a policy that the public does not consciously associate with gender.

These results make clear, however, that one important route to the gendered perception of issues — what I call gender implication — is a correspondence in structure between elite frames and mass schemas. These results further imply that gendered issue perceptions can be largely or entirely symbolic and metaphorical: the gender implication of health care opinion in 1993–94 turned not on the fact that women and men have different health problems. Rather, gender implication occurred because the frames deployed structured reform as interfering metaphorically with intimate power relations within the private sphere of health care provision.

Finally, the health care reform case adds significantly to our understanding of group implication more broadly. It does so in two ways. First, association of racial attitudes with some policy attitudes has been well documented, especially for welfare and crime. My Social Security analysis extends our knowledge of racialization significantly. On the other hand, these sorts of symbolic associations with gender predispositions have not been previously documented. The gender implication of health care reform makes clear, therefore, that gender attitudes may be mobilized implicitly by appropriately structured issue frames. This finding tells us something about the potential for gender to play an important role in political attitudes; it also makes clear the ways in which racialization is part of the more-general phenomenon of group implication.

Second, the health care example adds to the overall analysis of group implication because it represents an interrupted time series: a relatively abrupt change in framing that was associated with a relatively abrupt change in mass opinion. When framing changed in 1993 and 1994, opinion reacted in ways my theory predicts. When the issue faded from the national agenda after the failure of the Clinton effort, the group implication among the public faded as well. In contrast, the racial framing of Social Security and welfare has been quite stable over time, and the public has reacted by consistently racializing both issues. The health care case strengthens the overall causal argument by demonstrating a reaction among the public to a change in elite rhetoric. This evidence strengthens the argument that framing — and the specific patterns of congruence between frames and schemas — underlies group implication.

7

Race and Gender Frames in American Politics

I have shown that citizens' thoughts and feelings about race and about gender can be subtly evoked by appropriately structured political rhetoric. Once evoked, those thoughts and feelings are applied by people to the evaluation of political issues, even issues that on their face have nothing to do with race or gender. Thus, citizens' ideas about race and gender can underlie opinion on issues well beyond race and gender relations themselves. This process is controlled by the interaction between the structure of citizens' cognitive representations of race and gender — their race and gender schemas — and the structure that political elites lend to issues through framing. Frames impose structure on political issues, and when that structure matches the cognitive representation, or schema, for a social category (such as race or gender), that schema will likely govern comprehension and evaluation of the issue. Thus, when the structure of the race schema in people's minds matches the structure of an issue as it is framed in political discourse, then the schema may be evoked to perceive the issue, and people's thoughts and feelings about race relations will be mapped analogically to their evaluation of the issue. If, on the other hand, the frames for an issue structure it to be congruent with the gender schema, then citizens' thoughts and feelings about gender relations may become the source for evaluation of the issue.

American race and gender schemas share important characteristics. Each deals with difference, regulates relations between individuals and groups, includes strong normative implications, and contains a dimension along which individuals vary in their evaluations of the state of racial or gender affairs. Nevertheless, the two schemas have different structures in essential ways, which means that differently structured issue frames will evoke one or the other. Both schemas are apt to serve as sources for political reasoning because both are important psychologically and socially and because both have rich structures that include strong normative evaluations.

* * *

Chapter 4 presented experimental evidence of this process of group implication at work. This evidence demonstrates the basic mechanisms of group implication separately for racialization and gendering. The basic experimental strategy was to compare three randomly assigned groups of participants. The first, baseline, group read a single newspaper article about each of three ostensibly nonracial political issues: grandparent visitation, Social Security privatization, and government economic intervention. For the test of racialization, a second group had their racial schemas primed (by answering several questions about race relations) and then read a newspaper article about each of the issues. These articles were designed to structure each issue to be congruent with the race schema without mentioning race explicitly. For the test of gendering, a third group had their *gender* schemas primed and then read an article about each issue that structured it to be congruent with the gender schema, generally without mentioning gender explicitly.

For racialization, the results were strong. For two issues — grandparent visitation and Social Security privatization — those in the race condition were significantly more likely than those in the baseline condition to align their position on the issue with their feelings about race relations, which indicated that they were drawing on their racial schema to evaluate the issue. For the third issue — government economic intervention — participants in both the baseline and race conditions associated the issue with their racial predispositions, suggesting that, for these participants at least, that issue was already racialized. Still, the article did strengthen the relationship between racial predispositions and opinion among types of participants who were less prone to racialize the issue naturally.

For gendering, the results were a bit more complicated, in part because the gender-condition articles varied systematically in the subtlety of the gender framing. I varied the subtlety to explore the expectation that subtle, implicit frames would be most effective at invoking gender implication. For Social Security, gender was not mentioned explicitly in the gender-condition article, and the gendering was quite subtle and symbolic, in line with the subtle racialization for all three issues. For this issue, results were as expected: participants in the gender condition — who were exposed to the combination of a subtle prime of the gender schema plus an article that structured the issue to match that schema — were much more likely to draw on their feelings about proper gender relations to evaluate the issue. For the visitation issue, the gender framing was somewhat less subtle. Although gender was not mentioned explicitly, the issue of visitation rights for grandparents is closely related to questions of family structure and gender relations. Thus, some participants in the baseline condition might be expected to apply their gender schema to the issue even without reading an article that framed the issue in gender terms. It seems that this situation occurred, which made it harder to detect the effect of gender framing. Nonetheless, the results were stronger for this issue once I was able to separate out some of the participants who were likely to gender the issue regardless of its framing. Finally, for government economic intervention, the gender framing was explicit — the article framed the issue directly in terms of its impact on women and on gender relations. This treatment was a complete failure: it did not induce participants to evaluate the issue in terms of their gender schemas at all. Although not conclusive, this failure is consistent with the theoretical expectation that gendering — like racialization — operates implicitly. Overall, then, with some variation and complication across the three issues, the gender results were also broadly supportive of expectations.

The experiments tested jointly the effect of accessibility and fit. Participants' feelings about race or gender affected their opinions when two conditions held: when their race or gender schemas were primed unobtrusively and when they read newspaper articles that structured political issues to be congruent with the race or gender schema. Although the experiment did not directly test the separate effects of prime (which makes the schema accessible) and fit between schema and issue, additional analysis suggests that both are important for group implication and that merely priming the relevant schema is not sufficient to induce group implication reliably.

Furthermore, in addition to demonstrating separately the potential for racial group implication and gender group implication, the experimental analyses also make clear that race and gender implication are distinct processes. The frames that induced gender implication did *not* cause race implication, and the race-implicating frames did not implicate gender considerations. This finding reinforces further the importance of structural alignment between frame and schema as well as the distinction between the two schemas.

*   *   *

The survey results in chapters 5 and 6 picked up where the experimental results left off. They demonstrate that implication takes place outside the laboratory in contemporary American politics, with effects that are politically important. Chapter 5 considered the racialization of the American public's support for spending on two programs: welfare and Social Security. The chapter began by reviewing the framing of these programs in political rhetoric over the past fifty years and by showing the ways that framing fits the structure of the racial schema. Just as welfare policy has been associated in political rhetoric with laziness and perverse incentives, Social Security has been linked symbolically with hard work and legitimately earned rewards. These values and attributes are linked symbolically with whiteness in most (white) Americans' racial schemas. This linkage has led to Social Security being viewed (implicitly) as a "white" program, just as welfare has been branded as symbolically "black."

Drawing on American National Election Studies data, I documented this racialization among American whites from 1984 through 2000. I found that racially conservative whites are consistently less supportive of spending on welfare, compared with racially liberal whites. Conversely, racial conservatives are relatively more supportive of spending on Social Security than are racial liberals. Moreover, this racialization occurs most strongly through white Americans' feelings about the white in-group: those who feel more warmly toward whites as a group are more supportive of Social Security spending. The magnitude of this racialization is approximately equal to that of welfare. White Americans view Social Security in part as a program for them, just as they view welfare as a program for the racial out-group. This racialization separates racial liberals and racial conservatives; it also substantially increases overall white support for Social Security and decreases support for welfare.

These findings confirm that consistently racialized rhetoric, even though quite subtle, can lead people to evaluate an issue in terms of the racial schema. This analysis brings to light a little-noted phenomenon that is interesting and important in its own right. It also demonstrates the generality of the mechanisms underlying the more commonly reported findings about the racialization of welfare opinion. This chapter, therefore, demonstrates the way that elite rhetoric and public opinion evolve together. It also reinforces the theoretical point that racialization — often studied in the context of welfare and crime opinion — is more subtle, more pervasive, and more implicit than the example of welfare alone might suggest.

Chapter 6 turned to gender and explored the ways that the health care reform debate of 1994 temporarily gendered opinion on health care policy. The chapter first examined the discourse surrounding health care reform to show that the rhetoric in 1994 framed the issue in terms of public and private spheres, with opponents asserting repeatedly that the plan would infringe on the proper division of labor within the private sphere of doctor and patient. I show how the frames surrounding health care reform in 1994 — and only in that year — were remarkably well structured to link health care with Americans' gender schemas.

The quantitative analysis draws on ANES data to demonstrate that opinion on government involvement in health care was only slightly gendered both before and after the period of proposed health care reform. In contrast, opinion was gendered in 1994, with gender conservatives more opposed to a government role in health care than gender liberals. Health care opinion became gendered among both men and women; however, the gendering of health care reform in 1994 was especially pronounced among Democratic identifiers — moving gender-conservative Democrats against the plan — and among those highly engaged with politics, who were most likely to be exposed to the relatively new framing patterns. This pattern of effects suggests that opponents' rhetoric was well suited to interfering with the Clintons' coalition-building efforts.

By expanding the story to include gendering, this chapter demonstrates that group implication is a general phenomenon: welfare is but one example of racialization, and racialization is but one example of group implication. In addition, this chapter shows how a change in rhetoric, which took place during 1992 through 1994, led to a change in the degree of gendering for the health care issue. This finding increases our confidence that framing by political elites really does drive group implication among the mass public.

*   *   *

In the rest of this chapter I step back from these results to consider their broader implications for several topics: the political psychology of political communication; the study of race and opinion; the study of gender and opinion; the intersectionality of race and gender; and, finally, group implication's place in American politics and democracy.

FRAMING: POLITICAL COMMUNICATIONS MEETS POLITICAL PSYCHOLOGY

Public-opinion literature is rife with demonstrations of framing effects. It is clear that issue frames matter: they can shift opinions and can alter the bases on which citizens construct them. But attempts to frame are not always successful. Framing experiments fail and, more important, so do political campaigns and other attempts to sway the public. Relatively little work exists that demonstrates systematically when framing will succeed and when it will fail.[1] My theory and empirical work help to fill that gap.

A central insight of this book is that framing is a two-sided process. On one side, frames lend structure to issues by highlighting some considerations over others and by linking those considerations into a coherent narrative. On the other side, cognitive schemas structure our understanding of social categories by linking together their various attributes into a coherent story in our minds. When these two *structures* match — even if the surface contents are unrelated — then the schema can be applied analogically to the framed issue. Once this analogy is created, inferences suggested by the schema are mapped to the issue, driving opinion. Equally important, this process can occur unconsciously. This perspective allows me to draw on the extensive work on the cognitive psychology on analogical reasoning and metaphor comprehension to explore the ways that exceedingly subtle issue frames can resonate with psychological schemas to affect opinion formation.

The Role of Cognitive Accessibility in Framing

This book also puts some major debates in political communication research in a new perspective. Price and Tewksbury develop a model of the psychological processes that underlie the media's effects on political cognition (1997). Some version of this basic model underlies much of the work on framing in political science and political communication. They argue that a particular consideration or predisposition will affect an evaluation on the basis of a two-step process: first, the consideration must be activated and come to mind, and second, it must be judged relevant to the issue at hand.

Price and Tewksbury suggest that the first stage, coming to mind, generally occurs outside of conscious thought and is largely controlled by cognitive accessibility. Those considerations that have been recently or frequently used are more likely to come to mind, as are considerations that are chronically accessible for an individual. Accessibility is only the beginning, however; an accessible schema may or may not be applied to the task at hand. At the second stage, a person may consciously consider whether an activated consideration is relevant to the evaluation and reject those that are judged irrelevant. This conscious consideration may or may not occur in any particular case; it is particularly unlikely to occur when we are distracted, unmotivated, or uninterested in the issue at hand.

In most of the work on framing and priming, the first stage is treated as largely unconscious and automatic, and the second is regarded as conscious and therefore controlled. Thus, considerations come to mind simply because they have been recently activated or because a frame activates them. Next, a person may evaluate the relevance of the consideration. This relevance judgment depends on a more or less carefully considered evaluation of a frame and its source.[2] Some citizens, some of the time, may devote careful thought to an issue and therefore override implicit framing — although given Americans' generally low levels of information, interest, and attention to politics, we should not overestimate the frequency of this type of thought. If the consideration is judged irrelevant to the issue at hand, it is rejected and does not affect opinion.[3]

This basic model underlies an important debate on framing mechanisms, which turns on the question of whether framing occurs by unconsciously altering accessibility or by triggering conscious evaluation of relevance. One line of work draws on social psychological research to argue that cognitive accessibility — not necessarily consciously perceived importance or relevance — moderates framing and priming effects. Mendelberg, for example, argues that accessibility is a key pathway for the impact of implicitly racial messages (2001), although she does not measure accessibility directly (see also Iyengar and Kinder 1987; Kinder and Sanders 1996; Zaller 1992). Valentino and colleagues do directly measure cognitive accessibility, and they find that implicit racial messages affect attitudes toward government spending and that these messages work by increasing the accessibility of racial predispositions (Valentino, Hutchings, and White 2002).

On the other hand, several other studies that also measure accessibility directly find that priming and framing do not affect accessibility. These studies find instead that frames alter opinion by changing people's conscious evaluation of the importance or relevance of considerations (Nelson, Clawson, and Oxley 1997; Miller and Krosnick 2000; Peterson 2004).

This debate seems to have powerful implications for our normative evaluation of framing. If frames influence opinion automatically by altering accessibility, then citizens may be relatively helpless victims of political elites' attempts to manipulate opinion through cynically devised issue frames. On the other hand, if citizens evaluate frames consciously, they may be more active and discerning consumers of the political spectacle, with some reasonable defenses against manipulation at least under some circumstances (see Druckman 2001a, 233–45 for a review of this debate with an emphasis on its implications for citizens' competence).

The normative stakes are perhaps put in clearest relief in Mendelberg's account of racialized campaign discourse (2001). In her model, white Americans hold ambivalent racial predispositions: they both support egalitarian norms and feel resentful toward African Americans. Implicit racial messages can make racial resentments automatically more accessible for political judgments; when those messages are explicit, on the other hand, citizens become aware of their racial character and consciously reject them in favor of racial egalitarianism.[4]

This debate assumes that the choice is between conscious processing—in which case judgments of importance or relevance can and do sometimes swamp accessibility effects—and unconscious processing, in which case framing's impact is moderated by accessibility and little more. I do not have direct cognitive data on accessibility and importance and therefore cannot speak directly to this controversy. Nevertheless, my theory and findings suggest that the association of "coming to mind" with unconscious thought and "judgments of relevance" with conscious thought oversimplifies matters. Rather, both stages can involve both automatic and controlled processes, and political frames can affect both automatic and controlled processes at both stages.[5]

First, consider explicit frames, which make clear the considerations they attempt to link with an issue. These frames bring considerations to mind by mentioning them explicitly. The explicit frame can also trigger controlled consideration of relevance if the person receiving the frame is interested and motivated enough to engage in conscious thought about the issue. Thus, we should not be surprised that explicit frames can affect conscious judgments of relevance; and for considerations that are likely to be highly accessible to begin with, they may not have much impact on accessibility.

Implicit frames might make considerations more cognitively accessible and therefore more likely to come to mind. Although accessibility is necessary for implicit framing to work, my model suggests that it is not sufficient. Without accessibility—either chronic or induced by recent use or the frame itself—a predisposition is unlikely to come to mind in the context of an issue. Even if a predisposition does come to mind, however, it will not inevitably be applied. It must also be applicable, and for implicit frames that applicability is governed by the structural congruence between the schema of the predisposition and the way the issue is framed and understood. In this case, control over applicability lies not in the conscious consideration in an individual but in the way the issue is framed in political rhetoric.

Thus, even for implicit frames the relevance stage plays a role. My theory suggests that in this case relevance is not judged consciously; rather, it is moderated by the structural fit between schema and issue. Thus, a successful implicit racial frame works not simply by making racial considerations cognitively accessible but also by structuring the issue to fit those considerations. And although a successful implicit gender frame may prime the gender schema, it will also shape the issue to fit that schema. It is this shaping or structuring of the issue that makes the schema "relevant" and allows for unconscious analogical reasoning from schema to issue.

This theory puts in perspective patterns from several studies of implicit racial priming. Although these studies do not discuss fit as I define it, some of their findings support the idea that fit plays an important role. For example, Hurwitz and Peffley find that racial attitudes affect opinion on crime policy, but only in cases when the policy involves a violent crime and a punitive response (1997). In another study, Peffley and colleagues find that whites' racial attitudes affect their evaluation of welfare recipients and criminals (Peffley, Hurwitz, and Sniderman 1997). Those links, however, are contingent on how the target — welfare recipient or criminal — are described. When the targets are described in stereotype-consistent terms (black dropout on welfare; foul-mouthed black criminal), then racial predispositions are engaged in evaluation. When the targets are described as white, *or as blacks who did not fit stereotypes,* racial predispositions are not engaged. Finally, Valentino and colleagues find that implicit racial images link racial predispositions with opinion on government spending, but only when those images are consistent with negative racial stereotypes of blacks and positive racial stereotypes of whites (2002). They find that implicitly racial messages that include *counter*-stereotypical portrayals actually reduce the impact of racial predispositions on opinion.

In all these cases, something more than "mere accessibility" is at work. If simply bringing race to mind is enough to engage it in opinion formation, we would not expect these patterns of results. Instead, the findings in all these studies are consistent with my theory of group implication. When issues are portrayed in ways that do not fit racial schemas — that is, counter-stereotypically — then the schema is less apt to be employed regardless of accessibility (and without need for conscious rejection); in this case racial ideology plays less of a role in opinion formation.

This perspective makes the normative judgment of framing more complex, if not necessarily ultimately more reassuring. On the one hand, there are important limits on the power even of implicit frames. Citizens do not simply respond blindly to implicit racial or gender (or other) cues in their environment and apply them, willy-nilly, to all manner of policy opinion. Rather, they will apply those considerations only to policies that share structural similarity with the predispositions. Thus, there are important limits to the power of frames, even for frames that operate by making considerations more accessible. That said, the evaluation of fit can itself be automatic and unconscious, and fit between schema and policy need not correspond to some more-considered evaluation of relevance. Just because a schema fits a policy cognitively certainly does not mean we would consider it the best way to evaluate that policy.

On the other hand, explicit frames may not be so easy for citizens to evaluate well. Even in cases where citizens consider consciously the relevance of a frame, they may do so without full awareness of the effects that frame has on their political cognition. Consider my analysis of the framing of Social Security in chapter 5. Certainly many citizens may think carefully whether those frames are relevant for Social Security. Given the extremely subtle nature of the racial group implication, though, they are likely to evaluate that relevance without realizing that the frame evokes racial considerations. Rather, they might think about whether considerations of hard work and just rewards are relevant to Social Security without noticing the ways those considerations help to shape the program in a way that associates it symbolically with whiteness. In a similar way, the health care frames in 1993–94 turned explicitly on matters of the government's appropriate role and of private doctor-patient relationships. It was only in their structure that these frames evoked gender schemas. Thus, even a citizen who thought carefully about their relevance would be unlikely to notice the gendered nature of the appeals.

This perspective raises doubts about citizens' ability to reject frames appropriately on the basis of conscious consideration of their relevance. Certainly people can and do reject frames as irrelevant, and in the case of explicit frames, they may be able to evaluate fairly well the true nature of the frame they reject. In the case of more-subtle group-implicating frames, on the other hand, what you think you see may not be at all what you get, cognitively. In this case most citizens will be left to evaluate the relevance of a frame on the basis of its explicit contents, without being aware of some of its more subtle psychological effects on opinion formation.[6]

Quality of Opinion, Deliberation, and Elite Domination

Much of the mass public has relatively little interest in and engagement with politics; this lack of background knowledge can make many political issues seem distant and abstract (Converse 1964, 1990; Kinder 1983; Delli Carpini and Keeter 1996). This distance means that political elites face a two-part communications challenge: for all but the raciest political issues, they must simultaneously incite interest and engagement with an issue while also conveying their arguments over policy in terms that do not presuppose much prior knowledge (Kinder and Herzog 1993).

We might expect group-implicating frames to increase citizens' sense of competence and engagement. Mapping an unfamiliar domain to a familiar one analogically makes people feel that they have mastered the unfamiliar one (Holyoak and Thagard 1995, 131). In the context of specifically political metaphors, Mio suggests that "simple metaphors that render complex issues understandable make the issues relevant to the general population. These make the public feel a part of the political process and supportive of decisions by the political elite" (1997, 118; see also Thompson 1996). We might expect this effect to be particularly true for analogies that draw on race or gender, because people have rich, well-developed schemas for both. Thus, when people implicitly draw on their race or gender schemas, those schemas are likely to generate visceral and powerful evaluations of the issue. I have focused on the effects of group-implicating frames on opinion itself; this process also likely contributes to a sense of engagement with the issue and with politics more generally.

Beyond facilitating engagement, these sorts of frames might do a reasonably good communications job. For example, insofar as the differences between gender egalitarians and traditionalists reflect different beliefs about how society should be structured more generally, gender-implicated frames could help citizens choose political leaders and issue positions that are consistent with those preferences. For this process to occur, the connection between those predispositions and the policy must be real in some sense, rather than simply rhetorical. That is, the analogy must be a good one, in the sense that inferences and judgments drawn from the source domain must be valid when mapped to the target policy.

Holyoak and Thagard suggest a set of criteria for judging analogical reasoning in general; these criteria are useful for considering whether and how group implication might lead to reasoned, "high quality" opinion (1995, especially chaps. 5 and 7). The first criterion is whether an analogy leads to the right answer. For many routine cases of analogical problem solving, a particular analogy will succeed or fail objectively—that is, it will generate an answer that is clearly right or wrong. Over time, we can observe performance and learn which analogies are best applied to which sorts of problems. For political judgments, as with many real-life decisions, there is no way to evaluate a track record. Rarely are there standards for evaluating policy choices that are external to the very choices and reasoning we are evaluating.

Without performance comparisons, we are left to evaluate the quality of the analogies themselves. Analogies *feel* apt insofar as there is structural congruence between the source of the analogy and the domain we are applying it to, and this congruence is the central aspect of fit that moderates the effectiveness of group implication. Nevertheless, every schema contains myriad attributes or features, only some of which will be mapped in any particular analogy. Moreover, the mapped features are most salient; we tend to be less aware of features that do not figure in the analogical mapping (Markman and Gentner 1993). This tendency means that we are prone to "false positives." An analogy may seem sound on its face, and we are unlikely to notice a broader lack of fit between source and target domains because the ill-fitting features are less salient.[7] This problem likely underlies Representative Barney Frank's imprecation of political metaphors: "If I was going to limit free speech, I would make it a misdemeanor to use metaphors in the discussion of public policy. They almost always mislead you, especially in foreign policy" (2007). One defense against this tendency is to consider multiple analogies for any given problem, to consider carefully what it is about each analogy that makes it apt, and to consider the effect of one analogy on another. And some evidence suggests that exposing people to multiple, competing frames can help them make more considered—and possibly "better"—political decisions (Druckman 2001b, 2004; Druckman and Nelson 2003; Sniderman and Theriault 2004).

Nonetheless, because they are implicit, group-implicating frames are unlikely to foster thoughtful consideration of the quality of the analogies at work. If anything, they may make this sort of consideration more difficult, because they can obscure the very nature of the predispositions they evoke. An appeal that openly draws on gender invites one's opponent to point out the gendered nature of the appeal and thereby opens the door for debate over its appropriateness. And even coded racial messages, such as the Bush campaign's 1988 "Willie Horton" commercials, may have had much of their power eliminated when their implicitly racial basis was pointed out (Mendelberg 2001; see, though, Huber and Lapinski 2006). The frames I have discussed in this book are so subtle, however, that it seems unlikely that citizens would agree, even if their racial or gendered structure were pointed out. And it is likely that group implication will go unnoticed even by political elites. For example, although the racial undertones of welfare discourse have been documented in both the scholarly and the political domains, there has been little if any notice of the racial nature of Social Security framing or of the gendered quality of the health care reform debate.

Ultimately, the question of whether a particular frame misleads citizens from their "true" interests or helps them to realize those very interests is itself a political question. When judging particular issue frames normatively, we do not have strong theoretical standards that are external to the political debate at hand. Consider the gendered framing of health care reform in 1993–94. Gender implication led citizens to evaluate Clinton's health care plan in terms of their preferences for autonomous decision making in the symbolic health care "family." In this context, gender traditionalists reacted to the federal government as an inappropriate and threatening interloper into the private domain. Whether this was a correct way to view the issue depends on whether this threat was real. In the wake of the reform's failure there has been a rise of corporate control by employers and insurance companies in lieu of a government role. Reform supporters, some of whom predicted this outcome, might take this as evidence of the misleading — and therefore inappropriate — nature of the gender-implicating frames. But political conservatives might argue that corporate bureaucracy is very different from and preferable to government bureaucracy and that the gender frame therefore led people to appropriate positions. Ultimately, then, evaluating the frame requires judgment about whether government control is worse than corporate control. And that, of course, is a fundamental point of contention in current American politics.

Thus, judging the degree to which particular frames capture the important crux of an issue — or obscure it — is internal to the political debate itself. This dilemma is central to democratic theory, and it is one I cannot fully resolve here.[8]

Broader Effects of Group Implication: Polarization and Net Opinion Shifts

I have focused on the polarizing aspect of group implication: the ability of gender group implication to drive apart the opinions of gender egalitarians and traditionalists and the ability of racial group implication to separate racial liberals from racial conservatives. This polarization is important in part because it is a central aspect of creating both issue coalitions and broader political alliances.

We saw one glimpse of this coalition formation in chapter 6: the gendering of health care reform was particularly powerful among Democrats and therefore likely moved gender-traditionalist Democrats against health care reform. More broadly, several scholars have documented the ways that Republicans have used the racialization of welfare and crime to break apart the New Deal Democratic coalition and to cement a modern majority (Edsall and Edsall 1992; Gilens 1999; Mendelberg 2001; Weaver 2006).

We might suspect that gender group implication also underlies current political coalitions, although there is less research on this point. For example, the modern Republican coalition of social conservatives, foreign policy hawks, and antitax foes of government was not inevitable, nor is it even necessarily coherent. This package of issue positions may seem more coherent to the mass public, however, because conservative framing in each of these areas is gendered. So-called culture issues such as abortion and gay rights deal explicitly with gender roles; an aggressive foreign policy is symbolically associated with masculinity; and my analysis of health care reform in chapter 6 demonstrates the ways that antigovernment framing can take on symbolic gendered aspects.[9]

Clearly, we need additional research to understand how and whether the deployment of group-implicating frames across multiple domains—such as social issues, foreign policy, and social welfare policy—helps to make the issues seem to fit coherently together. Insofar as they do, then the polarizing effects of frames can be just as important as their effect on the distribution of opinion.

Of course, the actual distribution of support or opposition to a policy matters, and it is worth considering the net effects of group implication. How much does group implication shift opinion one way or the other on policy? Of course, this possible effect depends on many factors, including the effectiveness of the implicating frames, citizens' exposure to those frames, and the distribution of predispositions among the public. In addition, a frame can create a positive association between gender egalitarianism and opinion, for example, by increasing support among egalitarians, by decreasing support among traditionalists, or by some combination of both; each of these would create the same line of polarization, but with different effects on the overall distribution of opinion.

These factors mean that there is no simple, context-free bottom line. Nevertheless, my results do allow me to make several generalizations. First, for the three cases I investigated—welfare, Social Security, and health care reform—my simulations suggest that group implication has important, if not overwhelming, effects on opinion. By making some plausible if hypothetical assumptions, I find that support for Social Security is likely increased by its association with whiteness; support for welfare is decreased by its association with blackness; and support for health care reform was likely decreased by its gendering.

Ultimately, framing is both art and science. The impact of group implication will depend in part on the skill with which the frames are constructed and delivered, so it is impossible to make any completely general statement about the net impact of group implication on opinion distributions. Nevertheless, the results of the national survey analyses suggest that group implication can frequently influence opinion in ways that matter politically.

THE STUDY OF RACE AND PUBLIC OPINION

My work is certainly not the first to show that racial considerations underlie both rhetoric and opinion on ostensibly race-neutral policy. These connections have been well documented at least for the cases of crime and welfare, as I have discussed. The contribution of my racial results is to show that processes underlying racialization are in fact quite general. In both the crime and welfare examples, the policies are associated with race in white Americans' minds by a combination of symbolic associations and conscious (if sometimes inaccurate) beliefs that both policies apply overwhelmingly to African Americans. My experimental results, which go far beyond policies traditionally considered even implicitly racial, make clear that the phenomenon is potentially quite general and does not require any beliefs about the racial nature of policy targets. The case of Social Security racialization makes clear that the symbolic associations alone racialize policies not just in the laboratory but also in actual American politics as well.

These results also speak to the subtle but powerful role of whiteness in contemporary American politics. That role is difficult for many whites to see because the trappings of white privilege are constructed as "normal" rather than racial. The Social Security case demonstrates that white

Americans' positive feelings about their own racial group have a clear impact on their views of a government program that evokes the values and traits associated with whiteness. At one level there is nothing wrong with associating a program with positive values. Nevertheless, insofar as those associations occur in conjunction with an implicit association with the white racial in-group, they will serve not just to increase the popularity of a particular social welfare program but also to add to the unconscious psychic rewards white Americans derive from their race (Roediger 1999; Dyer 1997; Harris 1995; Essed 1991).

The results for racial group implication also reinforce critiques of calls for "color blindness" as a solution to contemporary American racial conflict. Analysts of white privilege have demonstrated the ways that the historical development of policies and institutions means that even without explicitly racist policy today, many outcomes are nevertheless shaped by race. Thus, ostensibly color-blind policies can be racist — or at least have differential racial impact — in practice. This means that being "blind" to race, even if it could be done, ignores the ways that race continues to structure outcomes through the policies and practices of institutions in concert with historical patterns of accumulation and disaccumulation (M. Brown 2003; Bonilla-Silva 2003; Blum 2002). My work demonstrates that the history of American race relations also lives on unconsciously in our cognitive racial schemas. Thus, even in a world of seemingly color-blind political rhetoric, racial group implication can both draw on and reinforce the cognitive machinery that ensures that we are very much not blind to matters of race.

There is significant debate in the literature on racial attitudes about the relationship between conservative values on the one hand and racial prejudice on the other. Analysts who hold the symbolic-racism perspective argue that for many white Americans, values such as individualism and the work ethic have become wrapped up with antiblack affect and that this racial resentment underlies opinion on racial policies. Others argue that this approach conflates two very different opinion ingredients: racial prejudice and nonracial values (for a recent set of entries in this debate, see Sears, Sidanius, and Bobo 2000). Although my theory and data do not speak directly to these questions, my work is consistent with arguments from the symbolic-racism perspective. Specifically, my theory and findings show the ways that ostensibly race-free language can evoke racial schemas. My account certainly does not imply that values evoked by political discourse *cannot* be race free. Nevertheless, it does spell out a set of rhetorical and psychological mechanisms by which ostensibly race-free discourse can nevertheless draw on racial predispositions. The findings regarding group implication therefore suggest that it is rather difficult to divide "racial" from "nonracial" appeals, because the racial nature of an implicit appeal can be quite symbolic indeed.

THE STUDY OF GENDER AND PUBLIC OPINION

This book demonstrates that gender can matter for public opinion in ways that go beyond our current approaches. As I have discussed, much of the existing work on gender and public opinion discusses issues that deal rather directly with gender relations; with the gender gap across a somewhat wider range of issues; or with citizens' evaluations of male and female candidates. All of this work is important, and all of it gives us important insight both into politics and into gender. These approaches do not exhaust the ways that gender can matter for mass opinion, however.

We know from work in psychology and anthropology that the gender distinction is learned very early in life and that it then serves as the basis for understanding all manner of other social differences. It grows out of and reinforces a fundamental metaphor of dualism that pervades Western thought (Weinreich-Haste 1994), and it gives rise to all manner of other dualities, including public-private, rational-emotional, nature-culture, universal-particular, and more (Ortner 1974, 1996; Smith-Rosenberg 1986). This book takes up the study of gender and opinion in a way analogous to work on the racialization of opinion. In so doing, it allows us to build on that work and to explore the ways that people's gender beliefs — which do so much to animate conceptions of social life — can also structure political cognition in ways simultaneously broader and more subtle than a focus on the gender gap or "women's issues" allows.

Beliefs about appropriate gender relations are deeply held by many Americans. These beliefs include strong normative prescriptions for appearance, behavior, and interpersonal interactions. When group implication draws on these gender ideologies, then, these powerful beliefs can be translated into powerful beliefs about other issues. That this process can take place symbolically and metaphorically means that gender beliefs — like racial beliefs — can influence politics in ways that go beyond issues that deal directly with male and female. And just as racial group implication both draws on racial ideology and simultaneously reinforces it, so too does gender group implication reinforce our assumptions about gender in subtle but powerful ways.

INTERSECTIONALITY AND GROUP IMPLICATION

My approach has been to analyze race and gender side by side. I have shown how the same cognitive machinery and framing processes underlie both race and gender implication. At the same time important differences exist between the race and gender schemas, conditioned by the different historical development and different social structure of each stratification system. These differences mean that gender-implicating and race-implicating frames differ in important ways.

The experiments took up race and gender group implication separately and in turn. The survey analyses included separate, though parallel, analyses of group implication: chapter 5 explored the racial group implication of framing and opinion on Social Security and welfare, and chapter 6 took up the gender group implication of health care. This parallel treatment tells us much about how racialization and gendering each work and emphasizes the common mechanisms by which rhetorical frames engage psychological schemas. The same psychological process governs both racialization and gendering. At the same time the parallel analyses also draw attention to the important differences between race and gender: the different social constructions of race and gender give rise to different schematic structures for each; these in turn are evoked by differently structured issue frames.

Of course, race and gender are not independent either as social categories or in the imagery deployed in political discourse. *Intersectionality* refers to the ways that multiple dimensions of social stratification interact with each other to shape individual identity and experience. People's positions in the social structure shape their experience, their treatment by others, and therefore their understanding of social reality in important ways. A central point of work in intersectionality is that multiple dimensions of social categorization interact with one another. Thus, a person's race and gender identities are not alternatives to choose between, and their effects on experience and behavior are interactive and multiplicative. The experience of being, for example, a white woman is not the simple combination of "white experience" plus "female experience."[10] The tendency to think about race and gender separately limits our understanding of all intersectional categories, but is especially insidious insofar as it makes the experiences and perspectives of African American women particularly invisible, in what Kimberlé Crenshaw calls "a political vacuum of erasure and contradiction maintained by the almost routine polarization of 'blacks and women' into separate and competing political camps" (1992, 403).

Intersectionality also refers to the ways that cultural *images* of race and gender interact. Many powerful political symbols exist at the intersection of race and gender (and other) categories, either explicitly or implicitly. Thus, for example, the "soccer mom" is defined explicitly by her gender, but, equally important, she is also defined by her race (white) and class (suburban middle); the paradigmatic "violent black criminal" is not just racial but also has a specific gender (male) and age (young); the "welfare queen" is black, female, and poor. These sorts of images, and related rhetorical issue frames, need not draw only on racial schemas or gender schemas individually, but rather can draw on both simultaneously or on some more-specific schemas for the intersectional categories. When they do so, race and gender interact such that the impact of both is something more complex than the sum of the separate dimensions.

Substantial attention has been given to intersectionality in political and legal theory, history, and feminist studies (Collins 1990, 2005; Crenshaw 1992, 1997, 1998; Davis 1981; Frankenberg 1993; Higginbotham 1992; hooks 1981; Hurtado 1996; King 1988; Spelman 1988). In general there has been less attention from political scientists (Hancock 2007), though there is a small body of literature that takes intersectionality seriously in the study of public opinion. These works include qualitative studies of opinion formation (e.g., Fine and Weis 1998; Press and Cole 1999) and a small but growing number of quantitative studies (e.g., Clawson and Clark 2003; Ovadia 2001; Lien 1998; Soss and LeClair 2004; Gay and Tate 1998; Philpot and Walton 2007; Steinbugler, Press, and Dias 2006; Winter 1998). Nevertheless, most work on public opinion and political psychology treats race and gender separately and independently. We therefore have relatively little understanding of whether and how citizens in different intersectional categories perceive politics differently and little understanding of how all citizens understand and apply intersectional images when thinking about political issues.

These two questions suggest two ways to think about intersectionality in the context of group implication. First, what we know about intersectional identities suggests that the shape of race and gender schemas themselves may vary in important ways among different types of citizens. Second, imagery that implicitly evokes both race and gender together may operate psychologically in ways that are more complex than simply the sum of race implication and gender implication. Although I do not have enough direct evidence to speak to either of these issues conclusively, my theory and findings do provide some interesting ways to think about each and suggest avenues for future research.

Different Schemas for Different Intersectional Identities?

As I discuss in chapter 3, race and gender schemas develop from a variety of sources, including both cultural representations of race and gender and one's personal experiences. If a person's race and gender identities condition the experience of race and gender in important ways — as indeed they do — then we might expect some variation in the structure of schemas among citizens who fall into different race/gender categories. This variation in schema structure might well condition the effectiveness of group-implicating frames, because a particular frame might fit the structure of some citizens' schemas but not others.

Schema structures certainly do vary at least to some degree across race and gender (and across class, sexual identity, and other dimensions). The important empirical question for my work is the nature and degree of that variation. If different groups have schemas that share essentially the same structure, with minor modification, then they should react to group-implicating frames in essentially the same ways. On the other hand, different groups, such as white men, white women, black men, and black women, might each have entirely unique schemas. In this case a group-implicating frame might fit the schemas of one type of citizen — white men, say — but not other types of citizens. We can think of a continuum of schematic variation; at one end, essentially similar schema structures are elaborated slightly differently among different groups, and at the other end, schemas have entirely different structures across demographic groups.[11]

We should first carefully note that different beliefs about race or about gender do not necessarily imply different schematic structures. Both race

and gender schemas as I describe them in chapter 3 include an evaluative dimension. Racial liberals and racial conservatives share a structural
schema for race — awareness of group differences, differential outcomes,
negative emotional tenor, and the rest — even while disagreeing on the
causes and appropriateness of those arrangements. In today's United
States, African Americans fall overwhelmingly toward the liberal end of
the evaluative dimension (Dawson 1994; Sigelman and Welch 1991; Schuman et al. 1997). This circumstance by itself does not mean that African
Americans' racial schemas have a fundamentally different *structure* or
that they will not, therefore, respond to an implicit racial frame. The
key empirical question is whether the structure itself varies substantially
enough that a particular frame that resonates structurally with the schemas for some groups fails to do so for others.

Unfortunately, my work, like much of the empirical work on race and
gender attitudes, speaks only very indirectly to this question. Nevertheless, some speculation is in order. First, let us consider gender schemas.
As I discuss in chapter 3, I expect white men and women, at least, to share
a common gender schema structure. A defining characteristic of gender
ideology is that it is largely constructed in the family — that is, in intimate,
day-to-day contexts where men and women, and boys and girls, interact
regularly. As I have discussed, this fact provides incentive for gender ideologies to emphasize interdependence and warm emotions, rather than
hostility and competition. Because men and women develop and enact
these ideas together, they are also relatively constrained to develop similar notions of gender. Where American racial segregation allows for the
development of rather different worldviews among whites and blacks,
gender integration mitigates against radically different views.

Still, this gender schema structure grows out of the structural relationship between *white* women and men, so we might expect gender relations
to be understood in structurally different terms among African Americans.
For example, bell hooks argues that the construction of the public-private
distinction — a central structural component of the gender schema as
I describe it — is very different for black women compared with white
women (2000, 37–39). For black women, she argues, the private realm
is traditionally an escape *from,* rather than a central location of, gender
oppression. More broadly, black men and women have both been excluded
from the public sphere and the power it confers, so African American
gender relations and ideologies have developed within a different social

context than that of whites (e.g., Lewis 1977). These and other differences in the lived experience of gender probably mean that African American men and women have differently structured gender schemas compared with white men and women.[12] Even so, it is an empirical question whether those gender schemas are structured so differently that issue frames that evoke the (white) gender schema are rendered ineffective among African Americans. Unfortunately, this important empirical question is one that I lack sufficient data to address.[13]

Next, let us examine race schemas. As I argue in chapter 3, I expect that white men and women in today's United States likely have similarly structured race schemas. Racial ideology in contemporary America is structured in important ways through separation, in contrast with the construction of gender. The Kerner Commission argued in 1968 that America's pervasive racial segregation meant that most whites learned about race not from personal experience but from their exposure to the media's portrayal of race (1968). Given continued segregation, we should expect this situation to continue mainly to be the case (Massey and Denton 1993; Entman and Rojecki 2000). Thus, we might expect most white Americans to share fairly similar race schemas.[14] On the other hand, we should not necessarily expect nonwhite Americans to understand race in the same terms. The segregation involved in American race relations allows for rather different understandings of race to evolve among whites and blacks (Jackman 1994). Partly for this reason, my analyses of the racialization of welfare and Social Security focused on white Americans.

My limited empirical results are consistent with these expectations. White men and white women racialize both welfare and Social Security in essentially the same ways; this response suggests that both react to group-implicating rhetoric in similar ways.[15] Among African Americans, on the other hand, these programs are not clearly racialized.[16] It is hard to say whether this lack of racialization is because African Americans' race schemas are structured differently from whites' or because they do not respond to the group-implicating framing for other reasons.

It seems likely, therefore, that at least some important variation exists in schema structure between black and white Americans and perhaps across gender lines within race as well. And, of course, this work leaves aside the question of the structure of racial schemas among other racial groups in America. It is not clear whether Latinos, Asians, and other racial and ethnic groups in America have race schemas that go beyond the binary "black-white" structure I describe here or instead assimilate their own racial experience into that binary structure; this question is complicated by the fact that both Latino and Asian are extremely heterogeneous categories.[17]

It is worth concluding this discussion by speculating briefly on how schematic variation may influence the future evolution of group implication in American politics. If we assume that some significant structural variation exists across different groups in American society, over the long term this variation will change the context for group-implicating frames. As American society becomes more and more racially and ethnically diverse, the proportion of the population that shares the racial schema as I describe it may decrease, both because citizens of color may have differently structured schemas and because whites' schemas may shift in reaction to the changing demographics of race.[18] These changes would mean that different sorts of frames would resonate with race and gender schemas and that the political power of existing racializing and gendering discourse might be muted. As white Americans become a smaller proportion of the electorate, frames that fit their schemas — and only their schemas — would become less powerful. Over the even longer term, additional change might come from turnover among political elites. As political elites themselves grow more diverse over time, the sorts of frames they are likely to employ will change, because they would draw at least in part on their own schemas in crafting appeals. On the other hand, insofar as citizens and leaders of color simply fall at the racially liberal end of the binary race schema that I describe, these appeals would continue to resonate but would push these citizens in the opposite direction from racially conservative whites.

Why Group Implication Is Frequently Not *Intersectional*

Intersectionality draws attention to the ways that multiple dimensions of social stratification interact. A central theme of this literature, however, is that the discourses about race and gender in American society, culture, and politics systematically obfuscate the intersectionality of race and gender (and other dimensions, including class and sexuality). Attending to intersectionality is important precisely because it is so frequently invisible.

The dominant narratives and conceptual categories deployed by both political elites and citizens militate against Americans developing nuanced, intersectional understandings of their own social positions and of political and social issues that touch on race and gender; one or the other frequently gets prime attention. For example, Evelyn Brooks Higginbotham argues that "race not only tends to subsume other sets of social relations, namely gender and class, but it blurs and disguises, suppresses and negates its own complex interplay with the very social relations it envelops" (1992, 255). Conversely, Ruth Frankenberg explores the ways that race shapes the gender experience of white women; an important part of the story lies in the ways that the effects of whiteness are systematically hidden from view (1993). And in broader terms, Patricia Hill Collins shows the ways that "racism is a gender-specific phenomenon, and Black antiracist politics that do not make gender central are doomed to fail" (2005, 7); this gender specificity is especially pernicious insofar as it is frequently obscured. And a now common critique of early white feminist scholarship argues that this scholarship obscured the role of race (and class) in constructing what white middle-class feminists took to be the universal experience of gender (e.g., Spelman 1988).

Moreover, political debates over issues where race and gender intersect often devolve into framing battles of "race versus gender." In her discussion of the Anita Hill–Clarence Thomas hearings, Crenshaw shows how the debate turned in part on competition between two frames (1992). The first was based on gender and framed the Thomas-Hill interaction in terms of sexual harassment, understood metaphorically as rape. The second was a race-oriented frame deployed by Thomas that portrayed him as the victim of a "high-tech lynching." Crenshaw discusses the ways that the rape and lynching narratives are actually both simultaneously gendered *and* racialized. Nevertheless, each was deployed in a way that focused attention on one dimension and obscured the other.

Thus, the hearings presented the public with a choice between two narratives. The first, gendered, narrative framed the issue as (nonracialized) sexual harassment; this account made invisible the ways that race conditions the harassment and Hill's reactions to it. In the second, racial, narrative, Thomas deployed the lynching image to portray himself as the victim. Of course, lynching was a white reaction to black men's perceived sexual advances on white women; nevertheless, Thomas's lynching frame succeeded by emphasizing race and hiding gender. The racial frame transformed Thomas from a male oppressor to a black victim. Crenshaw argues that both narratives hid aspects of Hill's experience. Ultimately, Hill's ability to make her case was hindered by the lack of culturally available narratives that simultaneously draw on race and gender.

Crenshaw develops a related analysis of the controversy surrounding rappers 2 Live Crew (1997). In 1990 a Florida community tried to prosecute the group for obscenity over its explicitly misogynistic lyrics. The public debate devolved into a clash over whether the group was sexist or its accusers were racist. As with Thomas-Hill, this either/or debate was facilitated by the lack of nuanced understanding among both black and white political elites — and the broader public — of the ways that racism and sexism interact. As Crenshaw summarizes, "The controversies over the Central Park jogger case, the 2 Live Crew case, the St. John's rape trial . . . all present issues of gender violence in which racial politics are deeply implicated but in ways that seem impossible to capture fully within existing frameworks that separate racial politics from gender politics. These separations are linked to the overall problem of the way racism and sexism are understood and how these understandings inform organizing around antiracism and feminism" (247). To this list, of course, we could add the trials of O. J. Simpson (Morrison and Lacour 1997) and Kobe Bryant (Leonard 2004).

These examples involve issues that evoke race and gender explicitly, not the sorts of subtle gender and race implication I explore. Nevertheless, they suggest that the dominant culture will not frequently or easily develop intersectional frames. When these sorts of explicit debates separate race and gender in people's minds, they make it more likely that race and gender schemas will remain distinct and independent frameworks for understanding social reality. Because of this tendency we should expect many implicit frames to evoke either race or gender, not usually both.

Many of this book's empirical results reflect this independence. First, the experiments show that race and gender schemas are cognitively independent enough to be brought to mind separately. In the experiments the gender-implicating frames did not induce racialization of opinion, and the race-implicating treatments did not induce gendering of opinion. Second, my analyses of Social Security and health care reform reinforce this picture of separate race and gender implication. Although the experiment showed that it is possible to gender implicate Social Security, the analysis in chapter 5 found that this gendering has not, in fact, happened in American politics generally. Rather, the framing of Social Security has racialized — but not gendered — opinion among American whites. Similarly, health care policy and actual health outcomes both have important racial aspects. Nevertheless, the analysis in chapter 6 demonstrated that framing of health care does not generally associate it with race and that the gendering frames of 1993–94 did not create health care racialization.

Social Security and health care reform are two important social issues that might be amenable to frames that subtly draw on the intersectional nature of race and gender. For these two issues at least, intersectional frames were not promulgated widely by political leaders, and the policies were not understood by the public in intersectional terms. The theoretical literature on intersectionality suggests we should not be surprised that race and gender implication operated independently in these cases and likely in many others in American politics.

Truly Intersectional Imagery

At the same time, however, I found that welfare opinion is both racialized and gendered by the American public. My analysis — like most of the literature on welfare opinion — focused on racialization, but I did also find that welfare is associated with gender considerations. This finding is consistent with something we might have expected: although racialization and gendering frequently operate independently, they can sometimes act in concert.

Although political debates frequently treat race and gender separately, clearly instances occur where the two come together explicitly and implicitly. One of the most prominent examples of this intersectionality is in the discourse on welfare and welfare reform.[19] And although many citizens — and in particular white citizens — seem to have relatively autonomous race and gender schemas, it is clear they also have schemas for some intersectional categories.

Scholars have documented the simultaneously racialized and gendered nature of welfare policy itself: throughout their history American welfare programs have been designed and implemented with ideas about both the racialization and the feminization of poverty in mind (Quadagno 1994; Skocpol 1992; Gordon 1994; Weir, Orloff, and Skocpol 1988). Elite discourse on welfare has reflected both group frameworks. In elite framing and in the popular imagination, welfare recipients are not just poor, not just black, and not just female. The three categories come together in various ways, most recently since the 1980s in the image of the "welfare queen," the prototypical (and mythical) welfare recipient who crystallizes stereotypes of black laziness and of uncontrolled female sexuality. The power of the welfare queen image is more than the sum of its race and gender components individually (Hancock 2004; Zucchino 1997; Adair 2000).

We know relatively little about the political psychology involved in the perception of this sort of truly intersectional imagery. Do citizens implicitly choose either to racialize or to gender the issue, that is, do they perceive the issue through one or the other schema alone, or do they draw on both simultaneously? Or does something more complex happen? The existing evidence suggests the final option: something more complex (and politically important) takes place.

* * *

My analysis of the intersectionality of welfare opinion in chapter 5 is limited by the measures available from the ANES. The analysis suggests at least that citizens draw on both race and gender schemas when thinking about welfare. Racial conservatives oppose welfare, compared with racial liberals, and gender traditionalists oppose welfare, compared with gender egalitarians. My analysis considers race and gender predispositions independently of each other; I do not have measures that would allow me to assess whether people draw on more complex, intersectional schemas in addition to each individually.

My analysis is not alone in this regard; most work on welfare opinion has focused on racialization. One exception to this situation is illuminating, however. Soss and LeClair conducted a study in which they explored the independent impact on whites' welfare attitudes of a racial stereotype — black laziness — and of an intersectional stereotype — black female sexual irresponsibility (2004). Although both stereotypes influenced opinion, the intersectional stereotype's impact was about twice that of the solely racial laziness stereotype. These limited results suggest that intersectional frames can shape opinion powerfully and in ways that go beyond the independent effects of their race and gender aspects.

This feature of intersectional welfare imagery is troubling at a deeper level as well. There is reason to expect that intersectional images — such as the welfare queen — may shape not just opinion but also citizens' understanding of intersectional categories themselves. If so, then political rhetoric and framing that do invoke intersectional categories can have far-reaching consequences, well beyond the policy issue at hand at a particular moment.

To see why, I return to what happens psychologically when we encounter a metaphor. Glucksberg and colleagues argue that the interpretation of novel metaphors involves more than simple comparison of the target with the source of the metaphor (Glucksberg and Keysar 1990). Rather, they suggest, it involves categorization and category creation. When we interpret a novel metaphor, aspects of both source and target are combined into a new superordinate mental category that can have implications for *both* source and target.[20]

For example — in a favorite from this literature — when we interpret the metaphor, "my job is a jail," we do not simply transfer things we know about the concept "jail" to the concept "my job." Rather, we draw on what we know about both jobs and jails to make sense of the metaphor. Depending on the context of my statement, certain aspects of the category "jail" will be more relevant (that it is confining, unpleasant, and unrewarding, perhaps); others will be less relevant (made of concrete, with bars, and so forth). These relevant features help to create a superordinate category of "things that are confining and unrewarding" that includes both jails and my job.

When "jail" is used in a different metaphor, other features of jails may be more relevant. In her exploration of prison metaphors, Monika Fludernik cites a rather different example, from George Eliot's "Janet's Repentance" (1975): "A door had been opened in Janet's cold dark prison of self-despair, and the golden light of morning was pouring in its slanting beams through the blessed opening" (cited in Fludernik 2005, 235). This metaphor draws attention to the physical aspects of a prison cell (the door in particular), as well as drawing on not just the confining property of prisons but also the possibility for release from that confinement. Metaphors therefore "pick out structural elements in source and target domains that can be mapped onto one another and give rise to a blend in which the two coalesce into a new meaning" (Fludernik 2005, 234).

Seana Coulson discusses the way that meaning can emerge from the combination of the source and target of a metaphor with the example, "The surgeon is a butcher." This metaphor suggests, of course, that the surgeon is incompetent even though incompetence is not a feature we normally associate with either surgeons or butchers. Rather, this metaphor draws attention to the tools and methods of a butcher; these imply incompetence only when applied to the context of surgery (Coulson 2001, 161).

Thus, our very understanding of (and schema for) a new concept will be shaped in part by the context in which we generate and use that concept: "Rather than being retrieved as static units from memory to represent categories, concepts originate in a highly flexible process that retrieves generic information and episodic information from long-term memory to construct temporary concepts in working memory. . . . This concept construction process is highly constrained by goals, context, and recent experience" (Barsalou 1987, 101; cited in Glucksberg and Keysar 1990, 9).

What does this mean for intersectional group implication? It suggests that frames that evoke intersectional images can reflect back on our understanding of the intersectional category itself, in addition to affecting policy opinion. That is, Americans' very understanding of intersectional categories, such as "black woman" or "white man," can be influenced by the frames that invoke those categories in political debates. Intersectional frames that combine race and gender imagery will draw on race schemas and gender schemas and on the details of the policy dispute at hand to create a combined concept at the intersection of race and gender. The shape of this combined category will depend significantly on the particular context, that is, on particulars of the frame and on the policy itself. Once this takes place, the broader category will then be available for later application to new targets.

The preceding discussion points to an important way that political discourse not only draws on existing mental categories but also creates and shapes new categories and their associated schemas. Thus, when Ronald Reagan talked about pink-Cadillac-driving welfare queens, he drew on race, gender, and class stereotypes to tarnish welfare. Beyond this, though, the frame also shaped schemas for "poor black woman" by highlighting aspects of existing race, gender, and class schemas and by drawing on ideas about welfare policy. Evelyn Brooks Higginbotham summarizes these reciprocal effects: "For example, the metaphoric and metonymic identification of welfare with the black population by the American public has resulted in tremendous generalization about the supposed unwillingness of many blacks to work. Welfare immediately conjures up images of black female-headed families" (1992, 254). And in particular, we might add, the images of welfare that are promulgated in frames such as the "welfare queen" serve to reinforce particular understandings among the American public of poor black women (as promiscuous, maliciously dependent, and lazy) and of poor black men (as irresponsible, absent, lazy, and so on).

I do not want to overstate the power of political frames to shape a society's categories for thinking about race and gender and their intersections. Images such as the welfare queen draw on the long history of race and gender relations in America and therefore likely reshape them only at the margin. Our cognitive representations of these things — our schemas — will evolve slowly; they are the products of many things over the course of our lifetimes, including personal experience, childhood socialization, and myriad other sources of cultural representations of race and gender.

Nevertheless, political frames and images — especially those such as the welfare queen that catch on and structure debate over a long period — do have some power to reshape understandings of race, gender, and their intersections as well. Such frames and images can be quite important because they create subtle new associations with these categories that can carry forward to structure future use of those categories beyond the political issue at hand.

The most prominent examples of intersectional imagery in political discourse are largely negative — that is, they draw on negative imagery for subordinate intersectional groups and on positive imagery for dominant intersectional groups. Thus, negative images of poor black women frame welfare discourse, and negative images of young black men frame discourse on youth criminality. In contrast, positive stereotypes about middle-class white manhood likely underlie framing and opinion on white-collar crime (e.g., Shapiro 1990) and on the economic and social policies enacted after World War II as part of the GI Bill, policies that were implemented in ways that advantaged white men over white women and over women and men of color (e.g., Katznelson 2005). It remains to be seen whether intersectional frames can be developed and deployed that do not reinforce negative associations with subordinate categories and positive associations with superordinate ones.

DO WE LIKE RACE AND GENDER IMPLICATION?

I have suggested that group-implicating frames may increase citizens' sense of engagement and competence. The same could be said, however, of any frame that evoked a familiar source domain. That is, a frame that evoked an implicit or explicit analogy to some domain other than race or gender could also serve those purposes. For example, the Saddam as Hitler analogy promoted by President George H. W. Bush before the first Gulf War in 1991 had nothing to do with race or gender but may well have led citizens to feel like they understood an otherwise-complicated situation in an obscure part of the world (Spellman and Holyoak 1992). Thus, all sorts of frames that invoke all sorts of implicit or explicit analogies are possible. As I argued in chapter 3, race and gender schemas are well positioned to serve as the basis for implication for two reasons. First, they both contain a rich structure, emotional resonance, and strong evaluative implications. This means that they can serve as the basis for rich analogies and that, when they do, they will pack some evaluative punch. Second, both are highly salient for many Americans, so they are likely to be available cognitively when people encounter appropriately structured frames.

We should consider, then, the normative status of appeals that draw on citizens' race and gender predispositions. Should we be particularly concerned about these sorts of implicitly gendered or implicitly racialized appeals?

On the one hand, perhaps we should not. Polarizing along lines of race or gender predispositions is not the same as polarizing by race or gender themselves. Much of the discussion of racialization — and the broader discussion of prejudice and opinion — focuses on the role of racialization in unifying those with racially conservative or with prejudiced beliefs. Racially implicated discourse can unify and mobilize a coalition of racial egalitarians, just as it mobilizes racial conservatives. Similarly, a discourse that polarizes on gender ideology can mobilize gender traditionalists, gender egalitarians, or both.

Even so, these sorts of frames are troubling for a liberal democratic discourse. Despite the possibility for mobilization of racial or gender egalitarians, the potential for racially implicated frames to convey covert racist messages and gender-implicated frames to convey covert sexist predispositions remains disturbing. Although group-implicating communications strategies may facilitate productive democratic communication under some circumstances, they also hold the potential for obfuscation and misdirection, either inadvertent or at the hands of deceitful political leaders. It is clear from the historical record that covert racist appeals have, in fact, mobilized racial conservatives (Mendelberg 2001; Kinder and Sanders 1996; Edsall and Edsall 1992) and that covert (and not-so-covert) sexist appeals have been deployed against female candidates, as well as candidates who do not appear manly enough.[21]

These sorts of frames are more troubling at a deeper level. This book has focused on the impact of gender implication in the relatively short term and on the relatively narrow matter of policy opinions. Thus, I have treated gender and race predispositions as given — as a fixed resource that political leaders may draw on, either intentionally or accidentally. Thus, for most of the book the social and psychological structure of gender and race relations is fixed and defines the context within which political rhetoric has its effect. Over the longer term, of course, that very political rhetoric has an effect on that social and psychological context. Frames that draw on race or gender predispositions do not merely make use of those schemas. They also reinforce the salience of those same schemas and forge cognitive connections between those schemas and other aspects of politics and social life. Over time and across many issues, this racialized or gendered political discourse serves to reinforce a politics rooted in ascriptive differences more generally. In this way, race and gender implication — even in the context of nonracial and nongender issues — can add inertia to race and gender stratification systems in current American society, subtly impeding change.

Despite these concerns, there is reason to think that these sorts of appeals will not disappear easily. My model implies that one characteristic that makes particular political symbols useful politically is that they have a rich structure and high psychological salience. As a schema's structure becomes richer, it provides more ways to shape an issue in ways that fit it. And as a schema becomes more salient among the public, it becomes more likely to be engaged to understand an issue it fits. This argument suggests that less-well-articulated and less-focal schemas — such as schemas of social class in the United States — will fail to mobilize opinion across broad arrays of issues. Denser and more-focal schemas, such as race and gender, provide the tools and the electoral temptation to create broad political coalitions.

Appendix 1

This appendix presents the text of the constructed news articles that served as the treatment in the experiment described in chapter 4. The actual treatments were formatted to look like clippings from the *New York Times,* as shown in the (considerably reduced) example in figure A1.1.

VISITATION — RACE VERSION

CASE ON VISITATION RIGHTS HINGES ON PARENTAL AUTONOMY
Supreme Court to Examine Visitation Laws

WASHINGTON, Jan. 3—A Supreme Court case on whether grandparents, other relatives, and even non-relatives should be able to gain a court-ordered right to visit with children over the parents' objection has opened the door to a profound debate. Next week, the U.S. Supreme Court will begin hearing arguments in Troxel vs. Granville, a case that will determine the fate of laws that allow visitation rights with children for people who are not their parents.

The case started as an unremarkable custody dispute in bucolic northwestern Washington, an hour north of Seattle. But it took on new importance last September when the U.S. Supreme Court, which usually defers

Case on Visitation Rights Hinges on Defining Family

Supreme Court To Examine Visitation Laws

By LINDA GREENHOUSE

WASHINGTON, Jan. 3 – A Supreme Court case on whether grandparents, other relatives, and even non-relatives should be able to gain a court-ordered right to visit with children over the parents' objection has opened the door to a profound debate. Next week, the U.S. Supreme Court will begin hearing arguments in Troxel vs. Granville, a case that will determine the fate of laws that allow visitation rights with children for people who are not their parents.

The case started as an unremarkable custody dispute in bucolic northwestern Washington, an hour north of Seattle. But it took on new importance last September when the U.S. Supreme Court, which usually defers to state courts on matters of family autonomy, agreed to hear the case.

Highly Charged Arguments

"Here they really jumped into state family law in a very, very sensitive area," says University of Delaware law professor Andrew Pruitt, who is teaching this year at New York University. "However they decide, a lot of people are going to be very upset."

Between 1966 and 1986, all 50 states passed laws allowing petitions, under various circumstances, for court-ordered access when it is in the best interests of the child. These laws were designed to address concerns arising from rising divorce rates, to allow visitation for people, such as former boy-friends of single mothers, who had played a role in a child's life.

The 1973 Washington law at issue has the broadest visitation provisions in the nation, says Yale University family-law expert Amy Denison, and went far beyond grandparent visits. It allows courts to order child-visits with "any person," even a non-relative.

Denison says the statute was so broad that some people are concerned

that gay parents or single parents might have to contend with unwanted, court-ordered visits from intrusive third parties. On the other hand, she points out, supporters of "third-party visitation" fear the Supreme Court will go too far in blocking well-thought-out, court-approved visits with former stepparents and others who have a strong relationship with the child, such as ex-partners who cohabitated with the parent and child.

Richard Allard is executive director of the Parents' Rights Alliance of West Falls, Minnesota, which filed a brief opposing the visitation laws. "Do parents have the right to decide which friends or extended family their children will spend time with? That's the specific issue in the case of Troxel vs. Granville before the Supreme Court. It's a topic of obvious importance to millions of families," says Allard. "Without the absolute right to control how children are raised – including who visits their children – parents cannot possibly govern their children's upbringing properly." Allard considers the Washington law to be "over-broad," because it gives "any person at any time" the right to request court-ordered visitation. "This is unnecessarily meddling in the most intimate sphere of private, family life," he added.

Supporters of visitation laws counter that as family structures become more complex because of divorce, remarriage, and stepfamilies, children need legal protection to preserve family relationships. "The legal test comes as the traditional American family consisting of a father, a mother, and their children is changing," says Caregiver Law Center director Cynthia Collins, "and we are urging the Court to simply recognize those changes." Against this tide of

Continued on Page A10

Continued From Page A1

divorce, out-of-wedlock birth, same-sex unions, custody battles and paternity disputes, advocates have struggled successfully in recent years for laws allowing people to stay in touch with the children they have formed attachments with.

"Often, the child will have close relationships with people other than their parents, and those should receive legal recognition," said Ms. Collins. "People have to realize that with every divorce in this country, parents are no longer related to the same people their children are. Children have an inherent right to a relationship with their family as they define family through their own eyes, not the eyes of the adults."

Collins continued: "you think about where we were two or three decades ago, the 'Ozzie and Harriet' sort of intact family raising children, well, that just is not reflective of society, today. We have grandparents, live-in lovers, stepparents, persons that are not even biologically related to children that are raising them, and we need to have some understandings to which standards we're going to use to determine which rights they have."

"The bottom line is that parents are naturally best suited to make decisions for their children, on visitation matters just like any other," countered Henry Van Dorn of the Family Alliance of Nashville, Tenn. Although some parents may find themselves in unfortunate positions, that does not mean that "the states and the courts must endorse and sanction changes to the traditional family. That family still remains society's building block, and should be the place where visitation decisions are made."

FIGURE A1.1 Example of Experimental Treatment

to state courts on these sorts of disputes over personal responsibility, agreed to hear the case.

Highly Charged Arguments

"Here they really jumped into state family law in a very, very sensitive area," says University of Delaware law professor Andrew Pruitt, who is teaching this year at New York University. "However they decide, a lot of people are going to be very upset."

Between 1966 and 1986, all 50 states passed laws allowing petitions, under various circumstances, for court-ordered access when it is in the best interests of the child. These laws were designed to address concerns about rising rates of out-of-wedlock births, parental drug use and crime, teen pregnancy and child abuse.

The 1973 Washington law at issue has the broadest visitation provisions in the nation, says Yale University family-law expert Amy Denison, and went far beyond grandparent visits. It allows courts to order child-visits with "any person," even a non-relative.

Denison says the statute was so broad that some people are concerned that parents might have to contend with unwanted, court-ordered visits which arise over differences in parenting style between the parents and intrusive third parties. On the other hand, she points out, supporters of "third-party visitation" fear the Supreme Court will go too far in blocking well-thought-out, court-approved visits with other responsible relatives who could provide stability to a child's upbringing.

"Children depend on role models in their formative years to develop well-rounded personalities, and the absence of role models can have profound consequences for the emotional stability of children," says a legal brief filed by The Caregiver Law Center at Hunter College in New York. "We have an obligation to see that children have contact with those role models."

"There is, for some, a very fragmented family situation in which grandparents may be the only stable force in a child's life. They may be the only ones willing to teach a child the value of hard work and an education," said Leo Wallace, director of the Law Center.

Wallace said he recognizes that not all grandparents are perfect, but he worries about cases in which a grandparent has become the primary caregiver for a child whose parent is in jail or has drug problems. Often, he said, when the parent is released or recovers, he or she will take the child back and try to cut off contact with the grandparent. "All of a sudden, the only real parent that the kid has ever known is out of their life," Wallace said.

Wallace continued: "You think about where we were two or three decades ago, the 'Ozzie and Harriet' sort of intact family raising children, well, that just is not reflective of society, today. We have parents who have disappeared, or who have moved to some new city and taken up with some new partner, who can't be bothered to raise their children right, and we need to have some understandings about which standards we're going to use to determine which other relatives might be better-suited to raise the child."

"We may disagree with how some parents raise their children, but we have no right to impose our views of good parenting on those people," countered Henry Van Dorn of the Family Alliance of Chicago. He argued that the family integrity of the poor is at risk under a law that "opens the door for subjective value judgments concerning the court's view of family" under a standard that appraises the best interests of the child, because "poorer, less educated parents will always look worse in relation to older, seemingly more established and settled relatives."

VISITATION — GENDER VERSION

CASE ON VISITATION RIGHTS HINGES ON DEFINING FAMILY
Supreme Court to Examine Visitation Laws

WASHINGTON, Jan. 3 — A Supreme Court case on whether grandparents, other relatives, and even non-relatives should be able to gain a court-ordered right to visit with children over the parents' objection has opened the door to a profound debate. Next week, the U.S. Supreme Court will begin hearing arguments in Troxel vs. Granville, a case that will determine the fate of laws that allow visitation rights with children for people who are not their parents.

The case started as an unremarkable custody dispute in bucolic northwestern Washington, an hour north of Seattle. But it took on new importance last September when the U.S. Supreme Court, which usually defers to state courts on matters of family autonomy, agreed to hear the case.

Highly Charged Arguments

"Here they really jumped into state family law in a very, very sensitive area,'" says University of Delaware law professor Andrew Pruitt, who is teaching this year at New York University. "However they decide, a lot of people are going to be very upset."

Between 1966 and 1986, all 50 states passed laws allowing petitions, under various circumstances, for court-ordered access when it is in the best interests of the child. These laws were designed to address concerns arising from rising divorce rates, to allow visitation for people, such as former boy-friends of single mothers, who had played a role in a child's life.

The 1973 Washington law at issue has the broadest visitation provisions in the nation, says Yale University family-law expert Amy Denison, and went far beyond grandparent visits. It allows courts to order child-visits with "any person," even a non-relative.

Denison says the statute was so broad that some people are concerned that gay parents or single parents might have to contend with unwanted, court-ordered visits from intrusive third parties. On the other hand, she points out, supporters of "third-party visitation" fear the Supreme Court will go too far in blocking well-thought-out, court-approved visits with former stepparents and others who have a strong relationship with the child, such as ex-partners who cohabitated with the parent and child.

Richard Allard is executive director of the Parents' Rights Alliance of West Falls, Minnesota, which filed a brief opposing the visitation laws. "Do parents have the right to decide which friends or extended family their children will spend time with? That's the specific issue in the case of Troxel vs. Granville before the Supreme Court. It's a topic of obvious importance to millions of families," says Allard. "Without the absolute right to control how children are raised — including who visits their children — parents cannot possibly govern their children's upbringing properly." Allard considers the Washington law to be "over-broad," because it gives "any person at any time" the right to request court-ordered visitation. "This is unnecessarily meddling in the most intimate sphere of private, family life," he added.

Supporters of visitation laws counter that as family structures become more complex because of divorce, remarriage, and stepfamilies, children need legal protection to preserve family relationships. "The legal test comes as the traditional American family consisting of a father, a mother, and their children is changing," says Caregiver Law Center director Cynthia Collins, "and we are urging the Court to simply recognize those changes." Against this tide of divorce, out-of-wedlock birth, same-sex unions, custody battles and paternity disputes, advocates have struggled successfully in recent years for laws allowing people to stay in touch with the children they have formed attachments with.

"Often, the child will have close relationships with people other than their parents, and those should receive legal recognition," said Ms. Collins. "People have to realize that with every divorce in this country, parents are no longer related to the same people their children are. Children have an inherent right to have a relationship with their family as they define family through their own eyes, not the eyes of the adults."

Collins continued: "You think about where we were two or three decades ago, the 'Ozzie and Harriet' sort of intact family raising children, well, that just is not reflective of society, today. We have grandparents, live-in lovers, stepparents, persons that are not even biologically related to children that are raising them, and we need to have some understandings to which standards we're going to use to determine which rights they have."

"The bottom line is that parents are naturally best suited to make decisions for their children, on visitation matters just like any other," countered Henry Van Dorn of the Family Alliance of Nashville, Tenn. Although some parents may find themselves in unfortunate positions, that does not mean that "the states and the courts must endorse and sanction changes to the traditional family. That family still remains society's building block, and should be the place where visitation decisions are made."

VISITATION — BASELINE VERSION

CASE ON VISITATION RIGHTS
Supreme Court to Examine Visitation Laws

WASHINGTON, Jan. 3—A Supreme Court case on whether grandparents, other relatives, and even non-relatives should be able to gain a court-ordered right to visit with children over the parents' objection has opened the door to a profound debate. Next week, the U.S. Supreme

Court will begin hearing arguments in Troxel vs. Granville, a case that will determine the fate of laws that allow visitation rights with children for people who are not their parents.

The case started as an unremarkable custody dispute in bucolic northwestern Washington, an hour north of Seattle. But it took on new importance last September when the U.S. Supreme Court, which usually defers to state courts on matters of family law, agreed to hear the case.

Highly Charged Arguments

"Here they really jumped into state family law in a very, very sensitive area," says University of Delaware law professor Andrew Pruitt, who is teaching this year at New York University. "However they decide, a lot of people are going to be very upset."

Between 1966 and 1986, all 50 states passed laws allowing petitions, under various circumstances, for court-ordered access when it is in the best interests of the child.

The 1973 Washington law at issue has the broadest visitation provisions in the nation, says Yale University family-law expert Amy Denison, and went far beyond grandparent visits. It allows courts to order child-visits with "any person," even a non-relative.

Denison says the statute was so broad that some people are concerned that parents might have to contend with unwanted, court-ordered visits. On the other hand, she points out, supporters of "third-party visitation" fear the Supreme Court will go too far in blocking well-thought-out, court-approved visits.

The nine justices — six of them grandparents themselves — will hear arguments from Seattle attorneys on both sides. Family law specialist Mark Olson for the grandparents and appellate lawyer Catherine Smith for Wynn each will get 30 minutes. A decision is expected by July.

The fact that so many justices are grandparents is a wild card, experts say. "It's kind of interesting to speculate" whether they will identify in some manner with the grandparents in this case, Denison says. "Every now and then, justices emerge between the lines when they are deciding things that could affect them personally."

The case is one of the most closely watched of the term and has prompted friend-of-the-court briefs from many organizations and more than a dozen states.

SOCIAL SECURITY — RACE VERSION

BIPARTISAN COMMISSION CONSIDERS SOCIAL SECURITY REFORM

March 12 — "Social Security as we know it faces a cross-roads," William Greene said yesterday. This was a sentiment that many of the witnesses echoed as they testified before the National Commission on Retirement Policy. All agreed that the Social Security system will face major challenges over the next 30 years as the baby boom generation retires.

The commission — a nonpartisan, private group of legislators, economists, pension-system experts and business executives assembled by the Center for Policy Studies — has been working for most of the last year exploring the Social Security system. Its report, due out in May, is expected to be the most comprehensive package of recommendations to date for remaking Social Security in preparation for the baby-boom generation's retirement.

More Money Needed

All agreed that more money must be found for Social Security; they differed on the best source for the funds. Some witnesses argued for using some of the federal budget surplus to shore up Social Security. Others advocated transferring some Social Security funds into private retirement accounts for individual workers. This change would trade some reductions in guaranteed benefits for the higher, if less certain, returns of the financial markets. The change would also allow individuals a choice of investment options for the money accumulating in their government-administered accounts.

The commission's 24 members include Sen. John Breaux, D-La., and Reps. Charles Stenholm, D-Texas, and Jim Kolbe, R-Ariz. Breaux, along with Donald Marron, chairman and chief executive of Paine Webber Group, the Wall Street brokerage firm, and Charles Sanders, former chairman of Glaxo Inc., the pharmaceutical company.

Some Would Use Surplus

"As baby-boomers approach retirement, we need to devote some of the surplus to Social Security, to ensure that we are all taken care of," suggested

Mark Johnson, of the Coalition to Safeguard Our Retirement, a Washington advocacy group. With the first surplus since before World War II, "let us use that money, rather than creating some other new do-gooder government program." he continued. "There is no need to break — and no justification for breaking — the sacred covenant between those of us in the working generation and the retired generation of Americans by privatizing Social Security."

Johnson argued forcefully against privatizing social security. "Social Security is one of the few programs that actually works. It benefits all working Americans. It is a contract we've made with retired Americans and future retirees: if you've worked as a productive member of society, and you have contributed to the Social Security trust fund, then you can get yours back. You will be supported in your golden years."

Privatizing would put that at risk, he contended. "Of course, private investment is wonderful, and many seniors have their own investments. But the privatizers would divert our parents' and grandparents' social security trust fund to play the market. That puts the very benefits our elders have earned in jeopardy. I know that my father, for one, did not work for 53 years to see his retirement frittered away in the stock market."

Others Favor Privatization

The commission heard opposing views as well. "We can take care of Social Security by privatizing it. Then we can use the surplus for other priorities," testified Ellen Sarkin, of the Coalition for Privatization. "We need to use our prosperity to do more for those who — through no fault of their own — are being left behind. We need to spend the budget surplus on programs to create opportunity for less-fortunate Americans, and to battle pockets of poverty, rather than spending more of the federal budget on Social Security. Only privatization will let us do that."

One of the most outspoken advocates of privatization, Norman Whittier of the Poverty Research Institute, in St. Louis, said that "spending the surplus on rich retirees who are already doing well is fundamentally unjust. It is a basic fact of arithmetic that spending more on relatively well-off retirees will take away from spending on those who really need the help. By privatizing part of Social Security, we would be able to use surplus money instead to combat economic inequality throughout society."

SOCIAL SECURITY — GENDER VERSION

BIPARTISAN COMMISSION CONSIDERS SOCIAL SECURITY REFORM

March 12 — "Social Security as we know it faces a cross-roads," William Greene said yesterday. This was a sentiment that many of the witnesses echoed as they testified before the National Commission on Retirement Policy. All agreed that the Social Security system will face major challenges over the next 30 years as the baby boom generation retires.

The commission — a nonpartisan, private group of legislators, economists, pension-system experts and business executives assembled by the Center for Policy Studies — has been working for most of the last year exploring the Social Security system. Its report, due out in May, is expected to be the most comprehensive package of recommendations to date for remaking Social Security in preparation for the baby-boom generation's retirement.

More Money Needed

All agreed that more money must be found for Social Security; they differed on the best source for the funds. Some witnesses argued for using some of the federal budget surplus to shore up Social Security. Others advocated transferring some Social Security funds into private retirement accounts for individual workers. This change would trade some reductions in guaranteed benefits for the higher, if less certain, returns of the financial markets. The change would also allow individuals a choice of investment options for the money accumulating in their government-administered accounts.

The commission's 24 members include Sen. John Breaux, D-La., and Reps. Charles Stenholm, D-Texas, and Jim Kolbe, R-Ariz. Breaux, along with Donald Marron, chairman and chief executive of Paine Webber Group, the Wall Street brokerage firm, and Charles Sanders, former chairman of Glaxo Inc., the pharmaceutical company.

Some Favor Privatization

John Bowers, a steelworker from Monroeville, Penn., argued forcefully for privatizing social security. "I've provided for my family since I got married as a young man," he said in testimony before the commission. "I don't see why I should be forced to depend on the government to make decisions about my retirement."

His point was echoed by Philip Milkey, a policy analyst with Privatize Now, Inc., who testified that "those who oppose privatization are saying to America's workers, 'some bureaucrat in Washington can decide better than you how to invest your nest egg.' One of the best things about Americans," he continued, "is their independent initiative and self-reliance. We should harness that, not stifle it."

Milkey also said investing part of the fund in private stock-market accounts would lessen political control over benefits. "This means that retirees would no longer have to come before the Congress, hat in hand, asking for handouts. Instead, they could take control of their own fates — they could care for themselves and their families themselves, by making their own investment decisions."

Others Would Use Surplus

The commission heard opposing views as well. "We have to remember," said Ellen Sarkin of the investment firm Morgan Stanley Dean Witter, "that Social Security was designed not just as a retirement program, but as a social welfare program as well. It has succeeded in giving many people economic power they otherwise would not have had." She drew the attention of the commission to one often-overlooked group, women. "Before Social Security, most women were dependent on their husbands for support. In addition to providing retirement income for many, the program has given economic security, power, and freedom to many women at all levels of society. If we privatize the system, we put these gains at risk."

Responding to critics who argue that individuals can make better investment decisions than the Social Security Administration, researcher Martin Sobol of Vanderbilt University testified that "there is an inevitable trade-off between individual autonomy and fair social outcomes. The whole point of Social Security is that it constrains the natural tendency for inequality." By devoting the budget surplus to Social Security, rather than privatizing the system, "we can choose as a society to live with some constraints for the overall good."

SOCIAL SECURITY — BASELINE VERSION

BIPARTISAN COMMISSION CONSIDERS SOCIAL SECURITY REFORM

March 12 — "Social Security as we know it faces a cross-roads," William Greene said yesterday. This was a sentiment that many of the witnesses echoed as they testified before the National Commission on Retirement Policy. All agreed that the Social Security system will face major challenges over the next 30 years as the baby boom generation retires.

The commission — a nonpartisan, private group of legislators, economists, pension-system experts and business executives assembled by the Center for Policy Studies — has been working for most of the last year exploring the Social Security system. Its report, due out in May, is expected to be the most comprehensive package of recommendations to date for remaking Social Security in preparation for the baby-boom generation's retirement.

More Money Needed

All agreed that more money must be found for Social Security; they differed on the best source for the funds. Some witnesses argued for using some of the federal budget surplus to shore up Social Security. Others advocated transferring some Social Security funds into private retirement accounts for individual workers. This change would trade some reductions in guaranteed benefits for the higher, if less certain, returns of the financial markets. The change would also allow individuals a choice of investment options for the money accumulating in their government-administered accounts.

The commission's 24 members include Sen. John Breaux, D-La., and Reps. Charles Stenholm, D-Texas, and Jim Kolbe, R-Ariz. Breaux, along with Donald Marron, chairman and chief executive of Paine Webber Group, the Wall Street brokerage firm, and Charles Sanders, former chairman of Glaxo Inc., the pharmaceutical company.

Some Would Use Surplus

"As baby-boomers approach retirement, some of the surplus should be devoted to Social Security," suggested Mark Johnson, of the Coalition on Social Security, a Washington advocacy group. He advocated using "the first surplus since before World War II," to strengthen the retirement program.

Johnson argued forcefully against privatizing social security. "The stock market is doing well today, but that is sure to change at some point." Privatizing would put Social Security at risk, he contended. "Of course, private investment is wonderful, but we should not use Social Security funds to play the market."

Others Favor Privatization

The commission heard opposing views as well. "With the market rising 10 percent or more a year, there is no reason not to take advantage of that," testified Ellen Sarkin, of the Coalition for Privatization.

* * *

ECONOMY — RACE VERSION

ECONOMIC EXPANSION GENERATES DEBATE

Nov. 25 —The U.S. economy is experiencing unprecedented growth — a hefty 5.5 percent annual rate in the July–September period — and very low unemployment — just above 4 percent — according to the Commerce and Labor Departments. Oddly, this good economic news is sparking a sharp debate over the government's role in the economy.

"How can we keep the expansion rolling?" Mark Slepner, vice president of the Roberts and Slepner Investment Group, asked in a speech at the Sheraton New York in Midtown Manhattan yesterday. He suggested that the answer lies, almost paradoxically, in those parts of the country that have been left behind so far in the information age. "Places like the inner city of East St. Louis and the remote towns of Appalachia have poverty rates that are several times the national average," he said.

Some Areas Have Been Left Behind by the "New Economy"

He suggested that those at the bottom of the economic ladder are not benefiting much from the boom and, by some measures, are falling even farther behind. "In the giddily prosperous era of the so-called new economy, talking about high unemployment in depressed urban neighborhoods may seem an anachronism, like discussing rust-prevention meth-ods at an Internet company. But even as the rates of teenage pregnancy and crime are dropping, joblessness in many cities remains disturbingly intractable."

Average income for families in the bottom fifth of the income scale fell 5 percent between the late 1970's and the late 1990's, after adjusting for inflation. By contrast, income among the top fifth of families rose 33 percent, according to the Economic Policy Institute.

Slepner called for action to extend prosperity to all Americans. "As a society, we must answer an increasingly urgent question," he said. "What can we do to close the widening gap in income and skills that leaves too many Americans unable to participate fully in the American dream?"

He picked up a stack of large color photographs and spread them across a table. "The Dow Jones? They don't know from it," he said, pointing to individuals in the photos who have been so hounded for so long by pov-erty on the South Side of Chicago and in the Mississippi Delta, that they cannot imagine an economically viable future.

"We need programs to share get the prosperity with everyone — not just those lucky enough to have benefited already," he argued. "The way to deal with these problems is to put people to work. We need job programs, and we need to raise the minimum wage." Because the economy is doing so well, the necessary investments should be made now. "You fix the hole in the roof when the sun is shining," Slepner said, "not when it's raining. Those of us who are doing well have an obligation to help those who have been left behind through no fault of their own."

But others disagree. "We don't need the government to be more involved in the economy, because anyone who wants a job and is plau-sibly attractive to employers can find a job within a half-dozen weeks of searching," argues Philip Russell, of the research group Concerned Amer-icans, "and once those people are absorbed into the labor force, they will gain work experience that will prove attractive to future employers and help them weather the next recession. The private economy is providing opportunity for anyone willing to grasp it.

"On the other hand, if you can read and write only at a third-grade level, the economy has to get extremely strong for there to be a market for you at the minimum wage or any wage," he continued. "And while the economy can make a difference for many people, there are a lot of people for whom the economy is not the problem."

Russell suggested that more government effort would not affect the long-term unemployed — those who can't get hired even in the tightest labor markets — and the non-employed, a group that includes those who don't bother looking for work and thus aren't counted among the jobless.

"The strong economy has started to do for these people what Government programs have not accomplished: provide the opportunities for those who are willing to take them. If the economic boom continues for a few years, it will do wonders for the disadvantaged workers who need help the most."

ECONOMY — GENDER VERSION

ECONOMIC EXPANSION GENERATES DEBATE

Nov. 25 — The U.S. economy is experiencing unprecedented growth — a hefty 5.5 percent annual rate in the July–September period — and very low unemployment — just above 4 percent — according to the Commerce and Labor Departments. Oddly, this good economic news is sparking a sharp debate over the government's role in the economy.

"How can we keep this going?" Cynthia Slepner, vice president of the Roberts and Slepner Investment Group, asked in a speech at the Sheraton New York in Midtown Manhattan yesterday. She suggested that the answer lies, almost paradoxically, in parts of the work force that have been left out so far in the information age: women who do not work, or who work part time. "In order to continue supplying the economy with additional workers to fuel expansion, we need to encourage more people to enter the work force," she said.

Expanded Role for Working Women in the "New Economy"

This labor in reserve consists mainly of women. They are not so noticeable in the statistics; many hold jobs and are counted as employed. But nearly half the women working in the United States today do so only part-time, and millions are gradually stepping up to full-time schedules — making themselves available eight hours a day instead of five, or five days a week instead of three, or working through July and August instead of dropping out during their children's school vacation.

Nearly a million women a year since 1994 have upgraded their status

189

to full-time from part-time work. "The chance to increase family income draws these women further into the work force," she added.

Slepner called for action in several areas to extend continued prosperity to all American families. "If working women are going to continue contributing to their families' prosperity," she said, "they need to be able to enter the work force, and they need to be paid decently once they get there." She urged lawmakers to approve a plan to bolster government subsidies for child care. "This is one area where the government can help to ensure that all families have a good standard of living," she argued.

Other programs she supported included raising the minimum wage from its current rate of $5.15, and expanded support [for] pay equity programs. These programs "add to the prosperity of American families by ensuring that women earn a decent living once they enter the world of work."

She suggested that the government's economic goals should change: "Now that the economy has plenty of jobs available, we need to make it possible for all Americans to take those jobs."

But others disagree. "We don't need the government to be more involved in the economy. The government has no business pushing mothers — or anyone else — into the work force," said Philip Russell, of the lobbying group Concerned Americans. He cited a poll conducted by Glamour magazine, which found that 84 percent of women who were employed full or part time agreed with the statement "If I could afford it, I would rather be at home with my children."

"The real hardship women face is having to compromise staying home with family and working outside the home for financial reasons, not day care or pay equity," suggested Russell. "Women who choose to stay at home with their children have not received the respect and support they deserve. Ultimately, the family suffers from the 'me-first' workplace mentality fostered by government meddling."

He called for Washington to "get out of meddling with jobs and pay. Let families make their own decisions, and let them keep more of their paycheck. If you do that, American families will do just fine without any 'help' from the government."

ECONOMY — BASELINE VERSION

ECONOMIC EXPANSION GENERATES DEBATE

Nov. 25—The U.S. economy is experiencing unprecedented growth—a hefty 5.5 percent annual rate in the July–September period—and very low unemployment—just above 4 percent—according to the Commerce and Labor Departments. Oddly, this good economic news is sparking debate over the government's role in the economy.

The question is when there will be a recession, and how severe it will be. When it occurs, getting the American economy back on its feet could be surprisingly hard and painful.

Expanded Government Role When the Tide Turns

The odds are that the next recession will come sooner rather than later, and it will be different from other recessions since World War II. The response will be different, too. Many of the politicians, executives, financiers and prominent economists who have bet so heavily on the virtues of a market economy unhindered by government will probably look this time to government for extra help in mitigating the damage. Not just in cutting interest rates, but in stepped-up public spending as well as tax cuts.

"We will have to change the rhetoric," said Robert Pollin, an economist at the University of Massachusetts. "We can still say that markets play an important role, but they can't cure themselves. We will have to acknowledge that we need government for that. It's the stabilizer. And that acknowledgement will open up a broader debate about what government should do."

The strengths of this expansion are potentially destructive. They are chiefly consumer spending and business investment, both of which are based on debt. Unlike the 1980's expansion, which was driven by government borrowing, the current expansion is fueled by private-sector debt. Rising stock prices and, more recently, rising home prices, have encouraged the borrowing. Bubbles have developed in stock prices and real estate. And when they burst, particularly in the stock market, much of the collateral for the borrowing will disappear.

"I know of no time in the post–World War II period in which the welfare of the American economy, and for that matter the rest of the world, has hinged so much on the well-being of the American stock market," said Henry Kaufman, the Wall Street economist. "We have been running the economy on private credit rather than government debt on a very large and unusual scale."

When hard times come, households and companies will almost certainly pull back on spending, investing and borrowing—a nightmare for an economy that has become increasingly dependent on such voluntary activity. Government—mainly Federal, but also state and local—will suddenly be expected to take up the slack. As Alan Blinder, a Princeton University economist, put it, "In the event of a recession, people turn to Government en masse."

More government spending on housing, public works, education and income subsidies also seems likely to accompany the next recession, given the unusual nature of the current expansion and the downturn it is likely to produce. Thus the door may reopen to the sort of government intervention that was commonplace until the 1980's, and that John Maynard Keynes, the British economist, first spelled out in the 1930's.

Appendix 2

The following are the questions included in the experimental protocol. All variables were coded from zero to one, as explained in the text; individual scale items were reversed as necessary. Summary statistics appear at the end of this appendix.

PRIMING QUESTIONS

Respondents received one of the following three sets of questions just before reading the treatment news articles.

Race Primes

Now we would like to ask a few questions about your perceptions of the relationships between blacks and whites in America today. On the average, blacks have worse jobs, income, and housing than white people.

Do you think these differences are mainly due to discrimination?
Do you think these differences are because most blacks have less in-born ability to learn?
Do you think these differences are because most blacks don't have the chance for education that it takes to rise out of poverty?

Do you think these differences are because most blacks just don't have the
motivation or will power to pull themselves up out of poverty?

Overall, how would you explain these differences between blacks and
whites?

Gender Primes

Now we would like to ask a few questions about your perceptions of the
relationships between women and men in America today. On the average,
women are more likely than men to take care of children, and men are
more likely to work outside the home.

Do you think these differences are because women are biologically
better-suited to care for children, while men are better-suited for paid
work?

Do you think these differences are because women are taught from childhood how to care for children?

Do you think these differences are because the way society is set up,
women and men don't have much choice?

Do you think these differences are because it is God's will that women
care for children and men provide for them?

Overall, how would you explain these differences between men and
women?

Baseline (Partisanship) Primes

Now we would like to ask a few questions about your perceptions of the
relationships between the political parties in America today. On the average, Democratic and Republican politicians disagree about what policies
the government should have on many different matters.

Do you think these differences are because the parties have real and legiti-
mate philosophical differences?

Do you think these differences are because it is simply in people's nature
to disagree about most things?

Do you think these differences are due to false issues created by politicians, who are just in it for personal gain?

Do you think these differences are because the way our political system is set up, politicians don't have much choice but to disagree with each other?

Overall, how would you explain these differences between the parties?

PRIMARY POLICY OPINION QUESTIONS

Visitation

There has been some discussion of laws that allow grandparents and others to go to court for visitation rights with a child against the wishes of the child's parents. Do you favor or oppose a law in your state that would allow this?

Social Security

Individual accounts. One proposal for Social Security is to take about a third of the Social Security tax now paid by a worker and employer and put that money into a private individual savings account for retirement. Would you favor or oppose such a proposal?

Control of individual accounts. Let us suppose for a moment that part of the Social Security tax is put into an individual savings account for each worker, with the money invested in the stock market. Would you favor having the federal government manage all of the accounts, or would you prefer workers to manage their own funds?

Spending. (The Social Security spending question appears as part of the battery of questions on the federal budget; see "Federal budget" subheading below.)

Government Role in the Economy

Minimum wage. Do you favor raising the minimum wage for American workers from its current rate of $5.15, or do you think it should be left as it is?

Government jobs and standard of living. Some people feel the government in Washington should see to it that every person has a job and a good standard of living. Others think the government should just let each person get ahead on their own. Where would you place yourself on this scale?

RACE AND GENDER PREDISPOSITIONS

Racial Liberalism

Over the past few years, blacks have gotten less than they deserve.

Irish, Italians, Jewish and many other minorities overcame prejudice and worked their way up. Blacks should do the same without any special favors. (R) [Note: (R) indicates that an item was reverse-coded before inclusion in the combined scale.]

It's really a matter of some people not trying hard enough; if blacks would only try harder they could be just as well off as whites. (R)

Generations of slavery and discrimination have created conditions that make it difficult for blacks to work their way out of the lower class.

Sex Role Egalitarianism

A woman should not be president of the United States. (R)

A husband's job is to earn money; a wife's job is to look after home and family. (R)

The husband should be the head of the family. (R)

Women can handle job pressures as well as men.

The entry of women into traditionally male jobs should be discouraged. (R)

Fathers are not as able to care for their sick children as mothers are. (R)

Things work out best in a marriage if the husband stays away from housekeeping tasks. (R)

Women ought to have the same chances as men to be leaders at work.

When both husband and wife work outside the home, housework should be equally shared.

A marriage will be more successful if the husband's needs are considered first. (R)

A person should be more polite to a woman than to a man. (R)

Both the husband's and wife's earnings should be controlled by the husband. (R)

The husband should represent the family in community affairs. (R)

CONTROL VARIABLES

Ideology

We hear a lot of talk these days about liberals and conservatives. Here is a seven-point scale on which the political views that people might hold are arranged from extremely liberal to extremely conservative. Where would you place yourself on this scale, or haven't you thought much about this?

Limited Government

Respondents were asked to choose between two options for each of these items:

One, the main reason government has become bigger over the years is because it has gotten involved in things that people should do for themselves; or two, government has become bigger because the problems we face have become bigger. (R)

One, the less government the better; or two, there are more things that government should be doing. (R)

One, we need a strong government to handle today's complex economic problems; or two, the free market can handle these problems without government being involved.

Individualism

If people work hard they almost always get what they want.

Most people who do not get ahead in life probably work as hard as people who do. (R)

Hard work offers little guarantee of success. (R)

Party Identification

Generally speaking, do you usually think of yourself as a Republican, a Democrat, an independent, or what? [Response options: Strong Republican, Republican, Leaning to Republican, Independent, Leaning to Democrat, Democrat, Strong Democrat, Other]

Political Engagement

What job or political office do the following people hold? [Al Gore, William Rehnquist, Vladimir Putin, Dennis Hastert]

ADDITIONAL POLICY OPINION QUESTIONS

Government child care. Do you think government should provide child care assistance to low- and middle-income working parents, or isn't it the government's responsibility?

Affirmative action in hiring. Some people say that because of past discrimination blacks should be given preference in hiring and promotion. Others say that such preference in hiring and promotion of blacks is wrong because it gives blacks advantages they haven't earned. What about your opinion?

Federal budget. If you had a say in making up the federal budget this year, for which of the following programs would you like to see spending increased and for which would you like to see spending decreased? [List of programs: dealing with crime; AIDS research; public schools; assistance to poor people; programs that assist blacks; child care; financial aid for students; homelessness; assistance to the unemployed; Social Security; welfare; aid to big cities; protecting the environment; food stamps. Response options: "increase," "keep same," and "decrease."]

TABLE A2.1 Summary Statistics for Experimental Variables

	OVERALL		BASELINE		BY CONDITION RACE		GENDER	
	MEAN	N	MEAN	N	MEAN	N	MEAN	N
Favor visitation laws	0.558	311	0.544	108	0.589	104	0.540	99
Privatize Social Security	0.598	311	0.589	107	0.598	105	0.609	99
Government manage SS accounts	0.273	310	0.278	107	0.293	105	0.247	98
Increase Social Security spending	0.637	307	0.689	106	0.586	105	0.635	96
Raise minimum wage	0.732	310	0.736	108	0.716	104	0.745	98
Government jobs and standard of living	0.514	312	0.507	107	0.493	105	0.545	100
Racial liberalism	0.608	311	0.622	108	0.584	104	0.620	99
Gender egalitarianism	0.831	311	0.836	108	0.826	104	0.831	99
Ideology	0.611	273	0.623	96	0.595	86	0.614	91
Limited government	0.391	313	0.406	108	0.383	105	0.383	100
Individualism	0.640	311	0.631	108	0.668	104	0.620	99
Party identification (1 = Strong Democrat)	0.582	290	0.568	100	0.584	97	0.593	93
Political engagement scale	0.419	313	0.444	108	0.377	105	0.434	100
Government child care	0.711	311	0.694	108	0.693	105	0.750	98
Affirmative action in hiring	0.322	309	0.353	107	0.290	105	0.322	97
Crime spending	0.733	309	0.750	108	0.738	105	0.708	96
AIDS spending	0.790	309	0.782	108	0.805	105	0.781	96
Schools spending	0.938	308	0.949	108	0.913	104	0.953	96
Poor spending	0.731	307	0.745	108	0.707	104	0.742	95
Spending on blacks	0.551	305	0.551	108	0.558	104	0.543	93
Child care spending	0.782	309	0.778	108	0.786	105	0.781	96
Financial aid spending	0.845	310	0.819	108	0.848	105	0.871	97
Homeless spending	0.726	307	0.729	107	0.721	104	0.729	96
Unemployment spending	0.610	308	0.565	107	0.633	105	0.635	96
Welfare spending	0.505	308	0.505	107	0.486	105	0.526	96
Cities spending	0.459	306	0.472	106	0.428	104	0.479	96
Environment spending	0.739	310	0.718	108	0.714	105	0.789	97
Food stamps spending	0.527	310	0.519	108	0.514	105	0.552	97

Source: All entries based on my experimental data. See chapter 4 for details; all variables are coded from zero to one.

Appendix 3

I measure race and gender predispositions with scales derived from proven multiple-item measures drawn from the literature. In both cases, I need measures that capture as much as possible of the structure of the relevant schemas and of the respondents' position on the evaluative dimension each includes.

RACIAL PREDISPOSITIONS

For racial ideology, therefore, I need a measure that goes beyond prejudice or antiblack attitudes. That is, I need a measure that taps into the range of elements of the racial schema, including the sense of unequal outcomes, different attributes, zero-sum competition, and attributions — individual or structural — for this state of affairs. These various elements are reflected in racial resentment, a measure developed by Kinder and Sanders expressly to capture the complex ways that concerns of race have become written into modern political rhetoric (1996). The items that make up the scale are designed to be subtle and to evoke feelings about and attributions regarding blacks and whites and their achievements in American society. At the racially resentful end of the continuum is the argument that African Americans *could* do just as well as whites if they would only try harder. At the racially egalitarian end is the argument that African Americans have faced, and continue to face, external and systematic barriers to their achievement.

Like SRES for gender, racial resentment does not simply measure positive or negative feelings about racial groups and does not simply ask about endorsement of stereotypes. Rather, this measure captures the complexity of the structure of the racial schema and assesses beliefs about the relationship between racial groups. For example, one item asks respondents to agree or disagree with the statement "It's really a matter of some people not trying hard enough; if blacks would only try harder they could be just as well off as whites."

Racial resentment is reliable and valid (Kinder and Sanders 1996, appendix), and it—like symbolic racism from which it developed—has a proven track record in public-opinion research (Sniderman, Crosby, and Howell 2000; Mendelberg 2001; Kinder and Sanders 1996; Sears, Van Laar, and Carrillo 1997).[1]

I measured racial predispositions using a four-item racial resentment battery, drawn from the American National Election Studies. For clarity in the discussion that follows, I reversed this scale, and I call it "racial liberalism" rather than "racial resentment." I combined the items into a linear scale, which runs from zero (most racially conservative) to one (most racially liberal). The racial liberalism scale had a mean of 0.61, a standard deviation of 0.23, and an alpha of 0.84.

GENDER PREDISPOSITIONS

Similarly, to measure gender predispositions, I need to capture the elements of the gender schema, including the ideas of difference between the sexes, hierarchical arrangements between men and women, warm confluence of interests, and so on. The Sex Role Egalitarianism Scale (SRES), developed by Beere, King, and King fits these needs (King and King 1997; Beere et al. 1984). This scale is designed to measure beliefs about the appropriateness of the traditional gender arrangements in contemporary American society. To this end it measures attitudes about multiple domains, including marital, parental, employment, social-interpersonal-heterosexual, and educational; it also includes measures of various features of gender equality, including questions of differential ability, duty, rights, opportunities, and consequences. In addition, unlike many other measures of gender predisposition, the SRES measures beliefs and judgments about the role behaviors of both men and women, rather than only one or the other.

For example, respondents are asked the degree to which they agree or disagree with the statement "A husband's job is to earn money; a wife's job is to look after home and family." This item makes reference to the separate roles both men and women traditionally take and encapsulates the interaction between the domains of home and work. Another item, "Fathers are not as able to care for their sick children as mothers are," also contrasts men and women, this time in their traditional parental roles. (Complete question wording appears in appendix 2.)

At the same time, SRES stays away from other aspects of gender that are less relevant to my purposes. It does not measure individuals' gendered sense of self as masculine or feminine, matters of personal gender identity or consciousness, sexism and hostility toward women, or support for feminism. Although all these are certainly important aspects of gender, they are less relevant for my purpose, which is to measure respondents' gender schemas — that is, to measure their evaluation of the arrangements between the sexes in contemporary America. The SRES has demonstrated reliability (Beere et al. 1984) and validity (King and King 1986; King et al. 1994; Scandura, Tejeda, and Lankau 1995). It has been employed mostly in psychology and sociology in studies of (among other things) attitudes and behavior surrounding domestic violence (e.g., Crossman, Stith, and Bender 1990; Stith and Farley 1993; Fitzpatrick et al. 2004), rape (Ben-David and Schneider 2005; Yamawaki and Tschanz 2005), and occupational choice (Temple and Osipow 1994; Brutus et al. 1993).

The complete SRES includes two different sets of ninety-five items. To keep the survey reasonably short and to avoid tipping respondents off to my particular interest in gender attitudes, I include a subset of thirteen items (see appendix 2) from the complete scale. The items ask respondents to place themselves on a five-point Likert scale that runs from "strongly disagree" to "strongly agree," with "neutral" at the midpoint. I combined the thirteen items into a linear scale, which runs from zero (most gender traditionalist) to one (most egalitarian). The resulting scale had a mean of 0.83, a standard deviation of 0.13, and an alpha reliability coefficient of 0.87.

*   *   *

We should note that both the racial resentment scale and SRES were developed in part to address the declining relevance of traditional measures of racism and sexism (see Kinder and Sanders 1996, 291–94; Beere et al. 1984) and that both therefore reflect contemporary American racial and gender arrangements and debates. As Kinder and Sanders describe, "We attempt to spell out how racial hostility and American values have become fused in a particular way at a particular time in a particular society. If we have made an original theoretical contribution to the meaning of prejudice, it lies here, in our effort to specify how racial ideology is shaped by alterations in intellectual currents, changes in economic arrangements, and eruptions of political crisis" (1996, 294).

Similarly, the SRES was developed in part to address the changing social context of gender (McHugh and Frieze 1997). I think this is appropriate — as I discussed in chapter 3, it is precisely the current state of racial or gender discourse that conditions the structure of the racial and gender schemas, and it is this structure that may serve as the analogical basis for group implication.[2]

Appendix 4

One might worry that the experimental findings do not represent the effect of race or gender schemas but rather that the treatments evoke some other, correlated set of predispositions. Because participants were randomly assigned to conditions, I can be confident that the differences between the conditions were caused by the treatments. Nevertheless, we still might question what the treatments really are — what theoretical construct they really tap. I argue that they evoke race and gender predispositions, but one could contest that claim.

In particular, one might be concerned that the racial frames in fact engage ideological considerations. Given the close connection between racialized politics and the structure of American partisan conflict, this is a real possibility (Carmines and Stimson 1989; Edsall and Edsall 1992). Moreover, the debate over individual versus social locus of causality for economic outcomes — which forms part of the racial schema — underlies broader ideological disputes (Sniderman and Piazza 1993).

To address this concern, in this section I test whether the articles affected the relationship between opinion and ideological predispositions in addition to or instead of affecting the relationship between opinion and racial predispositions. I conducted this test separately using several different measures of ideology in addition to racial liberalism.[1] The first is a question that asks people to place themselves on an ideology scale that runs from "very conservative" through "moderate" to "very liberal." Though this item taps ideology on its face, it probably does not fully capture predispositions that we might consider ideological because many Americans are unfamiliar with ideological terms (Converse 1964). Therefore, I included, in turn, two other measures that capture elements of ideological conflict in terms that are more concrete. The first is a three-item measure of support for limited government based on the scales developed by Markus (1990, 2001); the second is a three-item scale measuring support for economic individualism and the American work ethic developed by Feldman (1988). Both are drawn from the American National Election Studies.

If the articles implicate aspects of ideology rather than racial predispositions, the racialization effect should disappear in these analyses and should be replaced by large effects for ideology in the race condition. Table A4.1 represents the basic racialization analysis, along with models that include each of the measures of ideology in turn. The results here are quite clear. Ideology, support for limited government, and economic individualism are all related to opinion for some issues (as revealed by the b_3 coefficients), and some are primed by some of the treatments as well (see the b_4 coefficients). Nevertheless, the racialization effects estimated in the basic model are essentially unaffected by the inclusion of these control variables. The estimates are noisier because I have included additional collinear variables in the model, which means that the racialization results are much less statistically significant. The estimated degree of racialization, however, is essentially the same across the various issues and control variables.

In fact, for the government jobs item, the estimate of racialization due to the treatment is *larger* than in the basic model. This result occurs because the economic items are strongly related to ideology in the baseline condition. Once this relationship is accounted for, the apparent baseline-condition racialization of the jobs item is reduced, and the effect of the treatment becomes stronger. Thus, for this issue, ideology *was* obscuring the results—but in the direction of hiding some racial framing in the race condition. In any case, the results make clear that racial predispositions do indeed underlie the effects; they are *not* simply a proxy for ideology in one form or another.[2]

For the gendering analysis, the clearest alternate explanation is that the treatments prime a generalized distrust of authority and government rather than gender predispositions. The relationship between citizens

TABLE A4.1 Racialization Results—Models with Ideology

	FAVOR VISITATION LAWS	PRIVATIZE SOCIAL SECURITY	INCREASE SOCIAL SECURITY SPENDING	RAISE MINIMUM WAGE	GOV'T JOBS AND STD OF LIVING
Hypothesized sign for b_2	−	+	−	+	+
Basic Model					
Racial liberalism (b_1)	0.524	−0.650^	1.158**	0.583	2.500***
Racial liberalism × race condition (b_2)	−1.168*	0.836^	−1.196*	1.231*	0.315
Model with Ideology					
Racial liberalism (b_1)	0.531	−0.583	0.821^	−0.227	1.702***
Racial liberalism × race condition (b_2)	−1.118^	1.082^	−0.967	1.463*	1.282^
Ideology (b_3)	0.192	−0.164	−0.101	1.224**	1.241**
Ideology × race condition (b_4)	−0.260	0.089	0.758	0.537	−1.310^
Model with Limited Government					
Racial liberalism (b_1)	0.418	−0.572	1.121**	0.431	2.441***
Racial liberalism × race condition (b_2)	−1.237*	0.830	−1.428**	1.284*	0.159
Limited govt (b_3)	−0.688*	0.464^	−0.319	−1.097***	−1.219***
Limited govt × race condition (b_4)	0.233	−0.271	−0.381	0.770^	0.300
Model with Individualism					
Racial liberalism (b_1)	0.562	−0.301	1.055*	0.512	2.060***
Racial liberalism × race condition (b_2)	−1.407*	0.949^	−1.404*	1.058^	0.616
Individualism (b_3)	0.092	0.879^	−0.255	−0.177	−1.155*
Individualism × race condition (b_4)	−0.791	0.623	−0.766	−0.679	0.625

Source: All entries based on my experimental data. See chapter 4 for details.
Note: Entries are ordered probit coefficients. B_2 is the change in the impact of racial liberalism on opinion between the race and baseline conditions; b_4 is the change in the impact of ideology on opinion between the conditions. Complete results appear in the Web appendix.
*** $p < 0.01$; ** $p < 0.05$; * $p < 0.1$; ^ $p < 0.2$ two-sided.

and government can be seen in familial terms (Lakoff 1996), so perhaps the gender treatments simply tap into beliefs about the importance of limiting the scope and power of authority in political terms, rather than more-symbolic specific feelings about authority in the context of gender. This situation is a particular concern for Social Security, because the gender article for that issue raises explicit concerns about "government bureaucrats" having too much power. To examine this possibility, I explored the effect of the gender treatments simultaneously on gender egalitarianism and support for limited government.[3]

TABLE A4.2   Gendering Results—Models with Limited Government

	FAVOR VISITA- TION LAWS	PRIVATIZE SOCIAL SECURITY	GOV'T MANAGE SS ACCOUNTS	INCREASE SOCIAL SECURITY SPENDING	RAISE MINIMUM WAGE	GOV'T JOBS AND STD OF LIVING
Hypothesized sign for b_2	+	−	+	+	+	+
			Basic Model			
Gender egalitarianism (b_1)	0.586	−0.576	−1.571**	0.684	0.503	0.746
Gender egalitarianism × gender condition (b_2)	0.748	−1.644^	1.823^	0.769	0.366	−0.273
			Model with Limited Government			
Gender egalitarianism (b_1)	0.662	−0.631	−1.601**	0.760	0.647	0.899
Gender egalitarianism × gender condition (b_2)	0.584	−1.502^	1.647^	0.542	0.141	−0.598
Limited govt (b_3)	−0.645*	0.509^	−1.142***	−0.437	−1.099***	−1.267***
Limited govt × gender condition (b_4)	−0.184	0.303	−0.206	−0.462	0.302	−0.588

Source: All entries based on my experimental data. See chapter 4 for details.
Note: Entries are ordered probit coefficients. B_2 is the change in the impact of gender egalitarianism on opinion between the gender and baseline conditions; b_4 is the change in the impact of limited government on opinion between the conditions. Complete results appear in the Web appendix.
*** $p < 0.01$; ** $p < 0.05$; * $p < 0.1$; ^ $p < 0.2$ two-sided.

The results, presented in table A4.2, indicate that the framed articles really are evoking the gender schema, not some broader concerns about the scope of government. Although endorsement of limited government is related to policy opinion for most of the issues in the baseline condition, the gender treatment had little or no effect on those relationships. Moreover, the gendering effect of the treatments is about the same when limited government is included in the model. This result suggests that the gender treatments really do tap into gender predispositions.[4]

The results of these additional analyses buttress the claim that my racial treatment really did implicate racial schemas and that my gender treatment really did implicate gender schemas.[5]

Appendix 5

This appendix presents the relevant coefficients for the models from which figures 4.9 and 4.10 were created.

TABLE A5.1   Racialization of Other Policy Issues

	BASELINE CONDITION (B_1)	RACE INTERACTION (B_2)	P-LEVEL FOR B_2
Food stamps spending	1.930	0.489	0.486
Schools spending	0.961	0.413	0.679
Cities spending	1.098	0.228	0.741
Financial aid spending	0.325	0.135	0.859
Environment spending	0.530	0.054	0.938
Government child care	1.744	−0.208	0.749
Crime spending	−0.393	−0.233	0.744
AIDS spending	0.505	−0.256	0.722

Source: All entries based on my experimental data. See chapter 4 for details.
Note: Entries are ordered probit coefficients from group implication models, depicted in figure 4.9. N varies from 209 to 212; full results appear in the Web appendix.

TABLE A5.2   Gendering of Other Policy Issues

	BASELINE CONDITION (B_1)	GENDER INTERACTION (B_2)	P-LEVEL FOR B_2
Homeless spending	−1.211	2.912	0.020
Government child care	−1.070	1.945	0.084
Child care spending	−0.224	1.519	0.222
Welfare spending	0.730	1.245	0.286
Financial aid spending	−1.146	1.002	0.471
Poor spending	0.185	0.996	0.413
Food stamps spending	1.114	0.957	0.419
Affirmative action in hiring	0.596	0.437	0.709
Environment spending	1.347	0.040	0.974
Crime spending	0.090	−0.286	0.815
Schools spending	−0.553	−0.308	0.874
Unemployment spending	1.759	−0.270	0.820
Cities spending	0.093	−0.446	0.702
AIDS spending	1.990	−0.528	0.673
Spending on blacks	1.346	−1.252	0.286

Source: All entries based on my experimental data. See chapter 4 for details.
Note: Entries are ordered probit coefficients from group implication models, depicted in figure 4.10. N varies from 201 to 206; full results appear in the Web appendix.

Notes

1 Daugman also discusses electronic/optical metaphors and network/ automata metaphors and argues strongly that the currently fashion- able computer metaphor be understood as just that: a metaphor, with strengths and weaknesses, rather than as a literal description of the brain. On the role of metaphors in cognitive science generally, see Gentner and Grudin (1985), Leary (1990), and Sternberg (1990). A related body of litera- ture explores the role of analogy and metaphor in the scientific enter- prise more broadly (e.g., T. Brown 2003; Mac Cormac 1976; Biela 1991). Holyoak and Thagard review this literature, emphasizing the way that the development of new analogies suggests new ways of understanding ambig- uous scientific phenomena (1995, chap. 8). In this context, one aspect of a Kuhnian paradigm is the range of metaphors it allows or embraces (1962).

2 Carmines and Stimson's work on issue evolution (1989) can be understood as an account of how ideas about race came to underlie a wide range of other political issues and partisan conflict generally. Their approach is related to mine in that they show how one issue (or issue domain) came to underlie the opinion in other areas. They treat issues as relatively straight- forward and independent matters, however; their interest is in whether one of these issues serves as the basis for thinking about the others (and about the parties). They do not explore the political psychology involved in this process. My work also grows out of that on symbolic racism, inso-

far as that literature seeks to understand the ways that racial symbolism
became enmeshed with rhetoric and cognition about such "nonracial"
values as individualism. But again, most work on symbolic racism does
not explore the microlevel psychological underpinnings of this process to
explain how and why this could happen.

CHAPTER 2

1 There is extensive research on the nature and role of racial predispositions on racial policy attitudes (e.g., Kinder and Sanders 1996; Schuman
et al. 1997; Dovidio and Gaertner 1986; Bobo 1988; Alvarez and Brehm
1997). There is important controversy on the exact nature of white Americans' racial predispositions and about the relative importance of nonracial
predispositions such as conservatism and commitment to the principle
of limited government (Sniderman, Tetlock, and Carmines 1993; Tetlock
1994; Sears, Hensler, and Speer 1979; McConahay 1986, 1982; Sniderman
and Piazza 1993; Sears 1988; Sniderman, Crosby, and Howell 2000; for a
recent set of entries from both (all?) sides of this debate, see Sears, Sidanius, and Bobo 2000). I do not speak directly to this debate. Nevertheless, my approach raises questions about our ability to distinguish racial
from nonracial appeals cleanly in all cases, and it suggests ways that nonracial considerations can become intertwined with our ideas about race.

2 Stereotypes are an example of schemas about social groups (Smith 1998,
404), although McHugh and Frieze (1997) draw a distinction between
schemas, which have structure, and stereotypes, which they define as
a simple unstructured list of attributes. Not all cognitive psychological research maintains this distinction, however, and I will draw on both
schema and stereotype research somewhat interchangeably in what follows.

3 This basic distinction goes by various other names, including automatic
versus controlled (Devine 1989; Fazio et al. 1986; Dovidio et al. 1997;
Dovidio and Fazio 1992; Fazio and Dunton 1997; Schneider and Shiffrin
1977); central versus peripheral (Petty and Cacioppo 1981, 1986); and
systematic versus heuristic (Chaiken 1980). These all grow out of Freud's
distinction between conscious and unconscious (1943), which itself has a
long history in Western thought (Whyte 1978).

4 Note that the term "framing" refers to (at least) two rather different phenomena. The first, dubbed "equivalence framing" by Druckman (2001a),
occurs when people's choices change when presented with formally
equivalent choice sets (Tversky and Kahneman 1981; Quattrone and Tversky 1988; Kahneman and Tversky 2000). My work builds on a second type
of frame, which Druckman calls "emphasis frames." These frames draw

attention to qualitatively different sets of considerations regarding an issue and so do not involve formally equivalent choices (Druckman 2001a, 2001b, 2004; Callaghan and Schnell 2005; Druckman and Nelson 2003; Bartels 2003). This latter tradition is itself vast, with works spanning several disciplines and methods, including theoretical accounts (Chong 1996, 2000; Price and Tewksbury 1997; Riker 1986; Nelson, Oxley, and Clawson 1997); experiments that vary question wording and explore the resulting changes in opinion (Kinder and Sanders 1996; Nelson and Oxley 1999; Krosnick and Kinder 1990; Nelson and Kinder 1996; Freedman 1999; Kinder and Sanders 1990; Berinsky and Kinder 2006; Sniderman and Theriault 2004); open-ended interview-based explorations of the ways people grapple with different issue frames (Chong 1993); and analyses that explore the relationships between different frames in political discourse and patterns of public opinion (Iyengar 1991; Gilens 1999; Patterson 1993; Pollock 1994; Jacoby 2000; Nelson, Clawson, and Oxley 1997). Others examine the frames that people develop in their own discussions of issues (Gamson 1992; Walsh 2004; Gamson and Lasch 1983; Gamson and Modigliani 1989). And one important line of research in the social movements literature emphasizes the role of frames in mobilizing discontent (Zald 1996; Snow, Rochford, and Worden 1986; Tarrow 1994).

5 See note 4.

6 Scholars of intersectionality have pointed to the ways that arguments over whether this and other issues are "about race" or "about gender" obscure the ways that race and gender work together to shape politics. I return to fuller consideration of this literature on intersectionality in the concluding chapter.

7 Mendelberg is careful to make clear that the distinction is in the receiver's awareness of the nature of the message, not necessarily in the sender's intentions. She demonstrates that conservative politicians often have incentives to craft implicitly racial appeals and argues that they are often aware of what they are doing. But she suggests that implicit appeals can be crafted incidentally as well.

8 There are important debates in the political psychology literature on the mechanisms of framing and on the role of implicit versus explicit appeals. I will return to these questions in the concluding chapter.

9 There are various accounts of the difference between metaphor and analogy. For example, Holyoak and Thagard argue that analogical reasoning underlies metaphor and that the distinction lies not in the cognitive processes involved but in the distance between the source and target. When source and target are quite similar to each other, the comparison is considered merely analogical; as the domains draw further apart, the comparison becomes metaphorical (1995, 220–21). On the fundamental

equivalence of analogical and metaphorical reasoning, see also Genter et al. (2001).

10 This was the format the College Board used for the analogy section of the Scholastic Aptitude Test before that section was dropped from the test in 2005. It reads, "Word is to sentence as hand is to _____"; the correct answer, of course, would be "arm."

11 William Jennings Bryan, "Cross of Gold" speech, Democratic National Convention, July 9, 1896.

12 Foreign-policy decision making has been a fertile ground for analysis of political metaphor and analogy, in part because the metaphors deployed tend to be overt and because scholars and practitioners often argue explicitly over the applicability of rival analogies. Several scholars have studied the use of metaphor and analogy in the foreign-policy discourse of political elites. Because this work grows out of a concern for understanding the cognitive processes that shape and limit the decision making of leaders (Jervis 1976), it focuses on the ways that analogies shape foreign-policy reasoning rather than on political communication between political leaders and citizens (e.g., Beer and De Landtsheer 2004; Khong 1992; Houghton 1996; Rohrer 1991; Rohrer 1995; Shimko 1994; Voss et al. 1992; Vertzberger 1986).

13 From another point of view, this third analogy could be seen as apt, albeit humorous. One line of research on humor, dating back to Aristotle, draws attention to the humorous effect created when metaphors draw creative, surprising connections with two different domains at once (see, for example, Attardo 1994).

14 Others schemas can be central as well. For example, one way to view the authoritarian personality is as a propensity to view the world through a lens of power and status (Adorno, Frenkel-Brunswick, and Levinson 1950). Similarly, McClelland and colleagues look at effects of seeing the world through particular motivational lenses, including achievement (McClelland and Atkinson 1976), power (Winter 1973), affiliation (Koestner and McClelland 1992), or intimacy (McAdams 1992).

CHAPTER 3

1 Throughout the text I describe popular beliefs about race and gender as "ideologies." I do this to emphasize that these predispositions form a more or less coherent and organized system, although perhaps one that people cannot articulate explicitly, and to provide aesthetic relief from the more cumbersome "predispositions." I do not intend to suggest, however, that American beliefs about race or gender are ideological in the sense used in the debates growing out of Converse (1964).

2 A huge social theory literature deals with the roles of social structure in constraining ideologies and human agency in altering them. Some theorists put more weight on the role of structure, emphasizing the ways that social structure and our understanding of it reproduce each other through time. For example, Gramsci explores the way the hegemony, or dominant ideology, constrains and limits the very ideas and strategies that people can conceive (1991). Althusser focuses on the reproduction of social structure, institutions, and consciousness (1971), and Bourdieu develops his concept of the *habitus*—a socially instantiated understanding of the world, which defines the universe of the possible within which actors develop their life strategies (1977). Others emphasize potential sources of ideological change. For example, Laclau and Mouffe argue that there are always internal contradictions in a worldview that allow actors to develop new concepts of the possible (1983). Sahlins emphasizes the role played by forces external to a society, as when European explorers appeared in the world of Pacific islanders (1981, 1985). And others put weight on the role of technological and economic developments in opening up new ways of conceiving of the world and closing off others (e.g., Marx 1948). Finally, others emphasize that there is no simple or deterministic way to choose between structure and agency and that even framing the question that way limits our understanding. Ortner, for example, draws attention to the ways that structure constrains, yet actors have more or fewer resources and opportunities in any given situation for developing new understandings (1996).

3 Hacking makes the point that "socially constructed" and "real" are not antonyms (1999).

4 Although different people certainly vary somewhat in their understanding of race and gender, I expect that there should be enough similarity in the abstract structure of race and gender schemas for appropriately structured political appeals to resonate with them and therefore have broad political impact. Nevertheless, we might expect schema structures to vary across groups, especially among members of nondominant groups in American society. I will return to this point in the concluding chapter.

5 Mary Jackman discusses the fact that racial ideologies differed in the antebellum American South. Under slavery, blacks and whites lived in close physical proximity and were much more interdependent; in this different structural context, racial ideologies were much more paternalistic and involved more positive emotional valence (1994, 84–85).

6 This discussion of the evaluative dimension owes much to Kinder and Sanders (1996); see also Entman and Rojecki (2000, chap. 2).

7 I use the terms "racially conservative" and "racially liberal" to refer to the two ends of the continuum of racial predispositions in order to avoid nec-

essarily associating racially conservative positions with prejudice. Prejudice certainly underlies these beliefs for some whites, but considerations of principle may underlie them for others (e.g., Sniderman and Carmines 1997). We should note, however, that this distinction is conceptually different from *political* conservatism and liberalism.

8 Devine's work on race schemas supports this idea (1989). She shows that everyone is aware of the culture's race stereotypes; differences in prejudiced *behavior* stem from the fact that some people consciously counteract the effects of the stereotypes on their perceptions and evaluations. On the other hand, we should not necessarily expect nonwhite Americans to understand race in the same terms. The spatial and task segregation involved in American race relations allows for rather different understandings of race to evolve among whites and blacks (Jackman 1994). In addition, as the subordinate group in America, people of color are compelled to pay more attention to race (Fiske 1993; Dawson 1994, 2001; Sigelman and Welch 1991). My analysis of racial group implication therefore focuses on whites; clearly, additional research on group implication among nonwhites is needed.

9 Gender is an extraordinarily multifaceted concept; Haslanger, for example, develops a typology of approaches to understanding gender (2000). Gender, she suggests, can refer to attributes of masculinity and femininity, both literally and symbolically, when applied to inanimate objects and concepts. A second and related sense of gender is in terms of roles that men and women typically play in American family and social life. Third, several varieties of gender identity exist, including public identity, psychological identity, self-concept, and political identity. All these faces of gender have both descriptive and normative aspects. This variety of concepts has spawned a corresponding variety of measures of sexism, gender stereotypes, gender role beliefs, and more (Glick and Fiske 1997; Signorella 1999; Morrison et al. 1999; McHugh and Frieze 1997; Campbell, Schellenberg, and Senn 1997; Swim and Cohen 1997; Ashmore, Del Boca, and Bilder 1995; King and King 1997; Beere 1990a, 1990b; Blaszczyk 2000). My approach is to step back from these various concepts to consider somewhat more abstractly the "ideology" of gender, especially as it relates to politics.

10 Moreover, the power of the idea of difference is reflected in the fact that much of the research on gender and public opinion has focused on the gender gap (e.g., Shapiro and Mahajan 1986; Conover 1988; Cook and Wilcox 1991; Rapoport 1981; Manza and Brooks 1998), a pattern not generally shared by the research on race and opinion or on class and opinion (see, though, Kinder and Winter 2001; Wilcox 1990). Ironically, the gender gap is probably an appealing analytic construct in part because it reflects

a binary separation of male and female opinion spheres. See Epstein (1988, chap. 2) on the role of binary gender distinctions in social scientific research.

11 This reality is reflected in the emphasis of the early feminist movement on consciousness raising—the process of developing a sense among women of themselves as a group with possible conflicts of interest with "their" men. Although all social movements must work to mobilize a sense of group injustice, this barrier to the sense of group identity was and is likely particularly acute for the feminist movement because gender is constructed as private and individual. Because of this situation, "gender hierarchies are recipes for the morselization of experience, for enabling people—both scholars and the individuals they study—to explain any individual outcome as the product of individual and idiosyncratic circumstance and not as a consequence of large-scale structural forces like discrimination" (Burns 2007, 107; see also Stewart and McDermott 2004; for an account of the different, intersecting challenges for organizing posed by race, class, and gender, see Smith 1995).

12 As I discussed earlier, this structure is in contrast to modern race relations, where spatial and task segregation leads blacks and whites to different understandings of race (Jackman 1994; Sigelman and Welch 1991).

13 This construction of gender develops in important ways out of the structural relationship between *white* women and men (Hurtado 1989; Higginbotham 1992; Collins 1990). Unfortunately, the limited number of nonwhite respondents in the data prevents me from exploring racial differences in this analysis. Clearly, more theoretical and empirical work is needed in understanding the intersections of race and gender in this area. I return to this point in the concluding chapter.

CHAPTER 4

1 An example of the articles' formatting appears as figure A1.1 in appendix 1.
2 The full text of the question wording for all measures appears in appendix 2.
3 There is no evidence that the order of the articles had any effect on the results.
4 The priming was achieved for respondents in the gender condition by having them answer four close-ended questions and one open-ended question about the nature and causes of differences between men and women. Those in the race condition were primed by parallel questions about differential economic success between blacks and whites. Those in the control condition answered parallel questions about the causes of differences between Democrats and Republicans.

5 Because race and gender predispositions are independent variables in the analysis, ideally I would have measured them *before* the treatments and opinion measures. To have done so, however, would have risked priming both race and gender for all participants, and therefore it might have interfered with the effectiveness of the treatments. The risk with measuring them afterward is that the treatments might affect their measurement. This seems relatively unlikely, though, because race and gender ideologies are acquired very young and are quite stable. Moreover, this approach is common in this sort of study (Valentino, Hutchings, and White 2002; Iyengar and Kinder 1987; Mendelberg 2001; Valentino 1999). And, I am happy to say, the treatments did not influence the level of the predisposition measures. Participants in the race condition were marginally less racially egalitarian (0.58 on average, compared with 0.62 for both the gender and baseline conditions). This difference is both substantively small and statistically insignificant ($p = 0.41$ for the ANOVA of racial liberalism on condition). Participants were indistinguishable on gender egalitarianism across the three conditions (mean levels 0.83, 0.83, and 0.84 in the race, gender, and baseline, respectively; $p = 0.88$).

6 In all, 135 of the participants completed the experiment as part of the requirements of the introductory psychology course, 133 were recruited on a volunteer basis from an upper-level psychology course, and 45 were recruited on a volunteer basis from an upper-level political science course. (Although some of the courses from which participants were recruited dealt in public opinion, psychology, or both, I found no evidence that the recruitment source influenced the results; in any case the study was conducted early in the semester before directly relevant material was covered in class.) Participants completed the experimental protocol in groups ranging in size from one to forty-five (mean group size was thirteen) in university classrooms. Participants were fully debriefed about the true purpose of the study after finishing the survey, and none indicated that they had suspected the true nature of the study. The University of Michigan's Institutional Review Board approved the study.

7 The racial breakdown was 76 percent white, 6.5 percent black, 13 percent Asian, 4 percent Hispanic/Latino, and 0.5 percent other. Respondents ranged from eighteen to thirty-two years of age, with 91 percent falling under age twenty-two.

8 The 2000 American National Election Study, using fairly similar question wording, found that 50 percent of respondents identified as Democrats, 38 percent as Republicans, and 12 percent as independents. The ANES sample was 56 percent female.

9 For racial predispositions, my respondents have practically the identical distribution as the 2000 ANES sample, using an identically worded

measure of racial resentment. My participants have a mean of 0.608 and a standard deviation of 0.234, compared with mean 0.605 and standard deviation of 0.241 for the ANES. The Sex Role Egalitarianism Scale does not appear in any recent national studies. From my survey, however, I can construct a measure of gender predispositions that parallels the ANES measure I deploy in chapter 6 and that correlates 0.61 with SRES. My participants average 0.764 (standard deviation 0.172) on this measure, quite similar to the national mean of 0.729 (standard deviation 0.175).

10 Anderson, Lindsay, and Bushman (1999) conducted a meta-analysis of studies that compared the relationships among variables in national and college samples; they found substantial comparability of effect sizes across a wide range of psychological domains.

11 For all issues except Social Security spending, the line plots the predicted probability that respondents choose the "agree" or "strongly agree" response. For the spending question, the line indicates the probability of choosing "increase."

12 I use ordered probit to estimate the opinion models. For gendering I estimate the following model for each policy: Opinion = b_0 + b_1 [gender egalitarianism] + b_2 [gender egalitarianism × gender condition] + b_3 [gender condition]. The effect of gender egalitarianism on opinion in the baseline condition is estimated by b_1; in the gender condition the corresponding effect is (b_1 + b_2). The coefficient b_2 is the difference between the effects of gender egalitarianism in the two conditions and is a direct measure of the impact of the treatment on that relationship. For racialization, the statistical model is run among respondents in the race and baseline conditions and is exactly parallel: Opinion = b_0 + b_1 [racial liberalism] + b_2 [racial liberalism × race condition] + b_3 [race condition]. Again, b_2 is the coefficient and allows us to evaluate the framing impact of the treatment, compared with the baseline.

13 In other words, I do not have expectations about b_1, the effect of predispositions in the baseline condition. The interaction (b_2) is the key—rather than the size of the effect in the race or gender condition (b_1 + b_2)—because I am interested in the degree to which my treatments change the ambient racialization of the issue. If an issue is racialized positively in the baseline condition (i.e., b_1 > 0), and my treatment acts to racialize it negatively, then the sum of b_1 and b_2 may be positive or negative.

14 The full results for all models appear in the Web appendix (address provided on copyright page of this book).

15 A related concern is that the results may be conditioned by the demographic categories in which respondents fall: in particular, perhaps men react differently from women and white participants differently from participants of color. I have no reason to expect that men and women have

racial schemas with systematically different structures, though of course they may differ in their average evaluation of race relations. Although the limited number of cases makes firm conclusions impossible, it is clear that there are no systematic, across-the-board differences between men and women in their reactions to the racializing frames. As I discuss in chapter 3, I am less confident that nonwhite Americans share a racial schema structure with whites. The racialization results are actually slightly stronger among whites than among the total participant population, which may indicate that they are not as strong among nonwhites. (Nevertheless, there are far too few nonwhites to draw even speculative conclusions about African Americans or Latinos by themselves.) I maintain all participants in the racialization analyses to be conservative and to make it more strictly comparable to the gendering analyses that follow.

16 Because gender schematics are randomly distributed between conditions, this unmeasured heterogeneity does not bias the results; it just makes them less efficient and therefore makes it harder to detect the impact of the frame.

17 Among feminist identifiers, $b_1 = 3.352$, and $b_2 = -1.179$, both n.s. Among nonidentifiers, $b_1 = 0.056$ and $b_2 = 1.634$ (p = 0.096). Complete model results appear in the Web appendix.

18 Theoretically we might expect the racialization findings to be strengthened as well if we could weed out racial schematics. Unfortunately, the study included no measures that can serve, even badly, as measures of racial schematicity.

19 In contrast to the visitation issue, there is little evidence that gender schematicity is masking stronger effects for these issues: nonfeminist identifiers are no more affected by the treatments than are respondents as a whole.

20 As with the racialization analysis, one might also be concerned that the gender or race of respondents conditions the results (see note 15). For gender, I argue in chapter 3 that men and women should share gender schema structures—if not average evaluations—so I do not expect the gender of participant to affect the gendering results. As with the racialization analyses, there are too few cases to make firm conclusions, but there are no large and systematic differences between men and women in their reactions to the gendering frames. Similarly, there are no clear patterns of different effects for the frames among white and nonwhite respondents.

21 As I discuss above, this confound was created intentionally to maximize statistical power. Although randomly varying the prime independent of the fit would have allowed clear analysis of the separate roles of prime and fit, it would have divided the available data among at least seven condi-

tions rather than three. This probably would have left too few cases to allow any firm conclusions at all.

22 Several issues were highly racialized in the baseline, arbitrarily defined as having a b_1 coefficient greater than 2.0. These were issues that we would expect to be racialized: affirmative action, spending on programs to help blacks, and the like. These were excluded here because the strong baseline racialization creates a ceiling effect, limiting the scope for any additional impact of the prime.

23 That is, the model is: Opinion = b_0 + b_1 [racial liberalism] + b_2 [racial liberalism × race condition] + b_3 [racial liberalism × gender condition] + b_4 [gender egalitarianism] + b_5 [gender egalitarianism × gender condition] + b_6 [gender egalitarianism × race condition] + b_7 [race condition] + b_8 [gender condition].

24 In all cases, the comparisons are with the effect of the relevant predisposition in the baseline condition.

25 I did not include the economic opinion variables. Because gendering did not work for those issues, they do not represent a reasonable test of the effect of gendered frames on racial predispositions. Control of Social Security was not included because there were no expectations as to the effects of the racial treatment. The composite variable was created by averaging participants' responses to the three individual items. The Social Security privatization item was first reverse coded, because the expectations for the direction of racialization and gendering were opposite for that issue, compared with the other two.

CHAPTER 5

1 The discussion that follows draws heavily on chapter 5 from Gilens (1999).

2 That is, Aid to Dependent Children, later Aid to Families with Dependent Children, and still more recently Temporary Aid to Needy Families.

3 The welfare queen image also emphasizes gendered stereotypes as well, particularly of black female sexuality. I consider briefly the gendering of welfare later in this chapter and return to the intersectional—racialized and gendered—nature of the welfare queen image in chapter 7.

4 In fact, Clawson finds that the pictures of beneficiaries associated with national newsmagazine coverage of Social Security from 1992 through 2002 parallel the actual racial composition of recipients (and, therefore, of America as a whole): about 87 percent white, 10 percent African American, and 4 percent other (2003).

5 From President Reagan's remarks at a fundraising dinner for Senator Charles Percy in Chicago, January 19, 1983 (cited in Reagan 1984, 72, emphasis added).

6 Although conventional wisdom holds that Americans have little and declining confidence in Social Security, there is little evidence that this is actually the case. The public's confidence in the long-term solvency of Social Security is mixed and has increased somewhat from its low point in the 1970s (Baggette, Shapiro, and Jacobs 1995); see also Cook and Jacobs (2002); Jacobs and Shapiro (1998); Shaw and Mysiewicz (2004).

7 ANES data and complete information on data collection procedures are available at http://www.electionstudies.org.

8 The item does some violence to policy making for both programs: Social Security spending is not discretionary the way it is for some of the other programs in the battery, and the question ignores the prominent role of states in welfare financing and policy making. For my purposes, however, this is a strength precisely because these questions avoid the complications of welfare and Social Security policy making and specific reform proposals and instead tap respondents' general approval.

9 The questions ask respondents to rate whites and blacks (along with Asian and Hispanic Americans), in turn, on a seven-point scale that ranges from "hard working" to "lazy."

10 The battery asks respondents how much they agree with the following: (1) "Irish, Italian, Jewish and many other minorities overcame prejudice and worked their way up. Blacks should do the same without any special favors," (2) "Generations of slavery and discrimination have created conditions that make it difficult for blacks to work their way out of the lower class," (3) "It's really a matter of some people not trying hard enough; if blacks would only try harder they could be just as well off as whites," and (4) "Over the past few years, blacks have gotten less than they deserve."

11 That is, we are concerned that some omitted factor causes the observed effects, rather than the variable of interest. To bias our results and therefore be problematic, the omitted variable must both (a) affect opinion itself and (b) be correlated with race or gender predispositions. There is a long list of suspects that fit this bill, including ideology and partisanship, values, and demographics. So in this analysis I include a wide range of control variables to be as sure as possible that the effect I estimate really is that of racial predispositions and not some other omitted factor. Note that the logic of omitted variables is different for the experimental analysis in chapter 4. There I am not estimating simply the relationship between racial predispositions and opinion; rather, I am interested in the *difference* in that relationship between the baseline and race conditions. Thus, for the experimental analysis, the list of problematic omitted variables includes only those that (a) affect opinion, (b) are correlated with racial predispositions, and (c) affect opinion differently in the baseline

and race conditions. This list is shorter because of condition (c), which implies that something about the treatment framing engaged the omitted variable and linked it to opinion differently from its baseline association. So we must worry about things that might be engaged differentially by the treatment, not simply those that might cause opinion. Omitted variables that meet conditions (a) and (b) but not (c) will affect the estimate of b_1 (the baseline racialization) but *not* of b_2 (the change in racialization due to the treatment). Of course and as always, this logic applies in an analogous way to the gendering experiments. I deal with this concern in appendix 4.

12 The ANES sometimes includes a three-item scale that measures abstract support for limited government; unfortunately, these items do not appear before 1990 (Markus 1989, 2001). The pair of items I use are more concrete, and some might argue that they represent policy opinion variables. Nevertheless, there is precedent for using them as a predisposition (Kinder and Sanders 1996). Moreover, their use is conservative. Insofar as the scale picks up policy preferences beyond principled feelings about government, this may come at the expense of racial predispositions. For respondents who answered only one of the two items (between 10 and 20 percent in each study), I imputed scores based on the item they did answer. The substantive findings are the same when I substitute a dummy variable for these cases and when I substitute the abstract measure for the two-item scale.

13 Income is entered as a set of five dummy variables for percentiles of each year's income distribution; education as dummy variables for grade school, some high school, high school graduation, some college, and BA or more. Partisanship is entered as dummy variables for Democrats and Republicans, with independents as the omitted category; ideology is entered as dummy variables for liberal, conservative, and not ascertained, with moderate omitted. The results are unchanged by variation in the operationalization of these measures, or by the inclusion of controls for urban and rural residence. (These were omitted because they are not available for half of the respondents in 2000.)

14 Prior research has found that the elderly are less supportive of Social Security, compared with younger Americans, and that measures of imputed self-interest are inconsistently associated with opinion (Day 1990; Ponza et al. 1988; Rhodebeck 1993; Plutzer and Berkman 2005). This reinforces the point that inferring people's self-interest from demographics is difficult at best (Chong, Citrin, and Conley 2001).

15 The 1992 ANES asked respondents whether they or a family member receives Social Security or Medicare payments; this measure of self-interest was also essentially unrelated to opinion.

16 The estimated effects for racial resentment are almost identical in a model that omits the thermometer ratings. This basic pattern of results also holds when the racial resentment scale is replaced with one made up only of the first and third items. These two items contrast whites and blacks explicitly and are therefore arguably most relevant for my argument (see note 10).

17 All these findings are also reinforced by a series of confirmatory factor analysis models of opinion, which explore the simultaneous racialization of Social Security and welfare. These findings have been omitted in the interest of concision but are available from the author on request.

18 As always, complete results for these models are available in the Web appendix.

19 One explanation that does *not* seem to account for the pattern of racialized results is question-order effects. Specific policies might appear racialized insofar as they follow questions in the survey that invoke race either by association with those policies or by contrast with them. Examination of the survey instruments from 1984 to 2000, however, suggests no consistent pattern of the presence or absence of racialization after explicitly racial items.

20 The measurement of gender predispositions is discussed in chapter 6.

21 The models were run for self-identified Democrats, Republicans, and independents. Independents who then indicated on the follow-up question that they leaned toward one party or the other were not coded as partisan identifiers. The idea is that this sort of "leaning" is likely more endogenous to policy opinion than is the basic identification respondents indicate in the initial item. In any case the basic story is unchanged when leaners are categorized as party identifiers. The different years were collapsed for this analysis; separate analysis by year reveals no systematic differences over time, although the smaller number of available cases makes the individual estimates rather noisy.

22 Following Zaller, I make use of a fact-based information scale to measure political engagement (1992, appendix). This measure was normalized separately by year before pooling because it does not have a common metric from study to study. As with partisanship, there are no clear trends or patterns across the separate years, and confirmatory factor models yield entirely comparable results.

23 We should note that even an experiment using a nationally representative sample could not give us a realistic picture of Social Security and welfare opinion absent the group-implicating frames that have existed in political discourse over the past half-century. We could expose respondents to a different set of nonracial frames, but their opinion would still be influenced by their lifetime of experience with the real racialized framing.

24 Separately for each year, I used the models in table 5.1 to calculate predicted probabilities that each respondent would fall into each response category (decrease, keep the same, or increase) for welfare spending. I then used the mean of the probabilities in each category to calculate the average opinion, coding decrease as zero, keep the same as 0.5, and increase as one. This calculation reproduces the actual distribution of opinion, as presented in figure 5.1. Then I calculated a second set of probabilities, assuming each respondent rates blacks at one hundred on the thermometer scale. I used these simulated probabilities to calculate simulated opinion, again coding decrease as zero, keep the same as 0.5, and increase as one.

25 Simulated welfare opinion in 1996 averages 0.287, and simulated Social Security opinion averages 0.573.

CHAPTER 6

1 On the genesis of the administration's strategy and the ensuing political struggle, see Jacobs and Shapiro (2000) and Skocpol (1997). For a more policy-oriented discussion of the genesis of the reform plan itself, see Hacker (1997); broader accounts include Navarro (1994), who sets 1993 in the context of other reform efforts, and Oberlander (2003), who lays out the larger political context of the federal government's involvement in health policy administration.

2 See Luker (1984, 27–39) for a similar argument in the context of abortion policy.

3 This presumes, of course, that doctors are men and nurses are women. This circumstance is symbolically true and was literally the case during the nineteenth century. Even in 2004, 92 percent of nurses were women, and 71 percent of doctors were men (United States Department of Labor, Bureau of Labor Statistics 2005).

4 With minor variations, this item reads: "There is much concern about the rapid rise in medical and hospital costs. Some people feel there should be a government insurance plan which would cover all medical and hospital expenses for everyone. Others feel that all medical expenses should be paid by individuals, and through private insurance plans like Blue Cross or other company paid plans. Where would you place yourself on this [seven-point] scale, or haven't you thought much about this?"

5 With minor variations, this item reads: "Recently there has been a lot of talk about women's rights. Some people feel that women should have an equal role with men in running business, industry and government. Others feel that a women's place is in the home. Where would you place yourself on this [seven-point] scale, or haven't you thought much about this?"

6 A rating for "the women's movement" was included in 1992, 1994, 1996, and 2000; a rating for "feminists" was included in 1988, 1992, and 2000. The items that make up my scale are reasonably highly correlated with each other, and Cronbach's alpha for the combined scale is 0.49 (0.51 among women and 0.46 among men). This scale has a mean of 0.64 and a standard deviation of 0.23. It correlates quite highly with alternate gender measures from the ANES in the few years they are available and predicts opinion strongly on gendered issues such as abortion. A complete reliability and validity analysis appears in the Web appendix. In any case the results in this chapter are unchanged when the thermometer ratings alone are substituted for my gender ideology scale. The ANES did include a more complete gender ideology battery in 1992, though it did not appear in later years. Although some respondents questioned in 1992 were reinterviewed in 1994 and 1996, nonrandom panel attrition creates problems even for a supplemental analysis using this measure.

7 Because the dependent variable is measured on a seven-point scale, regression is a reasonable estimation strategy that makes interpretation particularly easy. In any case, and as usual, the substantive results are identical when estimated by ordered probit.

8 The effects of the other control variables are essentially the same in this model; complete results appear in the Web appendix.

9 Prior research on health care opinion is consistent with this finding. Schlesinger and Lee find, for example, that health care opinion is more associated with egalitarianism and less with racial feelings than other social welfare policy (1994). And Kinder and Winter find that opinion on health care is not particularly racialized by whites or by blacks (2001).

10 The reported models are run among all respondents in order to allow direct comparison of the gender effects with those reported above. All the conclusions are exactly the same when run among white respondents only. The results are also the same when the thermometer rating measures are replaced with racial resentment or with group stereotype measures.

11 Egalitarianism also shows an interesting pattern among the top two-thirds in political information. From 1988 to 1992 these respondents came to frame health care much more in terms of equality; they then abandoned the egalitarian frame for the implicit gendered frame in 1994. These findings for the moderating role of political information are consistent with those of Koch (1998), who also found that those with moderate information were the most influenced by the reform debate.

12 Of course, this exercise is entirely hypothetical and heuristic. If we imagine instead that gender egalitarians dropped as much as traditionalists between 1992 and 1994 (which would imply equalizing the slopes in figure

6.2 by rotating the right-hand end of the 1994 line *downwards*), average opinion in 1994 would have been 0.453.

13 Jacobs and Shapiro discuss the ultimately limited influence of public opinion on congressional action, although they do acknowledge the ways that fading public support contributed to the loss of an important group of moderate Republican legislators (2000, 125–48).

14 Although Wolbrecht (2000) demonstrates that parties' elites polarized on gender issues beginning in 1980, she does not explore the relationship between that polarization and mass opinion or the relationship among the public between gender attitudes and partisanship.

15 This conclusion is consistent with Burns and Kinder's (2003) findings that people's explanations for gender inequality predicted opinion much less pervasively than did their racial explanations.

CHAPTER 7

1 Work by Druckman and colleagues is a notable exception (Druckman 2001b, 2004; Druckman and Nelson 2003). This work focuses in particular on context factors and source characteristics that affect the impact of framing; my work explores characteristics of the frames themselves. Clearly, a complete account will require work from both of these perspectives and more.

2 A variety of factors increase the likelihood of active thought, including interest in the issue, not being rushed to make a decision, feeling that the issue is important, and having available cognitive resources (Petty and Cacioppo 1986).

3 Price and Tewksbury do allow for some judgment of relevance at the activation stage, depending on the "applicability" of the consideration to the issue. In their account, however, this process is not very substantive: "Assessing the applicability of constructs is a basic matter of coming to some understanding as to what a stimulus is and need not be a consciously evaluative process" (1997, 190–91). As I will discuss below, my model suggests that frames can have important effects on this stage of the process, even when they occur unconsciously.

4 Huber and Lapinski fail to replicate some of Mendelberg's experimental findings (2006). Nevertheless, they do not take issue with the basic psychological model. Rather, they find that only less-educated citizens are prone to unconscious racial priming, whereas only more-educated citizens reject explicit racial appeals. They demonstrate, that is, that the two processes may operate differently for different citizens, and they take issue, therefore, with Mendelberg's conclusion that we can undermine the political impact of implicit racial appeals by making them explicit.

5 In fact, cognitive processes probably lie on a continuum from conscious to unconscious (Bargh 1994; Conrey et al. 2005).

6 This argument is consistent with the broader finding that people generally do not have privileged access to their own cognitive functioning and often cannot report accurately the reasons for their beliefs and behaviors (Nisbett and Wilson 1977).

7 Some version of this cognitive process is probably necessary to allow analogical reasoning to take place at all. No analogy is perfect, just as few actual cases fit into a category precisely if considered in enough detail. It is precisely by ignoring some of this lack of fit, as long as there is some degree of fit, that we can use analogies productively. The key question is how much fit is enough.

8 See Bartels (2003) for an insightful development of the problems created for democratic theory by the fact that we lack context-independent theoretical grounds for evaluating particular issue frames and their effects.

9 On the role of gender ideas in the modern conservative coalition, see Lakoff (1996) and Ducat (2004).

10 Indeed, white female identity—like black male identity—may be particularly complex because it is positioned simultaneously at the superordinate location on one dimension and the subordinate dimension on another. On this point, Hurtado analyzes the way that white women and black men relate differently to the power held by white men (1996), and Fine and colleagues explore the sometimes-contradictory dynamics that lead white women and girls sometimes to support white men's privilege and sometimes to subvert it (2000).

11 George Lakoff discusses different dimensions along which whole conceptual systems—and therefore the schemas they contain—can vary (1987, chap. 18).

12 It is also likely that African Americans are nevertheless aware of the whites' construction of gender, if only because African Americans live in a white-dominated world and must navigate white politics, culture, and media. Susan Fiske makes the point that members of powerless groups must pay more attention to the powerful more than the reverse; this includes paying attention to the dominant group's constructions of race and gender (1993).

13 The health care gendering results in chapter 6 do not seem to hold up as well among African American respondents considered separately from whites. Still, the relatively small number of cases available in each year makes it difficult to draw strong conclusions on this point.

14 Of course, the experience of race for white Americans is significantly conditioned by gender. Frankenberg, for example, shows the ways that white women's construction of gender is significantly racialized (1993),

and Hurtado argues that whereas white men have racial privilege themselves, white women have *access to* racial privilege through intimate connections with men (1996, 1989). Both of these arguments suggest that
white men and women have somewhat different positions vis-à-vis race
and, therefore, may have somewhat differently shaped racial schemas.
As I discuss here, gender of respondent did not significantly condition
the racialization results in this book; nevertheless, of course, the question of whether these differences are great enough to affect the impact
of group-implicating frames in other cases is an empirical question that
requires more study.

15 The results are somewhat noisy from year to year, but they are consistent
with the claim of no systematic differences between men and women. Full
results are available from the author.

16 Results available from the author.

17 The future evolution and political significance of racial schemas among
these groups—and among whites and blacks—is a fascinating and important topic and one that is beyond the scope of this book (Cain, Kiewiet,
and Uhlaner 1991; Okamoto 2003; Garcia et al. 1989; Dominguez 1994;
De la Garza 1992; Villarreal and Hernandez 1991; Aoki and Takeda 2004;
Oliver and Wong 2003; Aoki and Nakanishi 2001; Kim 1999; Waters 1990;
Citrin, Reingold, and Green 1990; Lee 2003).

18 People are highly theory-driven and are therefore adept at fitting new
experiences into existing schemas. We should not, therefore, expect
demographic change to translate simply, easily, or automatically into new
and more complex racial schemas (Fiske and Taylor 1991). Nevertheless,
demographic changes could work in concert with parallel changes in
media portrayals and in leadership frames to forge change in racial schema
structure. We should expect this shift to occur particularly insofar as
demographic changes lead to changes in the social and economic relationships among racial groups.

19 Another important example is discourse on crime and prisons, which
joins together race and gender in the image of the black male criminal and
prisoner.

20 This account shares much with the "interaction" theory of metaphor
in the rhetorical context, which similarly suggests that metaphors can
involve the creation of something new that has implications for our
understanding of both target *and* source (e.g., Black 1962; Richards 1938).
Stepan applies this understanding of metaphor to an analysis of the ways
that race and gender concepts influence science (1986).

21 Nevertheless, some evidence indicates that gendered appeals have
mixed effects: under some circumstances at least, female candidates are
advantaged by gender stereotypes, being seen as more compassionate and

honest (Kahn 1996) and holding an advantage on so-called women's issues (Iyengar et al. 1997).

APPENDIX 3

1 Note, however, that racial resentment and symbolic racism have come under attack by critics who claim that it is not really racism—that it reflects general conservatism or commitment to the nonracial values of individualism and the work ethic (Sniderman and Carmines 1997; Tetlock 1994; Sniderman and Piazza 1993). I present some evidence in appendix 4 that the racial group implication picked up by racial resentment in my experiments really is racial. On the psychological coherence and stability of racial resentment, see Kinder and Sanders (1996). Mendelberg defends racial resentment and makes the point that although racial resentment has come under fire as a measure of *prejudice,* less controversy exists over its use as a measure of stereotypes (or racial predispositions) (2001, 192–31).

2 Nevertheless, we should also note that although these measures were chosen because they are theoretically appropriate measures of the structure of race and gender schemas, the results do not depend on this particular choice. See notes 2 and 4 in appendix 4.

APPENDIX 4

1 The model, estimated by ordered probit, is: Opinion $= b_0 + b_1$ [racial liberalism] $+ b_2$ [racial liberalism $\times$ race condition] $+ b_3$ [ideology] $+ b_4$ [ideology $\times$ race condition] $+ b_5$ [race condition].

2 Another related concern is that these results depend on the specific measure of racial liberalism I use. Unfortunately, the experiment did not include a range of other measures of racial predispositions. Still, I can construct a limited alternate measure of racial predispositions on the basis of policy opinions, using a question about support for racial affirmative action and a question about federal spending on programs to help blacks. This "policy racial liberalism" is certainly not ideal; nevertheless, the basic results hold (and are sometimes strengthened) when it is substituted for racial liberalism. Full results are available from the author.

3 As above, the model is Opinion $= b_0 + b_1$ [gender egalitarianism] $+ b_2$ [gender egalitarianism $\times$ gender condition] $+ b_3$ [limited government] $+ b_4$ [limited government $\times$ gender condition] $+ b_5$ [gender condition], estimated by ordered probit.

4 As with the racial results, a related concern is that these results depend on the specific measure of gender egalitarianism I use (see note 2 above). As

with racial predispositions, the experiment did not include any other gender predisposition scales. Nevertheless, I can construct an alternate measure on the basis of the thermometer ratings of feminists and the women's movement and a single item, drawn from the ANES, that asks respondents whether "women should have an equal role with men in running business, industry, and government" or "a woman's place is in the home." (This measure parallels the one I use in chapter 6.) With this measure the gendering results are somewhat messier but generally consistent with those reported above. Full results are available from the author.

5 A final concern is that the results may be conditioned by the demographic categories in which respondents fall: men may react differently from women; white participants may react differently from participants of color. For gender I argue in the theory chapter that men and women should share gender schema structures — if not average evaluations — so I do not expect the gender of the participant to affect the gendering results. Although the limited number of cases make firm conclusions impossible, it is clear that no systematic, across-the-board differences exist between men and women in their reactions to either the racializing or the gendering frames. As I discuss in chapters 3 and 7, I am less confident that nonwhite Americans share a racial schema structure with whites. The racialization results are actually slightly stronger among whites than among the total participant population (there are too few nonwhites to draw definitive conclusions among African Americans or Latinos by themselves). Nevertheless, I maintain all participants in the racialization analyses to be conservative and to make it more strictly comparable to the gendering analyses.

References

Adair, Vivyan C. 2000. *From Good Ma to Welfare Queen: A Genealogy of the Poor Woman in American Literature, Photography and Culture.* New York: Garland.

Adams, Greg D. 1997. "Abortion: Evidence of an Issue Evolution." *American Journal of Political Science* 41 (3): 718–37.

Adorno, Theodor W., Else Frenkel-Brunswick, and Daniel J. Levinson. 1950. *The Authoritarian Personality.* New York: W. W. Norton.

Althusser, Louis. 1971. *Lenin and Philosophy, and Other Essays.* London: New Left Books.

Alvarez, R. Michael, and John Brehm. 1997. "Are Americans Ambivalent towards Racial Policies?" *American Journal of Political Science* 41 (2): 345–74.

American National Election Studies. 2005. ANES Cumulative Data File, 1948–2004 (data set). Stanford, CA, and Ann Arbor: Stanford University and University of Michigan. http://www.electionstudies.org.

Anderson, Craig A., James J. Lindsay, and Brad J. Bushman. 1999. "Research in the Psychological Laboratory: Truth or Triviality?" *Current Directions in Psychological Science* 8 (1): 3–9.

Aoki, Andrew L., and Don T. Nakanishi. 2001. "Asian Pacific Americans and the New Minority Politics." *PS: Political Science and Politics* 34 (3): 605–10.

Aoki, Andrew L., and Okiyoshi Takeda. 2004. "Small Spaces for Different Faces: Political Science Scholarship on Asian Pacific Americans." *PS: Political Science and Politics* 37 (3): 497–500.

Ashmore, Richard D., Frances K. Del Boca, and Scott M. Bilder. 1995. "Construction and Validation of the Gender Attitude Inventory, a Structured

Inventory to Assess Multiple Dimensions of Gender Attitudes." *Sex Roles* 32 (11–12): 753–85.

Attardo, Salvatore. 1994. *Linguistic Theories of Humor.* Berlin: Mouton de Gruyter.

Baggette, Jennifer, Robert Y. Shapiro, and Lawrence R. Jacobs. 1995. "Social Security — An Update." *Public Opinion Quarterly* 59 (3): 420–42.

Ball, Robert M., and Thomas N. Bethell. 1998. *Straight Talk about Social Security: An Analysis of the Issues in the Current Debate.* New York: Century Foundation Press.

Bargh, John A. 1994. "The Four Horsemen of Automaticity: Awareness, Intention, Efficiency, and Control in Social Cognition." In *Handbook of Social Cognition,* ed. Robert S. Wyer and Thomas K. Srull, 1–40. 2nd ed. Tuxedo Park, NY: Lawrence Erlbaum Associates.

Bargh, John A., and Felicia Pratto. 1986. "Individual Construct Accessibility and Perceptual Selection." *Journal of Experimental Social Psychology* 22 (4): 293–311.

Barsalou, Lawrence W. 1987. "The Instability of Graded Structure: Implication for the Nature of Concepts." In *Concepts and Conceptual Development: Ecological and Intellectual Factors in Categorization,* ed. Ulric Neisser, 101–40. New York: Cambridge University Press.

Bartels, Larry M. 2003. "Democracy with Attitudes." In *Electoral Democracy,* ed. Michael MacKuen and George Rabinowitz, 48–82. Ann Arbor: University of Michigan Press.

Beauvoir, Simone de. 1989. *The Second Sex.* Trans. H. M. Parshley. New York: Vintage.

Beer, Francis A., and Christ'l De Landtsheer. 2004. *Metaphorical World Politics.* East Lansing: Michigan State University Press.

Beere, Carole A. 1990a. *Gender Roles: A Handbook of Tests and Measures.* New York: Greenwood Press.

———. 1990b. *Sex and Gender Issues: A Handbook of Tests and Measures.* New York: Greenwood Press.

Beere, Carole A., Daniel W. King, Donald B. Beere, and Lynda A. King. 1984. "The Sex-Role Egalitarianism Scale: A Measure of Attitudes toward Equality between the Sexes." *Sex Roles* 10 (7): 563–76.

Bem, Sandra L. 1981. "Gender Schema Theory: A Cognitive Account of Sex Typing." *Psychological Review* 88 (4): 354–64.

———. 1993. *The Lenses of Gender: Transforming the Debate on Sexual Inequality.* New Haven, CT: Yale University Press.

Ben-David, Sarah, and Ofra Schneider. 2005. "Rape Perceptions, Gender Role Attitudes, and Victim-Perpetrator Acquaintance." *Sex Roles* 53 (5): 385–99.

Bensonsmith, Dionne. 1999. "Welfare Queens and Other Metaphors: The Effects of Gender and Race Construction on Implementation and Bureaucratic Values." Paper presented at the Annual Meeting of the American Political Science Association, Atlanta.

Berger, Peter L., and Thomas Luckmann. 1966. *The Social Construction of Reality: A Treatise in the Sociology of Knowledge.* Garden City, NY: Doubleday.

Berinsky, Adam J., and Donald R. Kinder. 2006. "Making Sense of Issues through Media Frames: Understanding the Kosovo Crisis." *Journal of Politics* 68 (3): 640–56.

Biela, Adam. 1991. *Analogy in Science: From a Psychological Perspective.* Frankfurt: Peter Lang.

Black, Max. 1962. *Models and Metaphors.* Ithaca, NY: Cornell University Press.

Blanchette, Isabelle, and Kevin Dunbar. 2001. "Analogy Use in Naturalistic Settings: The Influence of Audience, Emotion, and Goals." *Memory and Cognition* 29 (5): 730–35.

Blaszczyk, Regina L. 2000. *Imagining Consumers: Design and Innovation from Wedgwood to Corning.* Baltimore: Johns Hopkins University Press.

Blum, Lawrence A. 2002. *"I'm Not Racist, but — ": The Moral Quandary of Race.* Ithaca, NY: Cornell University Press.

Bobo, Lawrence. 1988. "Group Conflict, Prejudice, and the Paradox of Contemporary Racial Attitudes." In *Eliminating Racism: Profiles in Controversy,* ed. Phyllis A. Katz, 85–116. New York: Plenum Press.

Bobo, Lawrence, and James Kluegel. 1993. "Opposition to Race-Targeting: Self-Interest, Stratification Ideology, or Racial Attitudes?" *American Sociological Review* 58 (4): 443–64.

Bonilla-Silva, Eduardo. 2003. *Racism without Racists: Color-Blind Racism and the Persistence of Racial Inequality in the United States.* Lanham, MD: Rowman and Littlefield.

Bourdieu, Pierre. 1977. *Outline of a Theory of Practice.* Cambridge: Cambridge University Press.

Brodkin, Karen. 1998. *How Jews Became White Folks and What That Says about Race in America.* New Brunswick, NJ: Rutgers University Press.

Brown, Michael K. 2003. *Whitewashing Race: The Myth of a Color-Blind Society.* Berkeley and Los Angeles: University of California Press.

Brown, Theodore L. 2003. *Making Truth: Metaphor in Science.* Urbana: University of Illinois Press.

Bruner, Jerome S. 1957. "Going Beyond the Information Given." In *Contemporary Approaches to Cognition,* ed. Howard E. Gruber and Kenneth R. Hammond, 41–69. Cambridge, MA: Harvard University Press.

Brutus, Stephane, Matthew Montei, Steve Jex, and Lynda King. 1993. "Sex Role Egalitarianism as a Moderator of Gender Congruence Bias in Evaluation." *Sex Roles* 29 (11): 755–65.

Burden, Barry C., and Anthony Mughan. 1999. "Public Opinion and Hillary Rodham Clinton." *Public Opinion Quarterly* 63 (2): 237–50.

Burns, Nancy. 2007. "Gender in the Aggregate, Gender in the Individual, Gender and Political Action." *Politics and Gender* 3 (1): 104–24.

Burns, Nancy, and Donald R. Kinder. 2003. "Explaining Gender, Explaining Race." Paper presented at the annual meeting of the American Political Science Association, Philadelphia.

Burrell, Barbara C. 1997. *Public Opinion, the First Ladyship, and Hillary Rodham Clinton.* New York: Garland.

Bush, George H. W. 1993. *Public Papers of the Presidents of the United States: George Bush.* Book 1: January 1–July 31, 1992. Washington, DC: U.S. Government Printing Office.

Cain, Bruce E., D. R. Kiewiet, and Carole J. Uhlaner. 1991. "The Acquisition of Partisanship by Latinos and Asian Americans." *American Journal of Political Science* 35 (2): 390–422.

Callaghan, Karen, and Frauke Schnell, eds. 2005. *Framing American Politics.* Pittsburgh: University of Pittsburgh Press.

Campbell, Bernadette, E. G. Schellenberg, and Charlene Y. Senn. 1997. "Evaluating Measures of Contemporary Sexism." *Psychology of Women Quarterly* 21 (1): 89–101.

Campbell, Donald T., and Julian C. Stanley. 1963. *Experimental and Quasi-Experimental Designs for Research.* Boston: Houghton Mifflin.

Carmines, Edward G., and James A. Stimson. 1989. *Issue Evolution: Race and the Transformation of American Politics.* Princeton, NJ: Princeton University Press.

Chaiken, Shelly. 1980. "Heuristic versus Systematic Information Processing and the Use of Source versus Message Cues in Persuasion." *Journal of Personality and Social Psychology* 39 (5): 752–66.

Chong, Dennis. 1993. "How People Think, Reason, and Feel about Rights and Liberties." *American Journal of Political Science* 37 (3): 867–99.

———. 1996. "Creating Common Frames of Reference on Political Issues." In *Political Persuasion and Attitude Change,* ed. Diana C. Mutz, Paul M. Sniderman, and Richard A. Brody, 195–224. Ann Arbor: University of Michigan Press.

———. 2000. *Rational Lives: Norms and Values in Politics and Society.* Chicago: University of Chicago Press.

Chong, Dennis, Jack Citrin, and Patricia Conley. 2001. "When Self-Interest Matters." *Political Psychology* 22 (3): 541–70.

Citrin, Jack, Beth Reingold, and Donald P. Green. 1990. "American Identity and the Politics of Ethnic Change." *Journal of Politics* 52 (4): 1124–54.

Clawson, Rosalee A. 2003. "The Media Portrayal of Social Security and Medicare and Its Impact on Public Opinion." Paper presented at the annual meeting of the American Political Science Association. Philadelphia.

Clawson, Rosalee A., and John A. Clark. 2003. "The Attitudinal Structure of African American Women Party Activists: The Impact of Race, Gender, and Religion." *Political Research Quarterly* 56 (2): 211–21.

Collins, Patricia Hill. 1990. *Black Feminist Thought: Knowledge, Consciousness, and the Politics of Empowerment.* Boston: Unwin Hyman.

———. 2005. *Black Sexual Politics: African Americans, Gender, and the New Racism.* New York: Routledge.

Conover, Pamela J. 1988. "Feminists and the Gender Gap." *Journal of Politics* 50 (4): 985–1010.

Conover, Pamela J., and Stanley Feldman. 1984. "How People Organize the Political World: A Schematic Model." *American Journal of Political Science* 28 (1): 95–126.

Conover, Pamela J., and Virginia Sapiro. 1993. "Gender, Feminist Consciousness, and War." *American Journal of Political Science* 37 (4): 1079–99.

Conrey, Frederica R., Jeffrey W. Sherman, Bertram Gawronski, Kurt Hugenberg, and Carla J. Groom. 2005. "Separating Multiple Processes in Implicit Social Cognition: The Quad Model of Implicit Task Performance." *Journal of Personality and Social Psychology* 89 (4): 469–87.

Converse, Philip E. 1964. "The Nature of Belief Systems in Mass Publics." In *Ideology and Discontent,* ed. David E. Apter, 206–61. New York: Free Press.

———. 1972. "Change in the American Electorate." In *The Human Meaning of Social Change,* ed. Angus Campbell and Philip E. Converse, 263–337. New York: Russell Sage Foundation.

———. 1990. "Popular Representation and the Distribution of Information." In *Information and Democratic Processes,* ed. John Ferejohn and James Kuklinski, 369–88. Chicago: University of Illinois Press.

Cook, Elizabeth A., and Clyde Wilcox. 1991. "Feminism and the Gender Gap — A Second Look." *Journal of Politics* 53 (4): 1111–22.

Cook, Fay L. 1992. *Support for the American Welfare State: The Views of Congress and the Public.* New York: Columbia University Press.

Cook, Fay L., and Lawrence R. Jacobs. 2002. "Assessing Assumptions about Attitudes toward Social Security: Popular Claims Meet Hard Data." In *The Future of Social Insurance: Incremental Action or Fundamental Reform?* ed. Peter Edelman, Dallas L. Salisbury, and Pamela J. Larson, 82–110. Washington, DC: National Academy of Social Insurance.

Coulson, Seana. 2001. *Semantic Leaps: Frame-Shifting and Conceptual Blending in Meaning Construction.* New York: Cambridge University Press.

Crenshaw, Kimberlé W. 1992. "Whose Story Is It, Anyway? Feminist and Anti-racist Appropriations of Anita Hill." In *Race-ing Justice, En-Gendering Power: Essays on Anita Hill, Clarence Thomas, and the Construction of Social Reality,* ed. Toni Morrison, 402–40. New York: Pantheon Books.

———. 1997. "Beyond Racism and Misogyny: Black Feminism and 2 Live Crew." In *Feminist Social Thought: A Reader,* ed. Diana T. Meyers, 246–63. New York: Routledge.

———. 1998. "Demarginalizing the Intersection of Race and Sex: A Black Feminist Critique of Antidiscrimination Doctrine, Feminist Theory, and Antiracist Politics." In *Feminism and Politics,* ed. Anne Phillips, 314–43. New York: Oxford University Press.

Crossman, Rita K., Sandra M. Stith, and Mary M. Bender. 1990. "Sex Role Egalitarianism and Marital Violence." *Sex Roles* 22 (5): 293–304.

Daugman, John G. 1990. "Brain Metaphor and Brain Theory." In *Computational Neuroscience,* ed. Eric L. Schwartz, 9–18. Cambridge, MA: MIT Press.

Davis, Angela Y. 1981. *Women, Race, and Class.* New York: Random House.

Davis, Darren W., and Brian D. Silver. 2004. "Civil Liberties vs. Security: Public Opinion in the Context of the Terrorist Attacks on America." *American Journal of Political Science* 48 (1): 28–46.

Dawson, Michael C. 1994. *Behind the Mule: Race and Class in African-American Politics.* Princeton, NJ: Princeton University Press.

———. 2001. *Black Visions: The Roots of Contemporary African-American Political Ideologies.* Chicago: University of Chicago Press.

Day, Christine L. 1990. *What Older Americans Think: Interest Groups and Aging Policy.* Princeton, NJ: Princeton University Press.

Degler, Carl N. 1971. *Neither Black nor White: Slavery and Race Relations in Brazil and the United States.* New York: Macmillan.

De la Garza, Rodolfo O. 1992. *Latino Voices: Mexican, Puerto Rican, and Cuban Perspectives on American Politics.* Boulder, CO: Westview Press.

———. 1998. "Interests Not Passions: Mexican-American Attitudes toward Mexico, Immigration from Mexico, and Other Issues Shaping U.S.-Mexico Relations." *International Migration Review* 32 (2): 401–22.

De la Garza, Rodolfo O., Angelo Falcon, and F. C. Garcia. 1996. "Will the Real Americans Please Stand Up: Anglo and Mexican-American Support of Core American Political Values." *American Journal of Political Science* 40 (2): 335–51.

Delli Carpini, Michael X., and Ester R. Fuchs. 1993. "The Year of the Woman? Candidates, Voters, and the 1992 Elections." *Political Science Quarterly* 108 (1): 29–36.

Delli Carpini, Michael X., and Scott Keeter. 1996. *What Americans Know about Politics and Why It Matters.* New Haven, CT: Yale University Press.

Derthick, Martha. 1979. *Policymaking for Social Security.* Washington, DC: Brookings Institution.

Devine, Patricia G. 1989. "Stereotypes and Prejudice: Their Automatic and Controlled Components." *Journal of Personality and Social Psychology* 56 (1): 5–18.

Devine, Patricia G., and Andrew J. Elliot. 1995. "Are Racial Stereotypes Really Fading? The Princeton Trilogy Revisited." *Personality and Social Psychology Bulletin* 21 (11): 1139–50.

Dickey, Nancy W., and Peter McMenamin. 1999. "Sounding Board: Putting Power into Patient Choice." *New England Journal of Medicine* 341 (17): 1305–8.

Dominguez, Jorge I. 1994. "Do 'Latinos' Exist?" *Contemporary Sociology* 23 (3): 354–56.

Doty, Richard M., Bill E. Peterson, and David G. Winter. 1991. "Threat and Authoritarianism in the United States, 1978–1987." *Journal of Personality and Social Psychology* 61 (4): 629–40.

Dovidio, John F., Nancy Evans, and Richard B. Tyler. 1986. "Racial Stereotypes: The Contents of Their Cognitive Representations." *Journal of Experimental Social Psychology* 22 (1): 22–37.

Dovidio, John F., and Russell H. Fazio. 1992. "New Technologies for the Direct and Indirect Assessment of Attitudes." In *Questions about Questions: Inquiries into the Cognitive Bases of Surveys,* ed. Judith M. Tanur, 204–37. New York: Russell Sage Foundation.

Dovidio, John F., and Samuel L. Gaertner, eds. 1986. *Prejudice, Discrimination, and Racism.* Orlando, FL: Academic Press, Inc.

Dovidio, John F., Kerry Kawakami, Craig Johnson, Brenda Johnson, and Adaiah Howard. 1997. "On the Nature of Prejudice: Automatic and Controlled Processes." *Journal of Experimental Social Psychology* 33 (5): 510–40.

Drimmer, Melvin. 1979. "Neither Black nor White: Carl Degler's Study of Slavery in Two Societies." *Phylon (1960–)* 40 (1): 94–105.

Druckman, James N. 2001a. "The Implications of Framing Effects for Citizen Competence." *Political Behavior* 23 (3): 225–56.

———. 2001b. "On the Limits of Framing Effects: Who Can Frame?" *Journal of Politics* 63 (4): 1041–66.

———. 2004. "Political Preference Formation: Competition, Deliberation, and the (Ir)Relevance of Framing Effects." *American Political Science Review* 98 (4): 671–86.

Druckman, James N., Donald P. Green, James H. Kuklinski, and Arthur Lupia. 2006. "The Growth and Development of Experimental Research in Political Science." *American Political Science Review* 100 (4): 627–35.

Druckman, James N., and Kjersten R. Nelson. 2003. "Framing and Deliberation: How Citizens' Conversations Limit Elite Influence." *American Journal of Political Science* 47 (4): 729–45.

Ducat, Stephen. 2004. *The Wimp Factor: Gender Gaps, Holy Wars, and the Politics of Anxious Masculinity.* Boston: Beacon Press.

Duncan, Birt L. 1976. "Differential Social Perception and Attribution of Intergroup Violence: Testing the Lower Limits of Stereotyping of Blacks." *Journal of Personality and Social Psychology* 34 (4): 590–98.

Dunning, David, and David A. Sherman. 1997. "Stereotypes and Tacit Inference." *Journal of Personality and Social Psychology* 73 (3): 459–71.

Dworkin, Andrea. 1983. *Right-Wing Women.* New York: Coward-McCann.

Dyer, Richard. 1997. *White.* New York: Routledge.

Edelman, Murray J. 1971. *Politics as Symbolic Action: Mass Arousal and Quiescence.* New York: Academic Press.

Edsall, Thomas B., and Mary D. Edsall. 1992. *Chain Reaction: The Impact of Race, Rights, and Taxes on American Politics.* New York: W. W. Norton.

Eliot, George. 1975 [1858]. *Scenes of Clerical Life.* New York: Garland Publishers.

Entman, Robert M., and Andrew Rojecki. 2000. *The Black Image in the White Mind: Media and Race in America.* Chicago: University of Chicago Press.

Epstein, Cynthia F. 1988. *Deceptive Distinctions: Sex, Gender, and the Social Order.* New Haven, CT: Yale University Press.

Essed, Philomena. 1991. *Understanding Everyday Racism: An Interdisciplinary Theory.* Newbury Park, CA: Sage Publications.

Evans, Sara M., and Barbara J. Nelson. 1989. *Wage Justice: Comparable Worth and the Paradox of Technocratic Reform.* Chicago: University of Chicago Press.

Fausto-Sterling, Anne. 1992. *Myths of Gender: Biological Theories about Women and Men.* 2nd ed. New York: Basic Books.

Fazio, Russell H., and Bridget C. Dunton. 1997. "Categorization by Race: The Impact of Automatic and Controlled Components of Racial Prejudice." *Journal of Experimental Social Psychology* 33 (5): 451–70.

Fazio, Russell H., David M. Sanbonmatsu, Martha C. Powell, and Frank R. Kardes. 1986. "On the Automatic Activation of Attitudes." *Journal of Personality and Social Psychology* 50 (2): 229–38.

Feldman, Stanley. 1988. "Structure and Consistency in Public Opinion: The Role of Core Beliefs and Values." *American Journal of Political Science* 32 (2): 416–40.

Feldman, Stanley, and Karen Stenner. 1997. "Perceived Threat and Authoritarianism." *Political Psychology* 18 (4): 741–70.

Feldman, Stanley, and John Zaller. 1992. "The Political Culture of Ambivalence: Ideological Responses to the Welfare State." *American Journal of Political Science* 36 (1): 268–307.

Fine, Michelle, Abigail J. Stewart, and Alyssa N. Zucker. 2000. "White Girls and Women in the Contemporary United States: Supporting or Subverting Race and Gender Domination?" In *Culture in Psychology,* ed. Corinne Squire, 59–72. Philadelphia: Routledge.

Fine, Michelle, and Lois Weis. 1998. "Crime Stories: A Critical Look through Race, Ethnicity, and Gender." *Qualitative Studies in Education* 11 (3): 435–59.

Fiske, Susan T. 1993. "Controlling Other People: The Impact of Power on Stereotyping." *American Psychologist* 48 (6): 621–28.

———. 1998. "Stereotyping, Prejudice, and Discrimination." In *The Handbook of Social Psychology,* ed. D. T. Gilbert, Susan T. Fiske, and Gardener Lindzey, 357–411. 4th ed. New York: McGraw-Hill.

Fiske, Susan T., and Patricia W. Linville. 1980. "What Does the Schema Concept Buy Us?" *Personality and Social Psychology Bulletin* 6 (4): 543–57.

Fiske, Susan T., and Laura E. Stevens. 1993. "What's So Special about Sex? Gender Stereotyping and Discrimination." In *Gender Issues in Contemporary Society,* ed. Stuart Oskamp, 173–96. Newbury Park, CA: Sage.

Fiske, Susan T., and Shelley E. Taylor. 1991. *Social Cognition.* 2nd ed. New York: McGraw-Hill.

Fitzpatrick, Marcia K., Dawn M. Salgado, Michael K. Suvak, Lynda A. King, and Daniel W. King. 2004. "Associations of Gender and Gender-Role Ideology with Behavioral and Attitudinal Features of Intimate Partner Aggression." *Psychology of Men and Masculinity* 5 (2): 91–102.

Fludernik, Monika. 2005. "The Metaphorics and Metonymics of Carcerality: Reflections on Imprisonment as Source and Target Domain in Literary Texts." *English Studies* 86 (3): 226–44.

Frable, Deborah E., and Sandra L. Bem. 1985. "If You Are Gender Schematic, All Members of the Opposite Sex Look Alike." *Journal of Personality and Social Psychology* 49 (2): 459–68.

Frank, Barney. 2007. Remarks at the National Press Club, January 3. http://www.house.gov/frank/pressclub07.html.

Frankenberg, Ruth. 1993. *White Women, Race Matters: The Social Construction of Whiteness.* Minneapolis: University of Minnesota Press.

Fraser, Nancy. 1989. "Women, Welfare, and the Politics of Need Interpretation." In *Unruly Practices: Power, Discourse, and Gender in Contemporary Social Theory,* ed. Nancy Fraser, 144–60. Minneapolis: University of Minnesota Press.

Freedman, Paul. 1999. "Framing the Abortion Debate: Public Opinion and the Manipulation of Ambivalence." Ph.D. diss., Department of Political Science, University of Michigan.

Freud, Sigmund. 1943. *A General Introduction to Psycho-Analysis.* Trans. Joan Rivere. Garden City, NY: Garden City Publishing.

Freyre, Gilberto, Samuel Putnam, and James Hendrickson. 1946. *The Masters and the Slaves* (Casa-Grande and Senzala): *A Study in the Development of Brazilian Civilization.* New York: Alfred A. Knopf.

Galbraith, John K. 1960. *The Affluent Society.* Boston: Houghton Mifflin.

Gamson, William A. 1992. *Talking Politics.* Cambridge: Cambridge University Press.

Gamson, William A., and Kathryn E. Lasch. 1983. "The Political Culture of Social Welfare Policy." In *Evaluating the Welfare State: Social and Political Perspectives,* ed. Shimon E. Shapiro and Ephraim Yuchtman-Yaar, 397–415. New York: Academic Press.

Gamson, William A., and Andre Modigliani. 1987. "The Changing Culture of Affirmative Action." In *Research in Political Sociology,* ed. Richard D. Braungart, 137–77. Greenwich, CT: JAI Press.

———. 1989. "Media Discourse and Public Opinion on Nuclear Power: A Constructionist Approach." *American Journal of Sociology* 95 (1): 1–37.

Garcia, F. C., John A. Garcia, Angelo Falcon, and Rodolfo O. de la Garza. 1989. "Studying Latino Politics: The Development of the Latino National Political Survey." *PS: Political Science and Politics* 22 (4): 848–52.

Gay, Claudine, and Katherine Tate. 1998. "Doubly Bound: The Impact of Gender and Race on the Politics of Black Women." *Political Psychology* 19 (1): 169–84.

Gentner, Dedre. 1983. "Structure-Mapping: A Theoretical Framework for Analogy." *Cognitive Science* 7 (2): 155–70.

Gentner, Dedre, Brian Bowdle, Phillip Wolff, and Consuelo Boronat. 2001. "Metaphor Is Like Analogy." In *The Analogical Mind: Perspectives from Cognitive Science,* ed. Dedre Gentner, Keith J. Holyoak and Boicho N. Kokinov, 199–254. Cambridge, MA: MIT Press.

Gentner, Dedre, and Jonathan Grudin. 1985. "The Evolution of Mental Metaphors in Psychology: A 90-Year Retrospective." *American Psychologist* 40 (2): 181–92.

Gilens, Martin. 1988. "Gender and Support for Reagan: A Comprehensive Model of Presidential Approval." *American Journal of Political Science* 32 (1): 19–49.

———. 1999. *Why Americans Hate Welfare: Race, Media, and the Politics of Antipoverty Policy.* Chicago: University of Chicago Press.

Gingrich, Newt. 1998. "Delivers Remarks on Taxes and Social Security." Remarks to the House Republican Caucus, August 6. CQ Transcriptions. http://www.fdch.com/politicalproducts.htm.

Glick, Peter, and Susan T. Fiske. 1997. "Hostile and Benevolent Sexism: Measuring Ambivalent Sexist Attitudes toward Women." *Psychology of Women Quarterly* 21 (1): 119–35.

———. 1999. "Sexism and Other 'Isms': Independence, Status, and the Ambivalent Content of Stereotypes." In *Sexism and Stereotypes in Modern Society: The Gender Science of Janet Taylor Spence,* 193–221. Washington, DC: American Psychological Association.

———. 2001. "An Ambivalent Alliance: Hostile and Benevolent Sexism as Complementary Justifications for Gender Inequality." *American Psychologist* 56 (2): 109–18.

Glucksberg, Sam. 1998. "Understanding Metaphors." *Current Directions in Psychological Science* 7 (2): 39–43.

Glucksberg, Sam, Patricia Gildea, and Howard Bookin. 1982. "On Understanding Nonliteral Speech: Can People Ignore Metaphors?" *Journal of Verbal Learning and Verbal Behavior* 21 (1): 85–98.

Glucksberg, Sam, and Boaz Keysar. 1990. "Understanding Metaphorical Comparisons: Beyond Similarity." *Psychological Review* 97 (1): 3–18.

Goffman, Erving. 1977. "The Arrangement between the Sexes." *Theory and Society* 4 (3): 301–31.

Goldner, Virginia, Peggy Penn, Marcia Sheinberg, and Gillian Walker. 1998. "Love and Violence: Gender Paradoxes in Volatile Attachments." In *The Gender and Psychology Reader,* ed. Blythe Clinchy and Julie K. Norem, 549–72. New York: New York University Press.

Gordon, Linda. 1990. *Woman's Body, Woman's Right: Birth Control in America.* Rev. ed. New York: Penguin.

———. 1994. *Pitied but Not Entitled: Single Mothers and the History of Welfare, 1890–1935.* New York: Free Press.

Gotanda, Neil. 1995. "A Critique of 'Our Constitution Is Color-Blind'." In *Critical Race Theory: The Key Writings That Formed the Movement,* ed. Kimberlé Crenshaw, Neil Gotanda, Gary Peller, and Kendall Thomas, 257–75. New York: New Press.

Gramsci, Antonio. 1991. *Prison Notebooks.* New York: Columbia University Press.

Green, Donald P., and Jonathan A. Cowden. 1992. "Who Protests: Self-Interest and White Opposition to Busing." *Journal of Politics* 54 (2): 471–96.

Greenwald, Anthony G., and Mahzarin R. Banaji. 1995. "Implicit Social Cognition: Attitudes, Self-Esteem, and Stereotypes." *Psychological Review* 102 (1): 4–27.

Gurin, Patricia, Arthur H. Miller, and Gerald Gurin. 1980. "Stratum Identification and Consciousness." *Social Psychology Quarterly* 43 (1): 30–47.

Gusfield, Joseph R. 1981. *The Culture of Public Problems: Drinking-Driving and the Symbolic Order.* Chicago: University of Chicago Press.

———. 1996. *Contested Meanings: The Construction of Alcohol Problems.* Madison: University of Wisconsin Press.

Guy, Mary E. 1995. "Hillary, Health Care, and Gender Power." In *Gender Power, Leadership, and Governance,* ed. Georgia Duerst-Lahti and Rita M. Kelly, 239–56. Ann Arbor: University of Michigan Press.

Hacker, Jacob. 1997. *The Road to Nowhere: The Genesis of President Clinton's Plan for Health Security.* Princeton, NJ: Princeton University Press.

Hacking, Ian. 1999. *The Social Construction of What?* Cambridge, MA: Harvard University Press.

Hamilton, David L., and Tina K. Trolier. 1986. "Stereotypes and Stereotyping: An Overview of the Cognitive Approach." In *Prejudice, Discrimination, and Racism,* ed. John F. Dovidio and Samuel L. Gaertner, 127–64. Orlando, FL: Academic Press, Inc.

Hancock, Ange-Marie. 2004. *The Politics of Disgust: The Public Identity of the Welfare Queen.* New York: New York University Press.

———. 2007. "When Multiplication Doesn't Equal Quick Addition: Examining Intersectionality as a Research Paradigm." *Perspectives on Politics* 5 (1): 63–79.

Harrington, Michael. 1962. *The Other America: Poverty in the United States.* New York: Macmillan.

Harris, Cheryl I. 1995. "Whiteness as Property." In *Critical Race Theory: The Key*

Writings That Formed the Movement, ed. Kimberlé Crenshaw, Neil Gotanda, Gary Peller, and Kendall Thomas, 276–91. New York: New Press.

Harris-Lacewell, Melissa. 2004. *Barbershops, Bibles, and BET: Everyday Talk and Black Political Thought.* Princeton, NJ: Princeton University Press.

Haslanger, Sally. 2000. "Gender and Race: (What) Are They? (What) Do We Want Them to Be?" *Nous* 34 (1): 31–55.

Haste, Helen. 1993. *The Sexual Metaphor.* New York: Harvard University Press.

Higginbotham, Evelyn Brooks. 1992. "African-American Women's History and the Metalanguage of Race." *Signs* 17 (2): 251–74.

Higgins, E. T., Gillian A. King, and Gregory H. Mavin. 1982. "Individual Construct Accessibility and Subjective Impressions and Recall." *Journal of Personality and Social Psychology* 43 (1): 35–47.

Hirschfeld, Lawrence A. 1996. *Race in the Making: Cognition, Culture, and the Child's Construction of Human Kinds.* Cambridge, MA: MIT Press.

Hofstadter, Douglas R. 2001. "Epilogue: Analogy as the Core of Cognition." In *The Analogical Mind: Perspectives from Cognitive Science,* ed. Dedre Gentner, Keith J. Holyoak, and Boicho N. Kokinov, 499–538. Cambridge, MA: MIT Press.

Holmes, Robyn M. 1995. *How Young Children Perceive Race.* Thousand Oaks, CA: Sage Publications.

Holtzman, Linda. 2000. *Media Messages What Film, Television, and Popular Music Teach Us about Race, Class, Gender, and Sexual Orientation.* Armonk, N.Y.: M. E. Sharpe.

Holyoak, Keith J., Dedre Gentner, and Boicho N. Kokinov. 2001. "The Place of Analogy in Cognition." In *The Analogical Mind: Perspectives from Cognitive Science,* ed. Dedre Gentner, Keith J. Holyoak, and Boicho N. Kokinov, 1–19. Cambridge, MA: MIT Press.

Holyoak, Keith J., and Paul Thagard. 1995. *Mental Leaps: Analogy in Creative Thought.* Cambridge, MA: MIT Press.

hooks, bell. 1981. *Ain't I a Woman: Black Women and Feminism.* Boston: South End Press.

———. 2000. *Feminist Theory: From Margin to Center.* 2nd ed. Cambridge, MA: South End Press.

Houghton, David P. 1996. "The Role of Analogical Reasoning in Novel Foreign-Policy Situations." *British Journal of Political Science* 26 (4): 523–52.

Huber, Gregory A., and John S. Lapinski. 2006. "The 'Race Card' Revisited: Assessing Racial Priming in Policy Contests." *American Journal of Political Science* 50 (2): 421–40.

Huddy, Leonie. 2001. "From Social to Political Identity: A Critical Examination of Social Identity Theory." *Political Psychology* 22 (1): 127–56.

Huddy, Leonie, Francis K. Neely, and Marilyn R. LaFay. 2000. "Trends: Support for the Women's Movement." *Public Opinion Quarterly* 64 (3): 309–50.

Hurtado, Aída. 1989. "Relating to Privilege: Seduction and Rejection in the Subordination of White Women and Women of Color." *Signs* 14 (4): 833–55.

———. 1996. *The Color of Privilege: Three Blasphemies on Race and Feminism.* Ann Arbor: University of Michigan Press.

Hurwitz, Jon, and Mark Peffley. 1997. "Public Perceptions of Race and Crime: The Role of Racial Stereotypes." *American Journal of Political Science* 41 (2): 375–401.

———. 2005. "Playing the Race Card in the Post–Willie Horton Era: The Impact of Racialized Code Words on Support for Punitive Crime Policy." *Public Opinion Quarterly* 69 (1): 99–112.

Iyengar, Shanto. 1991. *Is Anyone Responsible?: How Television Frames Political Issues.* Chicago: University of Chicago Press.

Iyengar, Shanto, and Donald R. Kinder. 1987. *News That Matters: Television and American Opinion.* Chicago: University of Chicago Press.

Iyengar, Shanto, Nicholas A. Valentino, Stephen Ansolabehere, and Adam F. Simon. 1997. "Running as a Woman: Gender Stereotyping in Women's Campaigns." In *Women, Media, and Politics,* ed. Pippa Norris, 77–98. New York: Oxford University Press.

Jackman, Mary R. 1994. *The Velvet Glove: Paternalism and Conflict in Gender, Class, and Race Relations.* Berkeley and Los Angeles: University of California Press.

Jacobs, Lawrence R., and Robert Y. Shapiro. 1995. *The News Media's Coverage of Social Security.* Washington, DC: National Academy of Social Insurance.

———. 1998. "Myths and Misunderstandings about Public Opinion toward Social Security." In *Framing the Social Security Debate: Values, Politics, and Economics,* ed. R. D. Arnold, Michael J. Graetz, and Alicia H. Munnell, 355–88. Washington, DC: Brookings Institution.

———. 2000. *Politicians Don't Pander: Political Manipulation and the Loss of Democratic Responsiveness.* Chicago: University of Chicago Press.

Jacoby, William G. 2000. "Issue Framing and Public Opinion on Government Spending." *American Journal of Political Science* 44 (4): 750–67.

Jamieson, Kathleen H., and Joseph N. Capella. 1994. "Media in the Middle: Fairness and Accuracy in the 1994 Health Care Reform Debate." Philadelphia: Annenberg Public Policy Center, University of Pennsylvania.

Jervis, Robert. 1976. *Perception and Misperception in International Politics.* Princeton, NJ: Princeton University Press.

Kahn, Kim F. 1996. *The Political Consequences of Being a Woman: How Stereotypes Influence the Conduct and Consequences of Political Campaigns.* New York: Columbia University Press.

Kahneman, Daniel, and Amos Tversky. 2000. *Choices, Values, and Frames.* Cambridge: Cambridge University Press.

Katz, Phyllis A. 1982. "Development of Children's Racial Awareness and Intergroup Attitudes." In *Current Topics in Early Childhood Education,* ed. Lilian G. Katz, 17–54. Vol. 4. Norwood, NJ: Ablex.

Katznelson, Ira. 2005. *When Affirmative Action Was White: An Untold History of Racial Inequality in Twentieth-Century America.* New York: W. W. Norton.

Kaufmann, Karen M., and John R. Petrocik. 1999. "The Changing Politics of American Men: Understanding the Sources of the Gender Gap." *American Journal of Political Science* 43 (3): 864–87.

Kerner Commission. 1968. *Report of the National Advisory Commission on Civil Disorders.* Washington, DC: U.S. Government Printing Office.

Khong, Yuen F. 1992. *Analogies at War: Korea, Munich, Dien Bien Phu, and the Vietnam Decisions of 1965.* Princeton, NJ: Princeton University Press.

Kim, Claire J. 1999. "The Racial Triangulation of Asian Americans." *Politics and Society* 27 (1): 105–38.

Kinder, Donald R. 1983. "Diversity and Complexity in American Public Opinion." In *Political Science: State of the Discipline,* ed. Ada W. Finifter, 389–425. Washington, DC: American Political Science Association.

Kinder, Donald R., and Don Herzog. 1993. "Democratic Discussion." In *Reconsidering the Democratic Public,* ed. George E. Marcus and Russell L. Hanson, 347–77. University Park: Pennsylvania State University Press.

Kinder, Donald R., and Tali Mendelberg. 1995. "Cracks in American Apartheid: The Political Impact of Prejudice among Desegregated Whites." *Journal of Politics* 57 (2): 402–24.

Kinder, Donald R., and Thomas R. Palfrey. 1993. "On Behalf of an Experimental Political Science." In *Experimental Foundations of Political Science,* ed. Donald R. Kinder and Thomas R. Palfrey, 1–39. Ann Arbor: University of Michigan Press.

Kinder, Donald R., and Lynn M. Sanders. 1990. "Mimicking Political Debate with Survey Questions: The Case of White Opinion on Affirmative Action for Blacks." *Social Cognition: Special Issue: Thinking about Politics: Comparisons of Experts and Novices* 8 (1): 73–103.

———. 1996. *Divided by Color: Racial Politics and Democratic Ideals.* Chicago: University of Chicago Press.

Kinder, Donald R., and Nicholas Winter. 2001. "Exploring the Racial Divide: Blacks, Whites, and Opinion on National Policy." *American Journal of Political Science* 45 (2): 439–56.

King, Deborah K. 1988. "Multiple Jeopardy, Multiple Consciousness: The Context of a Black Feminist Ideology." *Signs* 14 (1): 42–72.

King, Lynda A., and Daniel W. King. 1986. "Validity of the Sex-Role Egalitarianism Scale: Discriminating Egalitarianism from Feminism." *Sex Roles* 15 (3): 207–14.

———. 1997. "Sex-Role Egalitarianism Scale: Development, Psychometric Properties, and Recommendations for Future Research." *Psychology of Women Quarterly* 21 (1): 71–87.

King, Lynda A., Daniel W. King, D. B. Carter, Carol R. Surface, and Kim Stepanski. 1994. "Validity of the Sex-Role Egalitarianism Scale: Two Replication Studies." *Sex Roles* 31 (5): 339–48.

Koch, Jeffrey W. 1998. "Political Rhetoric and Political Persuasion: The Changing Structure of Citizens' Preferences on Health Insurance during Policy Debate." *Public Opinion Quarterly* 62 (2): 209–29.

Koestner, Richard, and David C. McClelland. 1992. "The Affiliation Motive." In *Motivation and Personality: Handbook of Thematic Content Analysis,* ed. Charles P. Smith, 205–10. New York: Cambridge University Press.

Krosnick, Jon, and Donald Kinder. 1990. "Altering the Foundations of Support for the President through Priming." *American Political Science Review* 84 (2): 497–512.

Kuhn, Thomas S. 1962. *The Structure of Scientific Revolutions.* Chicago: University of Chicago Press.

Kuklinski, James H., Robert C. Luskin, and John Bolland. 1991. "Where Is the Schema? Going Beyond the 'S' Word in Political Psychology." *American Political Science Review* 85 (4): 1341–65.

Laclau, Ernesto, and Chantal Mouffe. 1983. *Hegemony and Socialist Strategy: Toward a Radical Democratic Politics.* New York: Verso.

Lakoff, George. 1996. *Moral Politics: What Conservatives Know That Liberals Don't.* Chicago: University of Chicago Press.

———. 1997. *Women, Fire, and Dangerous Things: What Categories Reveal about the Mind.* Chicago: University of Chicago Press.

Lakoff, George, and Mark Johnson. 1980. *Metaphors We Live By.* Chicago: University of Chicago Press.

Lakoff, George, and Mark Turner. 1989. *More Than Cool Reason: A Field Guide to Poetic Metaphor.* Chicago: University of Chicago Press.

Lau, Richard R. 1989. "Construct Accessibility and Electoral Choice." *Political Behavior* 11 (1): 5–32.

Lavine, Howard, Diana Burgess, Mark Snyder, John Transue, John L. Sullivan, Beth Haney, and Stephen H. Wagner. 1999. "Threat, Authoritarianism, and Voting: An Investigation of Personality and Persuasion." *Personality and Social Psychology Bulletin* 25 (3): 337–47.

Leal, D. L., M. A. Barreto, J. Lee, and R. O. de la Garza. 2005. "The Latino Vote in the 2004 Election." *PS: Political Science and Politics* 38 (1): 41.

Leary, David E. 1990. *Metaphors in the History of Psychology.* New York: Cambridge University Press.

Lee, Taeku. 2003. "Pan-Ethnic Identity, Linked Fate, and the Political Significance of 'Asian Americans'." Working paper, University of California, Berkeley.

Leinbach, Mary D., Barbara E. Hort, and Beverly I. Fagot. 1997. "Bears Are for Boys: Metaphorical Associations in Young Children's Gender Stereotypes." *Cognitive Development* 12 (1): 107–30.

Lenz, Gabriel S. 2006. "What Politics Is About." Ph.D. diss., Department of Politics, Princeton University.

Leonard, David J. 2004. "The Next M. J. or the Next O. J.? Kobe Bryant, Race, and the Absurdity of Colorblind Rhetoric." *Journal of Sport and Social Issues* 28 (3): 284–313.

Levy, Gary D. 2000. "Individual Differences in Race Schematicity as Predictors of African American and White Children's Race-Relevant Memories and Peer Preferences." *Journal of Genetic Psychology* 161 (4): 400–419.

Lewis, Diane K. 1977. "A Response to Inequality: Black Women, Racism, and Sexism." *Signs* 3 (2): 339–61.

Lewontin, Richard C., Steven P. R. Rose, and Leon J. Kamin. 1984. *Not in Our Genes: Biology, Ideology, and Human Nature.* New York: Pantheon Books.

Lien, Pei-Te. 1998. "Does the Gender Gap in Political Attitudes and Behavior Vary across Racial Groups?" *Political Research Quarterly* 51 (4): 869–94.

Lipsitz, George. 2006. *The Possessive Investment in Whiteness: How White People Profit from Identity Politics.* Rev. ed. Philadelphia: Temple University Press.

Lodge, Milton, Kathleen M. McGraw, Pamela J. Conover, Stanley Feldman, and Arthur H. Miller. 1991. "Where Is the Schema? Critiques." *American Political Science Review* 85 (4): 1357–80.

Lorber, Judith, and Susan A. Farrell, eds. 1991. *The Social Construction of Gender.* Newbury Park, CA: Sage.

Luker, Kristin. 1984. *Abortion and the Politics of Motherhood.* Berkeley and Los Angeles: University of California Press.

Mac Cormac, Earl R. 1976. *Metaphor and Myth in Science and Religion.* Durham, NC: Duke University Press.

MacKinnon, Catharine A. 1987. *Feminism Unmodified: Discourses on Life and Law.* Cambridge, MA: Harvard University Press.

Mansbridge, Jane J. 1986. *Why We Lost the ERA.* Chicago: University of Chicago Press.

Manza, Jeff, and Clem Brooks. 1998. "The Gender Gap in U.S. Presidential Elections: When? Why? Implications?" *American Journal of Sociology* 103 (5): 1235–66.

Marcus, George E., John L. Sullivan, Elizabeth Theiss-Morse, and S. L. Wood. 1995. *With Malice toward Some: How People Make Civil Liberties Judgments.* New York: Cambridge University Press.

Markman, Arthur B., and Dedre Gentner. 1993. "All Differences Are Not Created Equal: A Structural Alignment View of Similarity." In *Proceedings of the Fifteenth Annual Conference of the Cognitive Science Society,* 682–86. Hillsdale, NJ: Erlbaum.

Markus, Gregory B. 1990. "Measuring Popular Individualism." American National Election Studies Pilot Study Report, no. nes002282, Ann Arbor, MI.

———. 2001. "American Individualism Reconsidered." In *Citizens and Politics:*

Perspectives from Political Psychology, ed. James H. Kuklinski, 401–32. New York: Cambridge University Press.

Markus, Hazel R., and Robert B. Zajonc. 1985. "The Cognitive Perspective in Social Psychology." In *Handbook of Social Psychology,* ed. Gardner Lindzey and Elliot Aronson, 137–230. 3rd ed. New York: Random House.

Marx, Anthony W. 1998. *Making Race and Nation: A Comparison of South Africa, the United States, and Brazil.* New York: Cambridge University Press.

Marx, Karl. 1948. *Capital: A Critical Analysis of Capitalist Production.* New York: International Publishers.

Massey, Douglas S., and Nancy A. Denton. 1993. *American Apartheid: Segregation and the Making of the Underclass.* Cambridge, MA: Harvard University Press.

Mathews, Donald G., and Jane S. De Hart. 1990. *Sex, Gender and the Politics of ERA: A State and Nation.* New York: Oxford University Press.

Mayer, Jeremy D. 2002. *Running on Race: Racial Politics in Presidential Campaigns, 1960–2000.* New York: Random House.

McAdams, Dan P. 1992. "The Intimacy Motive." In *Motivation and Personality: Handbook of Thematic Content Analysis,* ed. Charles P. Smith, 224–28. New York: Cambridge University Press.

McCabe, Amy E., and Laura A. Brannon. 2004. "An Examination of Racial Subtypes versus Subgroups." *Current Research in Social Psychology* 9 (8): 109–23.

McClelland, David C., and John W. Atkinson. 1976. *The Achievement Motive.* New York: Irvington Publishers.

McConahay, John B. 1982. "Self-Interest versus Racial Attitudes as Correlates of Anti-Busing Attitudes in Louisville." *Journal of Politics* 44 (3): 692–720.

———. 1986. "Modern Racism, Ambivalence, and the Modern Racism Scale." In *Prejudice, Discrimination, and Racism,* ed. John F. Dovidio and Samuel L. Gaertner, 91–125. New York: Academic Press.

McDermott, Rose. 2002. "Experimental Methods in Political Science." Annual Review of Political Science 5:31–61.

McHugh, Maureen C., and Irene H. Frieze. 1997. "The Measurement of Gender-Role Attitudes: A Review and Commentary." *Psychology of Women Quarterly* 21 (1): 1–16.

Mendelberg, Tali. 1997. "Executing Hortons: Racial Crime in the 1988 Presidential Campaign." *Public Opinion Quarterly* 61 (1): 134–57.

———. 2001. *The Race Card: Campaign Strategy, Implicit Messages, and the Norm of Equality.* Princeton, NJ: Princeton University Press.

Mettler, Suzanne. 1998. *Dividing Citizens: Gender and Federalism in New Deal Public Policy.* Ithaca, NY: Cornell University Press.

Miller, Joanne M., and Jon A. Krosnick. 2000. "News Media Impact on the Ingredients of Presidential Evaluations: Politically Knowledgeable Citizens Are Guided by a Trusted Source." *American Journal of Political Science* 44 (2): 301–15.

Mio, Jeffery S. 1997. "Metaphor and Politics." *Metaphor and Symbol* 12 (2): 113–33.

Morrison, Melanie A., Todd G. Morrison, Gregory A. Pope, and Bruno D. Zumbo. 1999. "An Investigation of Measures of Modern and Old-Fashioned Sexism." *Social Indicators Research* 48 (1): 39–50.

Morrison, Toni. 1992. *Race-ing Justice, En-Gendering Power: Essays on Anita Hill, Clarence Thomas, and the Construction of Social Reality.* New York: Pantheon Books.

Morrison, Toni, and Claudia B. Lacour. 1997. *Birth of a Nation'Hood: Gaze, Script, and Spectacle in the O. J. Simpson Case.* New York: Pantheon Books.

Murray, Charles A. 1984. *Losing Ground: American Social Policy, 1950–1980.* New York: Basic Books.

Navarro, Vicente. 1994. *The Politics of Health Policy: The US Reforms, 1980–1994.* Oxford: Blackwell.

Nelson, Thomas E., Rosalee A. Clawson, and Zoe M. Oxley. 1997. "Media Framing of a Civil Liberties Conflict and Its Effect on Tolerance." *American Political Science Review* 91 (3): 567–83.

Nelson, Thomas E., and Donald R. Kinder. 1996. "Issue Frames and Group-Centrism in American Public Opinion." *Journal of Politics* 58 (4): 1055–78.

Nelson, Thomas E., and Zoe M. Oxley. 1999. "Issue Framing Effects on Belief Importance and Opinion." *Journal of Politics* 61 (4): 1040–67.

Nelson, Thomas E., Zoe M. Oxley, and Rosalee A. Clawson. 1997. "Toward a Psychology of Framing Effects." *Political Behavior* 19 (3): 221–46.

Nisbett, Richard E., and Timothy D. Wilson. 1977. "Telling More Than We Can Know: Verbal Reports on Mental Processes." *Psychological Review* 84 (3): 231–59.

Nobles, Melissa. 2000. *Shades of Citizenship: Race and the Census in Modern Politics.* Stanford, CA: Stanford University Press.

Oberlander, Jonathan. 2003. *The Political Life of Medicare.* Chicago: University of Chicago Press.

Okamoto, Dina G. 2003. "Toward a Theory of Panethnicity: Explaining Asian American Collective Action." *American Sociological Review* 68 (6): 811–42.

Oliver, J. E., and Janelle Wong. 2003. "Intergroup Prejudice in Multiethnic Settings." *American Journal of Political Science* 47 (4): 567–82.

Omi, Michael, and Howard Winant. 1994. *Racial Formation in the United States from the 1960s to the 1990s.* 2nd ed. New York: Routledge.

Ong, Paul M. 1994. *The State of Asian Pacific America: Economic Diversity, Issues and Policies: A Public Policy Report.* Los Angeles: LEAP Asian Pacific American Public Policy Institute and UCLA Asian American Studies Center.

O'Reilly, Kenneth. 1995. *Nixon's Piano: Presidents and Racial Politics from Washington to Clinton.* New York: Free Press.

Ortner, Sherry B. 1974. "Is Female to Male as Nature Is to Culture?" In *Woman,*

Culture, and Society, ed. Michelle Z. Rosaldo and Louise Lamphere, 67–88. Stanford, CA: Stanford University Press.

————. 1996. *Making Gender: The Politics and Erotics of Culture.* Boston: Beacon Press.

Ovadia, Seth. 2001. "Race, Class, and Gender Differences in High School Seniors' Values: Applying Intersection Theory in Empirical Analysis." *Social Science Quarterly* 82 (2): 340–56.

Patel, Kant, and Mark E. Rushefsky. 1995. *Health Care Politics and Policy in America.* Armonk, NY: M. E. Sharpe.

Patient Advocacy. 1994. Managed Care Discussion. http://www.patientadvocacy .org/main/managedcare/mcrl_fvf.html (accessed February 1999; site now discontinued).

Patterson, James T. 2000. *America's Struggle against Poverty in the Twentieth Century.* Rev. ed. Cambridge, MA: Harvard University Press.

Patterson, Thomas E. 1993. *Out of Order.* New York: Alfred A. Knopf.

Peffley, Mark, and Jon Hurwitz. 2002. "The Racial Components of 'Race-Neutral' Crime Policy Attitudes." *Political Psychology* 23 (1): 59–75.

Peffley, Mark, Jon Hurwitz, and Paul M. Sniderman. 1997. "Racial Stereotypes and Whites' Political Views of Blacks in the Context of Welfare and Crime." *American Journal of Political Science* 41 (1): 30–60.

Peterson, David A. M. 2004. "Certainty or Accessibility: Attitude Strength in Candidate Evaluations." *American Journal of Political Science* 48 (3): 513–20.

Petrocik, John R. 1996. "Issue Ownership in Presidential Elections, with a 1980 Case Study." *American Journal of Political Science* 40 (3): 825–50.

Petty, Richard E., and John T. Cacioppo. 1981. *Attitudes and Persuasion: Classic and Contemporary Approaches.* Dubuque, IA: W. C. Brown Co..

————. 1986. *Communication and Persuasion : Central and Peripheral Routes to Attitude Change.* New York: Springer-Verlag.

Phillips, Anne. 1991. *Engendering Democracy.* Cambridge: Polity Press.

Phillips, Webb, and Lera Boroditsky. 2003. "Can Quirks of Grammar Affect the Way You Think? Grammatical Gender and Object Concepts." *Proceedings of the Twenty-fifth Annual Meeting of the Cognitive Science Society,* 928–33. Boston: Cognitive Science Society.

Philpot, Tasha S., and Hanes Walton. 2007. "One of Our Own: Black Female Candidates and the Voters Who Support Them." *American Journal of Political Science* 51 (1): 49–62.

Plutzer, Eric, and Michael Berkman. 2005. "The Graying of America and Support for Funding the Nation's Schools." *Public Opinion Quarterly* 69 (1): 66–86.

Pollock, Philip H., III. 1994. "Issues, Values, and Critical Moments: Did 'Magic' Johnson Transform Public Opinion on AIDS?" *American Journal of Political Science* 38 (2): 426–46.

Ponza, Michael, Greg J. Duncan, Mary Corcoran, and Fred Groskind. 1988. "The Guns of Autumn? Age Differences in Support for Income Transfers to the Young and Old." *Public Opinion Quarterly* 52 (4): 441–66.

Press, Andrea L., and Elizabeth R. Cole. 1999. *Speaking of Abortion: Television and Authority in the Lives of Women.* Chicago: University of Chicago Press.

Price, Vincent, and David Tewksbury. 1997. "News Values and Public Opinion: A Theoretical Account of Media Priming and Framing." In *Progress in Communication Sciences: Advances in Persuasion,* ed. George A. Barnett and Franklin J. Boster, 173–212. Greenwich, CT: Ablex Publishing Corporation.

Quadagno, Jill S. 1994. *The Color of Welfare: How Racism Undermined the War on Poverty.* New York: Oxford University Press.

Quattrone, George A., and Amos Tversky. 1988. "Contrasting Rational and Psychological Analyses of Political Choice." *American Political Science Review* 82 (3): 720–36.

Rapoport, Ronald B. 1981. "The Sex Gap in Political Persuading: Where the 'Structuring Principle' Works." *American Journal of Political Science* 25 (1): 32–48.

Reagan, Ronald. 1984. *Public Papers of the Presidents of the United States: Ronald Reagan.* Book 1: January 1–July 1, 1983. Washington, DC: U.S. Government Printing Office.

Reichmann, Rebecca L. 1999. *Race in Contemporary Brazil: From Indifference to Inequality.* University Park: Pennsylvania State University Press.

Rhodebeck, Laurie A. 1993. "The Politics of Greed? Political Preferences among the Elderly." *Journal of Politics* 55 (2): 342–64.

Richards, Ivor A. 1938. *Philosophy of Rhetoric.* Oxford: Oxford University Press.

Riker, William H. 1986. *The Art of Political Manipulation.* New Haven, CT: Yale University Press.

Roediger, David R. 1999. *The Wages of Whiteness: Race and the Making of the American Working Class.* Rev. ed. New York: Verso.

———. 2005. *Working toward Whiteness: How America's Immigrants Became White, the Strange Journey from Ellis Island to the Suburbs.* New York: Basic Books.

Rohrer, Tim. 1991. "To Plow the Sea: Metaphors for Regional Peace in Latin America." *Metaphor and Symbolic Activity* 6 (3): 163–81.

———. 1995. "The Metaphorical Logic of (Political) Rape: George Bush and the New World Order." *Metaphor and Symbolic Activity* 10 (2): 113–31.

Runkle, Jennifer. 1998. "Development and Initial Validation of a Measure of Race Schematicity." Ph.D. diss., Department of Psychology, Illinois Institute of Technology.

Sagar, H. A., and Janet W. Schofield. 1980. "Racial and Behavioral Cues in Black and White Children's Perceptions of Ambiguously Aggressive Acts." *Journal of Personality and Social Psychology* 39 (4): 590–98.

Sahlins, Marshall D. 1981. *Historical Metaphors and Mythical Realities: Structure in the Early History of the Sandwich Islands Kingdom.* Ann Arbor: University of Michigan Press.

———. 1985. *Islands of History.* Chicago: University of Chicago Press.

Sanbonmatsu, Kira. 2002. *Democrats, Republicans, and the Politics of Women's Place.* Ann Arbor: University of Michigan Press.

Sapiro, Virginia. 1986. "The Gender Basis of American Social Policy." *Political Science Quarterly* 101 (2): 221–38.

———. 2003. "Theorizing Gender in Political Psychology Research." In *Oxford Handbook of Political Psychology,* ed. David O. Sears, Leonie Huddy, and Robert Jervis, 601–34. New York: Oxford University Press.

Sapiro, Virginia, and Joe Soss. 1999. "Spectacular Politics, Dramatic Interpretations: Multiple Meanings in the Thomas/Hill Hearings." *Political Communication* 16 (3): 285–314.

Scandura, Terri A., Manuel J. Tejeda, and Melenie J. Lankau. 1995. "An Examination of the Validity of the Sex-Role Egalitarianism Scale (SRES-KK) Using Confirmatory Factor Analysis Procedures." *Educational and Psychological Measurement* 55 (5): 832–40.

Schiltz, Michael E. 1970. *Public Attitudes toward Social Security, 1935–1965.* Washington, DC: U.S. Social Security Administration Office of Research and Statistics.

Schlesinger, Mark. 2004. "Reprivatizing the Public Household? Medical Care in the Context of American Public Values." *Journal of Health Politics, Policy and Law* 29 (4–5): 969–1004.

Schlesinger, Mark, and Taeku Lee. 1994. "Is Health Care Different? Popular Support of Federal Health and Social Policies." In *The Politics of Health Care Reform: Lessons from the Past, Prospects for the Future,* ed. James A. Morone and Gary S. Belkin, 297–374. Durham, NC: Duke University Press.

Schneider, Walter, and Richard M. Shiffrin. 1977. "Controlled and Automatic Human Information Processing: I. Detection, Search, and Attention." *Psychological Review* 84 (1): 1–66.

Schuman, Howard, Charlotte Steeh, Lawrence Bobo, and Maria Krysan. 1997. *Racial Attitudes in America: Trends and Interpretations.* Rev. ed. Cambridge, MA: Harvard University Press.

Sears, David O. 1986. "College Sophomores in the Laboratory: Influences of a Narrow Data Base on Social Psychology's View of Human Nature." *Journal of Personality and Social Psychology* 51 (3): 515–30.

———. 1988. "Symbolic Racism." In *Eliminating Racism: Profiles in Controversy,* ed. Phyllis A. Katz, 53–84. New York: Plenum Press.

Sears, David O., Carl P. Hensler, and Leslie K. Speer. 1979. "Whites' Opposition to 'Busing': Self-Interest or Symbolic Politics?" *American Political Science Review* 73 (2): 369–84.

Sears, David O., Richard Lau, Tom Tyler, and Harris Jr. Allen. 1980. "Self-Interest vs. Symbolic Politics in Policy Attitudes and Presidential Voting." *American Political Science Review* 74 (3): 670–84.

Sears, David O., Jim Sidanius, and Lawrence Bobo, eds. 2000. *Racialized Politics: The Debate about Racism in America.* Chicago: University of Chicago Press.

Sears, David O., Colette Van Laar, and Mary Carrillo. 1997. "Is It Really Racism? The Origins of White Americans' Opposition to Race-Targeted Policies." *Public Opinion Quarterly* 61 (Spring): 16–53.

Sen, Amartya K. 1990. "Rational Fools: A Critique of the Behavioral Foundations of Economic Theory." In *Beyond Self-Interest,* ed. Jane J. Mansbridge, 25–44. Chicago: University of Chicago Press.

Shapiro, Robert Y., and Harpreet Mahajan. 1986. "Gender Differences in Policy Preferences: A Summary of Trends from the 1960s to the 1980s." *Public Opinion Quarterly* 50 (1): 42–61.

Shapiro, Susan P. 1990. "Collaring the Crime, Not the Criminal: Reconsidering the Concept of White-Collar Crime." *American Sociological Review* 55 (3): 346–65.

Shaw, Greg M., and Sarah E. Mysiewicz. 2004. "Trends: Social Security and Medicare." *Public Opinion Quarterly* 68 (3): 394–423.

Sherif, Muzafer. 1988. *The Robbers Cave Experiment: Intergroup Conflict and Cooperation.* Middletown, CT: Wesleyan University Press.

Shimko, Keith L. 1994. "Metaphors and Foreign Policy Decision Making." *Political Psychology* 15 (4): 655–71.

Sidanius, Jim, and Felicia Pratto. 1999. *Social Dominance: An Intergroup Theory of Social Hierarchy and Oppression.* Cambridge: Cambridge University Press.

Sigel, Roberta S. 1996. *Ambition and Accommodation: How Women View Gender Relations.* Chicago: University of Chicago Press.

Sigelman, Lee, and Susan Welch. 1991. *Black Americans' Views of Racial Inequality: The Dream Deferred.* Cambridge: Cambridge University Press.

Signorella, Margaret L. 1999. "Multidimensionality of Gender Schemas: Implications for the Development of Gender-Related Characteristics." In *Sexism and Stereotypes in Modern Society: The Gender Science of Janet Taylor Spence,* 107–26. Washington, DC: American Psychological Association.

Skocpol, Theda. 1992. *Protecting Soldiers and Mothers: The Political Origins of Social Policy in the United States.* Cambridge, MA: Belknap Press of Harvard University Press.

———. 1996. *Boomerang: Clinton's Health Security Effort and the Turn against Government in U.S. Politics.* New York: W. W. Norton.

———. 1997. *Boomerang: Health Care Reform and the Turn against Government.* 2nd ed. New York: W. W. Norton.

Smith, Barbara E. 1995. "Crossing the Great Divides: Race, Class, and Gender in Southern Women's Organizing, 1979–1991." *Gender and Society* 9 (6): 680–96.

Smith, Eliot R. 1998. "Mental Representation and Memory." In *The Handbook of Social Psychology,* ed. Daniel T. Gilbert, 1:391–445. 4th ed. Boston: McGraw-Hill.

Smith, Robert C., and Richard Seltzer. 2000. *Contemporary Controversies and the American Racial Divide.* Lanham, MD: Rowman and Littlefield.

Smith-Rosenberg, Carroll. 1986. *Disorderly Conduct: Visions of Gender in Victorian America.* New York: Oxford University Press.

Sniderman, Paul M., and Edward G. Carmines. 1997. *Reaching beyond Race.* Cambridge, MA: Harvard University Press.

Sniderman, Paul M., Gretchen C. Crosby, and William G. Howell. 2000. "The Politics of Race." In *Racialized Politics: The Debate about Racism in America,* ed. David O. Sears, Jim Sidanius, and Lawrence Bobo, 236–79. Chicago: University of Chicago Press.

Sniderman, Paul M., and Michael G. Hagen. 1985. *Race and Inequality: A Study in American Values.* Chatham, NJ: Chatham House.

Sniderman, Paul M., and Thomas L. Piazza. 1993. *The Scar of Race.* Cambridge, MA: Belknap Press of Harvard University Press.

Sniderman, Paul M., Philip Tetlock, and Edward G. Carmines. 1993. *Prejudice, Politics, and the American Dilemma.* Stanford, CA: Stanford University Press.

Sniderman, Paul M., and Sean M. Theriault. 2004. "The Structure of Political Argument and the Logic of Issue Framing." In *Studies in Public Opinion Attitudes, Nonattitudes, Measurement Error, and Change,* ed. Willem E. Saris and Paul M. Sniderman, 133–65. Princeton, NJ: Princeton University Press.

Snow, David A., E. B. Rochford, and Steven K. Worden. 1986. "Frame Alignment Processes, Micromobilization, and Movement Participation." *American Sociological Review* 51 (4): 464–81.

Soss, Joe, and Danielle LeClair. 2004. "Race, Sex, and the Implicit Politics of Welfare Reform." Paper presented at the annual meeting of the Midwest Political Science Association, Chicago.

Spellman, Barbara A., and Keith J. Holyoak. 1992. "If Saddam Is Hitler Then Who Is George Bush? Analogical Mapping between Systems of Social Roles." *Journal of Personality and Social Psychology* 62 (6): 913–33.

Spelman, Elizabeth V. 1988. *Inessential Woman: Problems of Exclusion in Feminist Thought.* Boston: Beacon Press.

Srull, Thomas K., and Robert S. Wyer. 1979. "The Role of Category Accessibility in the Interpretation of Information about Persons: Some Determinants and Implications." *Journal of Personality and Social Psychology* 37 (10): 1660–72.

———. 1980. "Category Accessibility and Social Perception: Some Implications for the Study of Person Memory and Interpersonal Judgments." *Journal of Personality and Social Psychology* 38 (6): 841–56.

Steinbugler, Amy C., Julie E. Press, and Janice J. Dias. 2006. "Gender, Race, and Affirmative Action: Operationalizing Intersectionality in Survey Research." *Gender Society* 20 (6): 805–25.

Stenner, Karen. 2005. *The Authoritarian Dynamic*. New York: Cambridge University Press.

Stepan, Nancy L. 1986. "Race and Gender: The Role of Analogy in Science." *Isis* 77 (2): 261–77.

Sternberg, Robert J. 1990. *Metaphors of Mind: Conceptions of the Nature of Intelligence*. New York: Cambridge University Press.

Sternberg, Robert J., Roger Tourangeau, and Georgia Nigro. 1993. "Metaphor, Induction, and Social Policy: The Convergence of Macroscopic and Microscopic Views." In *Metaphor and Thought*, ed. Andrew Ortony, 277–303. 2nd ed. New York: Cambridge University Press.

Stewart, Abigail J., and Christa McDermott. 2004. "Gender in Psychology." *Annual Review of Psychology* 55:519–44.

Stith, Sandra M., and Sarah C. Farley. 1993. "A Predictive Model of Male Spousal Violence." *Journal of Family Violence* 8 (2): 183–201.

Stockard, Jean. 1999. "Gender Socialization." In *Handbook of the Sociology of Gender,* ed. Janet S. Chafetz, 215–28. New York: Kluwer Academic/Plenum Publishers.

Sullivan, John L., James Piereson, and George E. Marcus. 1982. *Political Tolerance and American Democracy*. Chicago: University of Chicago Press.

Swim, Janet K., and Laurie L. Cohen. 1997. "Overt, Covert, and Subtle Sexism: A Comparison between the Attitudes toward Women and Modern Sexism Scales." *Psychology of Women Quarterly* 21 (1): 103–18.

Tajfel, Henri. 1957. "Value and the Perceptual Judgment of Magnitude." *Psychological Review* 64 (3): 192–204.

———. 1981. *Human Groups and Social Categories: Studies in Social Psychology*. New York: Cambridge University Press.

———. 1982. *Social Identity and Intergroup Relations*. New York: Cambridge University Press.

Tajfel, Henri, and John Turner. 1979. "An Integrative Theory of Intergroup Conflict." In *The Social Psychology of Intergroup Relations,* ed. William G. Austin and Stephen Worchel, 33–47. Monterey, CA: Brooks/Cole.

Tannenbaum, Frank. 1946. *Slave and Citizen: The Negro in the Americas*. New York: Alfred A. Knopf.

Tarrow, Sidney G. 1994. *Power in Movement: Social Movements, Collective Action, and Politics*. New York: Cambridge University Press.

Temple, Richard D., and Samuel H. Osipow. 1994. "The Relationship between Task-Specific Self-Efficacy Egalitarianism and Career Indecision for Females." *Journal of Career Assessment* 2 (1): 82–90.

Tetlock, Philip E. 1994. "Political Psychology or Politicized Psychology: Is the

Road to Scientific Hell Paved with Good Moral Intentions?" *Political Psychology* 15 (3): 509–29.

Thagard, Paul, and Cameron Shelley. 2001. "Emotional Analogies and Analogical Inference." In *The Analogical Mind: Perspectives from Cognitive Science,* ed. Dedre Gentner, Keith J. Holyoak, and Boicho N. Kokinov, 335–62. Cambridge, MA: MIT Press.

Thomas, Dan, Craig McCoy, and Allan McBride. 1993. "Deconstructing the Political Spectacle: Sex, Race, and Subjectivity in Public Response to the Clarence Thomas/Anita Hill 'Sexual Harassment' Hearings." *American Journal of Political Science* 37 (3): 699–720.

Thompson, Seth B. 1996. "Politics without Metaphors Is Like a Fish without Water." In *Metaphor: Implications and Applications,* ed. Jeffrey S. Mio and Albert N. Katz, 185–202. Mahwah, NJ: Erlbaum.

Tolleson Rinehart, Sue. 1992. *Gender Consciousness and Politics.* New York: Routledge.

Tolleson Rinehart, Sue, and Jyl J. Josephson, eds. 2005. *Gender and American Politics: Women, Men, and the Political Process.* 2nd ed. Armonk, NY: M. E. Sharpe.

Tourangeau, Roger, and Lance Rips. 1991. "Interpreting and Evaluating Metaphors." *Journal of Memory and Language* 30 (4): 452–72.

Tourangeau, Roger, and Robert J. Sternberg. 1981. "Aptness in Metaphor." *Cognitive Psychology* 13 (1): 27–55.

———. 1982. "Understanding and Appreciating Metaphors." *Cognition* 11 (3): 203–44.

Tversky, Amos, and Daniel Kahneman. 1981. "The Framing of Decisions and the Psychology of Choice." *Science* 211 (1): 453–58.

Twine, France W. 1998. *Racism in a Racial Democracy: The Maintenance of White Supremacy in Brazil.* New Brunswick, NJ: Rutgers University Press.

Tynes, Sheryl R. 1996. *Turning Points in Social Security: From "Cruel Hoax" to "Sacred Entitlement."* Stanford, CA: Stanford University Press.

United States Department of Labor. Bureau of Labor Statistics. 2005. *Women in the Labor Force: A Databook.* http://www.bls.gov/cps/wlf-databook-2005.pdf.

United States Social Security Administration. 1998. *Social Security: Toward a National Dialogue: Strengthening Public Understanding of the Issues.* Baltimore, MD: Social Security Administration.

———. 2000. *A Brief History of Social Security: Issued on Social Security's 65th Anniversary.* Baltimore, MD: Social Security Administration.

Valentino, Nicholas A. 1999. "Crime News and the Priming of Racial Attitudes during Evaluations of the President." *Public Opinion Quarterly* 63 (3): 293–320.

Valentino, Nicholas A., Vincent L. Hutchings, and Ismail K. White. 2002. "Cues That Matter: How Political Ads Prime Racial Attitudes during Campaigns." *American Political Science Review* 96 (1): 75–90.

Vertzberger, Yaacov Y. I. 1986. "Foreign Policy Decisionmakers as

Practical-Intuitive Historians: Applied History and Its Shortcomings." *International Studies Quarterly* 30 (2): 223–47.

Villarreal, Roberto E., and Norma G. Hernandez. 1991. *Latinos and Political Coalitions: Political Empowerment for the 1990s.* New York: Greenwood Press.

Voss, James F., Joel Kennet, Jennifer Wiley, and Tonya Y. E. Schooler. 1992. "Experts at Debate: The Use of Metaphor in the U.S. Senate Debate on the Gulf Crisis." *Metaphor and Symbolic Activity* 7 (3–4): 197–214.

Walsh, Katherine C. 2004. *Talking about Politics: Informal Groups and Social Identity in American Life.* Chicago: University of Chicago Press.

Warren, Jonathan W., and France W. Twine. 1997. "White Americans, the New Minority? Non-Blacks and the Ever-Expanding Boundaries of Whiteness." *Journal of Black Studies* 28 (2): 200–218.

Waters, Mary C. 1990. *Ethnic Options: Choosing Identities in America.* Berkeley and Los Angeles: University of California Press.

Weaver, Vesla. 2006. "Frontlash: Racial Unrest, Civil Rights, and the Origins of Contemporary Criminal Justice Policies." Paper presented at the annual meeting of the American Political Science Association, Philadelphia.

Weinreich-Haste, Helen. 1994. *The Sexual Metaphor.* Cambridge, MA: Harvard University Press.

Weir, Margaret, Ann S. Orloff, and Theda Skocpol, eds. 1988. *The Politics of Social Policy in the United States.* Princeton, NJ: Princeton University Press.

Weisberg, Herbert F., and Arthur H. Miller. 1980. "Evaluation of the Feeling Thermometer: A Report to the National Election Study Board Based on Data from the 1979 Pilot Survey." Technical report to the American National Election Studies Board of Overseers, Ann Arbor, MI.

West, Candace, and Don H. Zimmerman. 1987. "Doing Gender." *Gender and Society* 1 (2): 125–51.

Whyte, Lancelot L. 1978. *The Unconscious before Freud.* New York: St. Martin's Press.

Wilcox, Clyde. 1990. "Race Differences in Abortion Attitudes: Some Additional Evidence." *Public Opinion Quarterly* 54 (2): 248–55.

Wilcox, Clyde, Lee Sigelman, and Elizabeth Cook. 1989. "Some Like It Hot: Individual Differences in Responses to Group Feeling Thermometers." *Public Opinion Quarterly* 53 (2): 246–57.

Winant, Howard. 2001. *The World Is a Ghetto: Race and Democracy since World War II.* New York: Basic Books.

Winter, David G. 1973. *The Power Motive.* New York: Free Press.

Winter, Nicholas J. G. 1998. "Separate Worlds? African American and White Men and Women's Views on the 'Core' Value of Equality." Paper presented at the annual meeting of the American Political Science Association, Boston.

———. 2005. "Framing Gender: Political Rhetoric, Gender Schemas, and Public Opinion on U.S. Health Care Reform." *Politics and Gender* 1 (3): 453–80.

———. 2006. "Beyond Welfare: Framing and the Racialization of White Opinion on Social Security." *American Journal of Political Science* 50 (2): 400–420.

Winter, Nicholas J. G., and Adam J. Berinsky. 1999. "What's Your Temperature? Thermometer Ratings and Political Analysis." Paper presented at the annual meeting of the American Political Science Association, Atlanta, GA.

Wittenbrink, Bernd, Pamela L. Gist, and James L. Hilton. 1997. "Structural Properties of Stereotypic Knowledge and Their Influences on the Construal of Social Situations." *Journal of Personality and Social Psychology* 72 (3): 526–43.

Wittenbrink, Bernd, James L. Hilton, and Pamela L. Gist. 1998. "In Search of Similarity: Stereotypes as Naive Theories in Social Categorization." *Social Cognition,* special issue: *Naive Theories and Social Judgment* 16 (1): 31–55.

Wolbrecht, Christina. 2000. *The Politics of Women's Rights: Parties, Positions, and Change.* Princeton, NJ: Princeton University Press.

Wong, Janelle. 2000. "The Effects of Age and Political Exposure on the Development of Party Identification among Asian American and Latino Immigrants in the United States." *Political Behavior* 22 (4): 341–71.

Wong, Janelle S., Pei-Te Lien, and M. M. Conway. 2005. "Group-Based Resources and Political Participation among Asian Americans." *American Politics Research* 33 (4): 545–76.

Yamawaki, Niwako, and Brian T. Tschanz. 2005. "Rape Perception Differences between Japanese and American College Students: On the Mediating Influence of Gender Role Traditionality." *Sex Roles* 52 (5): 379–92.

Zald, Mayer N. 1996. "Culture, Ideology, and Strategic Framing." In *Comparative Perspectives on Social Movements: Political Opportunities, Mobilizing Structures, and Cultural Framings,* ed. Doug McAdam, John D. McCarthy, and Mayer N. Zald, 261–74. New York: Cambridge University Press.

Zaller, John. 1992. *The Nature and Origins of Mass Opinion.* Cambridge: Cambridge University Press.

Zucchino, David. 1997. *Myth of the Welfare Queen: A Pulitzer Prize–Winning Journalist's Portrait of Women on the Line.* New York: Scribner.

Index

abortion, 44

accessibility, cognitive, 29–30, 40, 44, 59, 88, 143–44, 147–51

Affluent Society, The (Galbraith), 86

African Americans. *See* black Americans

age, as a variable, 99, 104, 127

agency, 215n2

alcoholism, 5, 6

alphabet, gendered, 1–2

Althusser, Louis, 215n2

American Medical Association, 123

American National Election Studies (ANES), 56, 84, 95, 120, 202, 206. *See also* survey analyses for health care reform; survey analyses for welfare and Social Security

analogies and metaphors: analogies vs. metaphors, 213n9; and cognitive science, 4–5, 6, 26–28; computer metaphors, 5, 211n1; and foreign-policy discourse, 24, 27, 214n12; and gold standard as thorns and cross, 25–26; hydraulic metaphors, 5; interaction theory of metaphor, 229n20; and intersectionality, 169–71; metaphors for the mind, 5; and political communication, 5–6, 24–28, 146; political metaphors, 5–6, 152, 153; prison metaphors, 169; Québec independence as divorce, 25; race and gender as metaphors, 18–19; reasoning by, 4–7, 19, 23–28, 152–53; Saddam-as-Hitler, 24, 27, 172

Anderson, Craig A., 219n10

ANES. *See* American National Election Studies (ANES)

Armey, Dick, 122

Asian Americans, 13, 163–64

Ball, Robert, 91

Banaji, Mahzarin R., 21

Bartels, Larry M., 228n8

Dunning, David, 20
Dunton, Bridget C., 29

economy, government's role in, 8,
56–57, 58, 66–67, 69, 71–73, 80, 142,
187–92
Edelman, Murray J., 5–6
education, as a variable, 99, 127
egalitarianism, 99, 100, 102, 104, 127,
130, 226n11
egalitarianism, gender. *See* gender
egalitarians
emotional ties between genders, 43,
45, 229n14
Epstein, Cynthia F., 217n10
Equal Rights Amendment, 18, 44
expectations: for newspaper articles
experiment, 61–63; survey analyses
for health care reform, 125; survey
analyses for welfare and Social
Security, 94–95

Fazio, Russell H., 29
Feldman, Stanley, 206
feminism, 72, 217n11
fish video experiment, 30–31
Fiske, Susan, 228n12
fit, structural: importance of, 72–76;
between schema and frame, 30–31,
48, 59, 83–84, 85, 141, 143–44, 146,
149–51; between Social Security
and race schema, 90, 92; between
welfare and race schema, 88–89
Fludernik, Monika, 169
frames: and cognitive accessibility,
147–51; defined, 6, 21–23; emphasis
frames, 212n4; equivalence frames,
212n4; explicit vs. implicit, 22–23,
30, 57–58, 149–51, 172; gendered,
50–53, 55–58, 68–73, 120–25; and
group implication, 31, 47–48, 61–63;

119–20, 139, 146, 151–56; and health
care reform, 10, 120–25, 136–39;
joined to schemas by analogy, 7,
23–26; in newspaper articles experiment, 50–58, 64–73; and opinions,
4, 22–23, 48, 49–51, 85–86, 119–20;
and political communication, 6, 11,
151–54; and political engagement,
113–14; and political issues, 2–3,
6–9, 11, 22–23, 80–81; and poverty,
86–89; power of, 49, 171–73; racialized, 50–58, 64–68, 86–94; and
Social Security, 9, 48–49, 53–56, 80,
90–94, 115–18, 151; and structural
fit, 30–31, 48, 59, 73–76, 83–84,
85, 141, 149–51; success/failure of,
80–81, 146; and welfare, 9, 86–89,
115–18
Frank, Barney, 153
Frankenberg, Ruth, 36, 165, 228n14
Freud, Sigmund, 212n2
Frieze, Irene H., 212n2

Galbraith, John Kenneth: *The Affluent
Society,* 86
gender: concept of, 216n9; emotional
ties between genders, 43, 45, 217n11;
identification and consciousness,
14, 217n11; and interdependence,
42–43; and opinion, 13–15, 17–19,
158–59; and poverty, 108–9; and
power and dominance, 42, 45; reality of, 36; and sex, 3
gender difference, 18, 41–44, 45, 46, 133
gender egalitarians, 43–44, 45, 50,
61–62, 230n4; and government's
economic role, 57; and health care
reform, 128, 129, 136, 145; and Social
Security, 55–56, 69–70, 109–10;
and visitation rights, 52–53; and
welfare, 168